MAVERICK UNCHANGED, UNREPENTANT

MAVERICK UNCHANGED, UNREPENTANT

RAM JETHMALANI

RAINLIGHT
RUPA

Published in Rainlight by
Rupa Publications India Pvt. Ltd 2013
7/16, Ansari Road, Daryaganj
New Delhi 110002

Sales centres:
Bengaluru Chennai
Hyderabad Jaipur Kathmandu
Kolkata Mumbai Prayagraj

Copyright © Ram Jethmalani 2013

The views and opinions expressed in this book are the author's own and the facts are as reported by him which have been verified to the extent possible, and the publishers are not in any way liable for the same.

All rights reserved.
No part of this publication may be reproduced, transmitted, or stored in a retrieval system, in any form or by any means, electronic, mechanical, photocopying, recording or otherwise, without the prior permission of the publisher.

P-ISBN: 978-81-291-2391-6
E-ISBN: 978-81-291-3350-2

Thirteenth impression 2025

15 14 13

The moral right of the author has been asserted.

Typeset by RECTO GRAPHICS, Delhi

Printed in India

This book is sold subject to the condition that it shall not, by way of trade or otherwise, be lent, resold, hired out, or otherwise circulated, without the publisher's prior consent, in any form of binding or cover other than that in which it is published.

*In discharge of my debt to the people of India,
with whose sympathy and love I have grown to be what I am,
and who, I believe, should know the truth about several things
that have happened in our country.*

Ram Jethmalani

Onward Maverick, Onward, go on, on, and on
Change Naught, Repent Nothing, till Devils all gone
But even then, Rest not, for their Legions rise again
Father to daughter, son to wife; and Yes, their children.

And when the Day of Judgement came, gods wished to know
From the Lord God of ALL, 'Where shall this Maverick go?
To Deepest Hell, Highest Heaven or Back to Earth again?'
'Send him Back,' said the Lord, 'Sorely Earth needs such men.'

—From 'Onward Maverick—Onward, On!'
Bhagwan Gidwani

Contents

Introduction		*xi*

Section 1: Tectonic Plates of the Subcontinent
1	Pakistan: In the Shadow of Jihad	3
2	Kashmir: Time to Move on	17
3	China: Counter the Dragon before It Is too Late	40

Section 2: The Mechanics of Power
4	Dynastic Democracy: Bravely Evaluate Your Leaders	51
5	Three Blind Mice and the Politics of the Ruling Party	81
6	Public Service: For Man, Mammon or Master?	118
7	Political Life	134

Section 3: When Conscience Flees
8	Transparency, RTI and the Lokpal Bill	155
9	Bhopal: A Tale of Two Tragedies	176
10	Black Money, State Collusion and National Fraud	190

Section 4: An Ode to Humanity
11	Fanaticism, Religion and the Contemporary World	213
12	A Refreshing Change: Kate and William	231

Postscript	233
Appendix	247
Selected Speeches	249
Acknowledgements	274

Introduction

My life has been inextricably woven with the law and the courts of justice. In the course of my practice, I have attained cerebral pleasure and excellence, notable victories, the kudos of clients and peers and the respect of judges. While all this is gratifying in the extreme I must confess to a tinge of regret. A lawyer's life exists in the fast lane; as one hurtles between research, conference and appearance, time ticks relentlessly. Law is an insanely jealous mistress as the old saying goes.

Lawyers with political aspirations are accordingly constrained by the demands of their profession. An elitist law practice fits ill with grassroot politics so necessary for mass leadership. In a sense my ability to marry a successful legal practice with an almost uninterrupted parliamentary career of 35 years has been because the politics of that period consisted of a battle between feudal forces wedded to a dynastic cult and the forces of Constitutional liberalism. My political prominence and parliamentary career commenced when I opposed the declaration of emergency in 1975 by the proponents of the dynasty, on the ground that it was a fraud on the Constitution. I was persecuted for that 'heresy' but I won my parliamentary spurs by successfully winning a seat in the elections that followed in the aftermath of the emergency. My political relevance persists till today as India's neo-monarchists continue to rear their ugly heads and perpetuate themselves in power by recourse to rampant self-aggrandisement, through loot of public resources and the public exchequer, and by subversion of all institutions.

A new, free and hopeful India was born at the zero hour of 15th August 1947, as the late Jawaharlal Nehru delivered his famous *Tryst with Destiny* speech. Two thousand princes and politicians gathered in the chamber of the Constituent Assembly and the nation's heart beat for every word he spoke. 'Long years ago,' he said, 'we made a tryst with destiny. And now the time has come when we shall redeem our pledge not wholly or in full measure, but substantially. At the stroke of the midnight hour, while the world sleeps, India will awake to life and freedom.'

Sixty-five years have gone by and the eloquent and inspiring words now jar the ears while the pledges that remain unredeemed and forgotten only bring tears to swollen eyes, and, to some, thoughts of suicide as the only escape from the hell into which almost all of us have landed. Life and freedom have been cornered by the privileged few: men without morals engaged in the sordid pursuit of polluted power and stolen wealth.

A handful of us, not involved in the sordid game, recall with sadness a bad omen that went unnoticed in the ecstasy of independence. Mahatma Gandhi was not in the celebrations but was sleeping in the modest house of a poor man in the suburbs of Calcutta, quelling the fires of communal hatred and violence. His prophetic vision did not prescribe a shining future. Now with scam after scam emphasizing a corrupt society to international glare, poverty rising, food scarcity, unaffordable cost of living, a foreign policy in shambles as we are surrounded by hostile neighbours, and democracy and freedom turning into a mirage, it is a tragic 'paradise lost'. Around the time we became independent, many other newly independent nations too were born. In the world of Islam none adopted secularism and they turned into theocracies of the most dangerous hue. Even Turkey, once a shining example of a secular state though its majority population was Islamic, is becoming more and more fundamentalist. It is well known that Hindus were opposed to the partition of the country on the basis of religion but their will did not prevail. If Hindus had retaliated they could have easily justified India becoming a Hindu state. But they gladly opted for a secular India. This could not be unless secularism was fully endorsed by the religion of the majority. Having been born and brought up in Sind, the cradle of Sufism, I have imbibed secularism through my genes. I do not need to be indoctrinated or educated by anyone.

The 25th Article of the Constitution of India defines our secularism. All religious dogma, beliefs or practices are subject to public order, health and morality. Interpreted rightly, Indian secularism mandates a life guided by reason and logic but inspired by love and compassion.

The ruling dispensation has refused to explain or practice true secularism. It has converted secularism into a term of political vituperation and abuse. 'We are secular and our opponents communal,' is the common refrain. Any hindu proud of his religion is at once condemned as a criminal. This is vote bank politics of the most vulgar and divisive kind. The Supreme Court in more than one binding judgment has accepted my view of Hinduism and Hindutva. But today, even the Supreme Court is attacked as being communal by persons who one would expect to be more judicious and fair.

All laws are made in the context of clime and circumstance. Like all biological species, they too must change in response to changes in the context, which means imperatives of social needs at a given time. Those who cling to unsuitable laws, claiming they are unalterable because sanctioned by some ancient scripture, I condemn as unalterable fools. Rajiv Gandhi proved to be one when, by a legislation, he reversed a secular and wise decision of the Supreme Court in the Shah Bano case; vote bank politics again. Repeatedly, it trumps and defeats India's secular spirit.

In the 21st century, as Kashmir and Assam stand charred by the fires of ethnic conflict, our tryst with destiny seems strikingly reminiscent of the bleeding social fabric that only the genteel but passionate Gandhi could heal; the utopia of Nehru's grandiloquence seems such a distant dream.

That is again the inexorable consequence of dynastic politics, where defence and perpetuation of dynasty are the cardinal principles of governance, while pursuit of the public good is an alien doctrine. Courtiers have neither the will nor capacity to resolve burning issues that demand public attention. There is ennui and paralysis in government action.

Manifestly, a dynastic party puts personality and charisma at a premium and policy and programme at a discount. Ideology in such circumstances is reduced to populist slogans and vacuous shibboleths. Some articles in this collection are devoted to exposing the true nature of the dynastic beast and the pitiable obsequiousness of its followers. Absence of ideology and the cult of personality entails that the adherents of a dynastic party are not wedded to it on a matter of principle or precept. A dynastic party's members are attracted by the opportunity of accumulating largesse that it affords them. Its regional satraps are leaders wedded to the patronage system. Public resources are thus allotted not on rational transparent criteria, but to crony capitalists. Auctions are the exceptions, and arbitrary exercise of discretion the rule. The economic advantage of the patronage system is shared between the ruler and the privileged class of people. This system, it is axiomatic, is inherently corrupt but is so entrenched that what objectively is tantamount to rampant corruption, appears to the party faithful to be a legitimate mode of governance. And once mammon becomes a governing credo, the scale of corruption is of little consequence; witness the quantum of losses certified by the CAG in the 2G, Commonwealth games, Civil Aviation ministry and Coalgate scams. The allure of mammon also trumps national honour (Commonwealth games); is blind to large scale tragedies (Bhopal); and dishonours the bravest among us (Adarsh).

The astronomical figures involved in the prominent scams of recent times, have necessitated recourse by the perpetrators of corruption to tax havens and the secrecy laws that hide away their ill gotten gains. So long as the fruits of corruption were restricted to small numbers, they could be retained by the beneficiaries locally in cash as 'Black Money'. The new volumes require to be stashed in secret accounts in accommodating jurisdictions. Global Financial Integrity (GFI) has estimated the volume of money illegally owned by Indian nationals in tax havens abroad as being of a magnitude of $ 500 billion to $ 1.5 trillion. While our present rulers and their acolytes in the media have poured scorn on these figures without any credible justification, it is significant that the present director of the CBI has affirmed these figures at an Interpol seminar on stolen assets and their recovery.

Three circumstances suggest that the highest and the mightiest in the land are the biggest culprits in the matter of holding illegal accounts and wealth abroad. The baffling decision of the Union of India to seek a review of the Supreme Court's decision in a case successfully filed by some public spirited citizens, including myself, for the appointment of a Special Investigating Team to be designated by the government to investigate and recover monies illegally stashed in foreign banks popularly known as the Black Money Case; the refusal of the government to comply with the Supreme Court's direction to reveal the names of the illegal account holders in the Liechtenstein Bank, disclosed by the German government, and the reluctance of the Indian government to co-operate with the Swiss government in complying with that government's protocol for disclosure of account holders in Swiss banks. In an article entitled 'Black Money, State Collusion and National Fraud' I posed 15 questions to the government pertaining to their conduct on this most serious national issue. Its silence to this day is ominous.

A corrupt and dynastic political party is antithetical to the rule of law and to carefully crafted constitutional checks and balances to prevent abuse of power. A tendency towards autocracy and consequent institutional subversion is inevitable with a party thus configured. The result is a prime minister bereft of real power, subservient to the dynastic head and a mute spectator to the loot and plunder of the nation's resources; a president who is a loyal camp follower and will faithfully rubber stamp the decisions ordained by the dynasty: witness how unhesitatingly President Fakhruddin Ali Ahmed signed the Proclamation of Emergency at Mrs. Gandhi's bidding in 1975 and ponder whether Mrs. Pratibha Patil, (besieged as she was by her co-operative sugar factory in liquidation, her co-operative bank bankrupt, and her family embroiled in the murder case of a popular intra-party rival in Jalgaon at the time of her nomination by Mrs. Sonia Gandhi), would have done otherwise; or for that matter whether President Pranab Mukherjee, whose many acts of subversion of the Constitution during the Emergency have been documented by the Shah Commission, is so radically transformed that he would now protect it; a judiciary accused of judicial overreach when it censures the government or brings its ministers to book while its inconvenient judgments are subjected to review or Presidential Reference; a CAG whose findings against the government's decisions are vilified as being patently erroneous, in excess of jurisdiction and even motivated, although that august body, the Constituent Assembly had opined that as the guardian of the nation's finances, the CAG was as important a Constitutional functionary as the justices of the Supreme Court; a CVC appointed despite the taint of corruption and over the protest of the leader of the Opposition, whose appointment was finally quashed by the Supreme Court; and a CBI whose only role on empirical evidence is to falsely implicate political opponents and wrongly exonerate the regime's members and cronies. The mass movements of Anna Hazare and Baba Ramdev for the creation of an all-powerful ombudsman like the Lokpal were surely doomed for failure in their expectation of a favourable response from a government fundamentally at odds with Constitutional values.

Finally, a caveat. The views reflected in all the articles published in this book are exclusively my own. Some of the essays deal with internal and external threats to our polity—Kashmir, Pakistan and China (I have recently also published a trilogy of articles on Assam which are available elsewhere), and my efforts to resolve these troublesome issues, or as in the case of China, my perception of the threat that that country constitutes to India, and how the dragon needs to be contained. I am aware that my stand, particularly on the contentious issues of friendship with Pakistan and the resolution of the Kashmir problem, may be at odds with that of the BJP on whose ticket I was elected to the Rajya Sabha. Mercifully, unlike the Congress party, there is tolerance of dissent within my party. I do not claim to be infallible but even my most trenchant critics would not deny that I speak and act out of personal conviction. I write also to stir debate and have the humility to retract my views when bested in such debates. If that makes me a maverick, I confess I relish the epithet.

In the meantime I proudly remain 'Unchanged and Unrepentant'.

Ram Jethmalani

Section 1
Tectonic Plates of the Subcontinent

1
Pakistan: In the Shadow of Jihad

I was born in Sindh which is now a part of Pakistan. I came to India during Partition, leaving behind my many Muslim friends including my partner in practice, the late Allah Bux Brohi. It was a heart-wrenching experience. While living in an Indian refugee camp I came to the firm conclusion that India and Pakistan must forget the tribulations of the tragic Partition and develop a relationship of trust and cooperation. I have ceaselessly striven to achieve this throughout my political career.

Terrorism, water disputes and the contentious Kashmir issue are undoubtedly behemoths that tower over the India-Pakistan relationship creating an environment of hostility and mistrust in the Asian subcontinent. The mutual dissonance and suspicion that India and Pakistan harbour towards each other has been an enduring concern of mine. I see no reason why obdurate positions and antagonistic approaches to diplomacy persist; why suspicion and forked speech* of egotistic politicians drown out the voice of the people; or why it is not possible to develop a relationship of mutual trust. If there is to be security in the 21st century, we need to transcend history and forge an alliance based on honour, sincerity and genuine desires of the people of our great nations.

Unfortunately, my dream has not been fulfilled. Instead of being friends, we have gone to war more than once and insane terrorism is continuously spilling the blood of innocent people.

---

*Forked speech is here derived from the phrase forked to ungue—meaning to mislead or deceive.

Pakistan, terrorism and double speak

Pakistan is often considered the nursery of global jihad. This is not a position achieved overnight, but one towards which it has steadily moved. A journey that commenced with the successes of the *mujahidin*, in support of whom Pakistan became a client state of one superpower in order to evict the other super power from Afghanistan in the Great Game *la deuxième partie*. Hoping to replicate that grand success with regard to Kashmir, Pakistan has assiduously built an infrastructure of jihad within the state. Those who had bloodied their hands in Kashmir were allowed to roam freely in Pakistan, to solicit contributions, use propaganda and recruit mercenaries. Eventually many of these jihadists began operating on sectarian lines, and slowly the monster forged in the fires of Afghan jihad started devouring its creator. Yet, the establishment played its game of duplicity which culminated in the surreptitious hosting of the Sheikh of Jihad, Osama bin Laden, in its very heartland.

No sensible, properly-instructed jury would have believed Pakistan's false defence, even if it was bolstered by the testimony of otherwise respectable witnesses. Pakistan has been receiving enormous sums of American money in consideration of the commitment that its armed forces and intelligence agencies have sincerely joined the war against Osama bin Laden and his criminal gangs. No one who has some understanding of circumstantial evidence can ignore the almost conclusively incriminating circumstance that the world's most-wanted terrorist lived for five years within less than a mile of the country's most prestigious defence academy. Add to this the reputation of the ISI as an intelligence network so efficient and pervasive that no dinner guest at a foreign journalist's house has ever gone unnoticed or unscrutinised, and you have an unconvincing and unpalatable story.

As a lawyer, I would convict Pakistan of lying on the basis of Prime Minister Yousaf Raza Gilani's statement to his Parliament. He accused the United States of violating Pakistan's sovereignty and threatened that any such incursion in future would invite Pakistan's retaliation in full force. A heavily paid ally in the war against Osama bin Laden would have sought forgiveness for national incompetence, thanked the US and promised more sincere and effective cooperation in future. But I would refrain from belabouring this point further, because I want India and Pakistan to be friends, I want Pakistan's democracy to strike strong roots, mastering its armed forces and enforcing a sincere resolve to banish the Taliban and Al Qaeda from Pakistani soil. I want it to be a respected member of the comity of nations, truly wedded to the last testament of Quaid-e-Azam Jinnah.

Nobody in the West believes that Osama bin Laden was living in Abbottabad, just 75 miles from the capital of Pakistan, without the knowledge of the government, top ministers and bureaucrats. Hillary Clinton's exoneration of Pakistan's higher ups has cut no ice with any except those determined to lie and needing false testimony of some 'credibility' to fortify a foolish falsehood. Pakistan's national anguish was summed up by a perceptive observer who wrote, 'If we did not know that he (bin Laden) was in Abbottabad for years with his wives and kids, we are a failed state; if we did know, we are a rogue state.'

India, and indeed the entire civilised world, should be concerned with the prospect of having as its neighbour a failed state unable to cope with its army, its murderous terrorists and a lethal nuclear arsenal. India must, therefore, be less critical and more sympathetic.

President Barack Obama has carried out many drone attacks inside Pakistan even after the killing of bin Laden. This is a clear statement to Pakistan that the US is not going to leave the Taliban and Al Qaeda to take control of Afghanistan. His announcement of troop-withdrawal from Afghanistan is not an abdication of the American responsibility of sustaining Afghanistan's democracy. He has obviously planned an alternative strategy for ensuring access to the landlocked country. It contains a gentle hint that this will be done—with Pak cooperation if possible, but without it if necessary.

Pakistan will do well to assess the price of confrontation with an erstwhile ally which has sunk billions of dollars to buy its cooperation. Speaker John Boehner has been brutally forthright: "I think this is a moment when we need to look each other in the eye and decide, 'Are we really allies? Are we going to work together?'"

Pakistan establishing a cordial relationship with India by signing a formal treaty of perpetual peace and eschewing terrorism and war will go a long way to allay American mistrust, strengthen democracy in Asia and put a healthy fright into the hearts of the bin Laden gangs. This will also remove Pakistan's excuse that its anti-terrorist effort on the western frontier is greatly curbed by its troops being tied up in the east for defence against Indian aggression. This has always been a false excuse. India has no territorial designs on Pakistan and is only too happy to have a fully democratic Jammu & Kashmir with as much autonomy as it can handle. It has joined its destiny with India through a freely enacted Constitution by its own sovereign Constituent Assembly.

Pakistan must understand that the US has its own western worries that are almost as serious as the Afghanistan involvement. Its people are weary of wars in which they do not see any serious threat to immediate and obvious American interests. They want US troops to return home from faraway lands where they are not even welcome. Europe is proving to be a big headache as well. The European Union is falling apart; survival of its common currency is becoming doubtful; and so are free movement across national borders and transatlantic collective security. A fracturing of the euro could drag down the global economy. A weakened NATO would mean the US will have to bear a bigger security burden. The debt crisis seems to defy the wisdom of European leaders. They have under-invested in their military infrastructure and are turning to Washington for bombs and military necessities. President Obama must wonder how much longer his voters will support financially draining alliances and wars big and small. India and Pakistan, singly and jointly, must also cater to US anxieties.

But, even as the world wearies of Pakistani claims of being at the forefront of the war against terror, the US continues to pours in billions of dollars in aid in return for assisting the operations against jihadists and to stop Pakistan from tumbling into an abyss.

It is legitimate to conclude that the source of money which enabled Osama bin Laden to live in a specially-built villa in Abbottabad possibly came from funds provided by donations originating in Saudi Arabia and spent under the watchful eye of the Pakistani Army. So, when the US conducted a highly secret operation and killed Osama bin Laden in Abbotabad, Pakistan, the world held its breath and waited to see what would happen next.

The Al Qaeda, as expected, reacted with venom, swearing to avenge the death of their leader. After all, the Al Qaeda is the most feared terrorist network in the world and it had to live up to its evil reputation. Silence would have meant accepting the validity of the murder of their most iconic leader. Whether threats of violence and bloodshed will come to be executed may be doubtful, yet they cannot be complacently ignored. The blood-curdling statements of retribution issued by Nasir al-Wahishi, the leader of the powerful Yemeni franchise of the Al Qaeda, serves as a chilling reminder of the fact that even after the death of Pakistan's closet friend Osama bin Laden, the war on terror is far from over. Nasir al-Wahishi, who heads Al Qaeda in the Arabian Peninsula, has warned that global jihad is all set to become 'more intense and harmful' as future attacks will be 'greater and worse'. As expected, the second generation of terror leaders has used the killing of Osama bin Laden as an excuse to call for a fresh wave of terror attacks. And let there be no doubt that such calls to avenge the killing of 'the Sheikh of Jihad' that have been sent out to every *mujahid* will tragically be answered with equal amounts of gore and flesh as innocent civilians in America and across the world will be made to pay a heavy price for 'a serious sin'.

Mohammad Ilyas Kashmiri, a Pakistani commando-turned-global-terrorist linked to multiple terror plots including the planning of a series of 'Mumbai style' attacks in key European cities was one of the main contenders for succeeding Osama bin Laden as the chief of Al Qaeda. As the US kept up its pressure on flushing out terrorists hiding in Pakistan, Kashmiri also met his end in a June 2011 US drone attack in South Waziristan, thereby providing another example of Pakistan's malfeasance. Given this background, it is important to ensure that there is no slack in counter-terrorism operations worldwide. Genuine cooperation from Pakistan is the need of the hour if these attempts are to be a success.

Unfortunately, sympathy for jihadists is deeply rooted in many sections of Pakistani society although we have repeatedly been led to believe that this is not so, and only some sections of the Pak Army and the ISI were involved in terrorist activities, and guiding and financing of terrorists. Yet, Pakistan's main right-wing party, Jamiat Ulema Islam Fazl (JUI-F), a Deobandi organization, did not hesitate to condone the death of the Al Qaeda chief in no less a place than the National Assembly of Pakistan. Maulvi Asmatullah of the JUI-F, stood up from his seat and offered prayers for Osama bin Laden. He was joined by the other legislators from his party as well as from the Opposition benches. Ata-ur Rehman, JUI-F leader Mulana Fazlur Rehman's brother, was the second legislator to join Asmatullah. 'God bless Osama bin Laden and rest his soul in peace,' the legislators had said in one voice.

I ask, can this be countenanced by a state unless it actively supports and sponsors the terror machinery?

These events are recent. Let us go back to the world before Osama bin Laden and 9/11 to examine Pakistan's relationship with terror, guised as jihad. Noteworthy are the words of Hafiz Mohammad Saeed, the founder of Lashkar-e-Taiba on 3 November 1999: 'Jihad is not about Jammu & Kashmir only. About 15 years ago, people might have found it ridiculous if someone told them about the disintegration of the USSR. Today, I announce the break-up of India, *Insha-Allah*. We will not rest until the whole of India is dissolved into Pakistan.' Hafiz Mohammad Saeed is reputed to be a professor of Islamic Studies, but he forgets the true message of Islam when incessantly spewing vitriol against India.

Pakistan's connivance is such that no action is taken even when the Lashkar-e-Taiba publishes such incendiary literature as a pamphlet titled *Why are we waging Jihad?* According to it 'Jihad is obligatory; it pronounces for taking back Spain where Muslims ruled for 800 years. The same goes for Nepal and Myanmar. Of course, the whole of India, including Jammu and Kashmir, Hyderabad, Bihar, Junagarh and Assam, also have to be retaken.' Such sentiments appear acceptable to the Pakistani establishment. This is why it also allowed on 17 October 2008, at the Jamia al Qudsia Mosque in Lahore, a Friday sermon that stated, 'India has blocked the Chenab waters and constructed the Baglihar Dam. The only reason all this has happened is because Jihad-e-Kashmir has been abandoned by the rulers. India understands only the language of jihad, which cannot be suppressed. In fact, with some support, jihad can break up India like the former USSR.' No action was taken against this Jamaat-ud-Dawa (JuD), ameer and hardly 40 days later, on 26 November 2008, a terrorist attack of mind-boggling proportions was carried out in Mumbai.

The Economist on November 19, 2011 reports, 'Water is the latest battle cry for *jihadis*, they shout that water must flow, or blood must flow.' It is reported that this notorious group threatens to blow up India's dams.

In 2010, a Pakistani extremist, Abdur Rehman Makki, addressed a rally saying that if India were to 'block Pakistan's waters, we will let loose a river of blood'. A Pakistani newspaper, Nawa-i-Waqt, wrote a venomous editorial: 'Pakistan should convey to India that a war is possible on the issue of water and this time the war will be a nuclear one.'

Is Pakistan going to put an end to these threats that do not become any civilized nation?

Its own worst enemy

What is happening in Pakistan is not Islam. The Holy Quran does not advocate or condone threats of aggression or destruction of Hindus and India. The great Prophet of Islam advised his followers to search for knowledge. He is the only one who declared that the ink of the scholar is more valuable than the blood of the martyr. As this is forgotten by the establishment, which I can almost say overtly supports jihadists, a ray of light and hope is provided only by some liberal persons from the media. For example, Pakistani anchor Kamran Khan on Geo TV had the courage to ask these questions: 'Why has it become a sin for us to call ourselves Pakistanis? Why is it that every terror attack anywhere in the world has a Pakistan connection? Why have our rulers followed a dual policy on terrorism if terrorists have bled us so badly?'

Kamran himself answered these questions: The enemy lies within, and 'conspiracy lollipops' won't work anymore, not after the Americans nabbed Osama bin Laden at a place which is a short drive from Islamabad.

Some of the most militant religious fundamentalists, knowing that they cannot realistically hope to overthrow liberal and democratic societies, nevertheless desire to punish them, and do so by acts of mass murder. The worst such attack to date being 9/11 in the United States, the Underground bombings in London, the train bombings in Madrid, and the attacks in Mumbai.

Moreover, there is the frightening prospect of nuclear weapons getting into the hands of terrorists or terrorist organizations. Society can no longer rest content with the comfortable religious belief that there is a sleepless and watchful deity that maintains an unblinking surveillance on earth all the time.

A greater danger however needs to be noticed. It is that a frightened society often resorts to self-repression. Society begins to cut down its own liberty in supposed self defence. Pakistani society today is conceding retreat to terrorism at no further cost to the terrorists. Already their society is full of conservatives, especially the religious-minded who see opportunity in the monitoring and surveillance that restrict personal freedoms. The creation of new commodities such as identities, privacy, and centrally collated personal data—such self-inflicting injuries to civil liberties—plays directly into the hands of the terrorists. It is no exaggeration that this is a very expensive act of destructive policy. Future generations will have to fight all over again for liberties which had once been achieved by the courage and perseverance of centuries. Pakistanis must recognize that dismantling civil liberties is not the solution they need. As Justice Thurgood Marshall of the US Supreme Court once remarked, 'History teaches us that grave threats to liberty often come in times of urgency, when constitutional rights seem too extravagant to endure.'

Thus, those who are willing to give up personal freedom in order to gain security will have neither personal freedom nor security and nor would they deserve them. Liberty doubtless carries risks and the courage to face the risks is what makes one worthy of having such liberty. I regret that the Pakistani press has internalised Pakistan's surrender of internal sovereignty to the jihadi militants. The sane and liberal elements in Pakistan are afraid to speak. The murder of Governor Salman Taseer is a tell-tale event showing the political degeneration of the entire nation. It is my humble and fervent appeal that this vulgar jingoism must stop.

Media glare and failures of diplomacy

India and Pakistan invariably fail to negotiate a reasonable detente to the main contentious issues between them. Diplomacy requires carefully calibrated and structured handling, and working up the diplomatic ladder to achieve negotiations that will be palatable to both nations. Unfortunately, diplomacy between the two countries has a history of grand gestures, media blaze and heavy-handed dealings that only lead to breakdowns like that of the bus diplomacy, various attempts at cricket diplomacy and the bungled Agra summit.

In recent times, the S.M. Krishna—S.M. Qureshi spat of 16 July 2010 put the clock back by a quarter of a century. Such spats make it difficult for the governments of India and Pakistan to start all over again—as the old saying goes one could make an omelette out of eggs, but not eggs out of an omelette. The meeting of the two ministers was an unmitigated disaster and should not have been held merely because a few months earlier at Thimphu, the two prime ministers had casually agreed upon it. The preparation required for a summit meeting of this kind had seen completely lacking. Although the time-tested technique of diplomacy, the one clothed in privacy and secrecy, has ceased to be fashionable, yet it remains, and must remain, a compulsory prelude to any successful summit meeting.

Intrusion by the media into every phase and level of the negotiation process changes the whole spirit and nature of diplomacy. The modern negotiator cannot escape the duality of his role. He must transact business simultaneously with his negotiating partner and public opinion of his own country under constant media glare. Before this unwanted intrusion, the intermediary stages of negotiations were totally sheltered from the domestic constituency of the negotiators as well as from the international news media. But we have been pushed into an era of what the media gleefully calls 'open diplomacy'. President Woodrow Wilson of the US, one of the earliest proponents of open diplomacy would be pleased. His famous Fourteen Points announced in 1919 open with , 'Open covenants openly arrived at, after which there should be no private international understandings of any kind. Diplomacy shall proceed always frankly and in the public view.'

Diplomats and scholars with professional training and experience regarded the intrusion of media as a major disruption of the diplomatic process. Negotiation presupposes bargaining. A negotiator must be prepared for the eventuality of emerging from the bargaining process with a position different from the one that he espoused in the beginning. If the initial positions are widely published, the negotiator is inhibited in his capacity to move on to other proposals. The legitimate mobility of negotiation is interpreted in the public mind as a failure of credibility.

It is important to understand that there is a built-in conflict of interest between the diplomat and the journalist. What one seeks to conceal, the other seeks to reveal, according to the guiding principle of his vocation. I would not, however, be harsh on Mr S.M. Qureshi for the July 2010 spat. His churlish reference to his Indian counterpart was the only way of demonstrating to his domestic supporters that he had scored a victory over India and its foreign minister. I am glad that Foreign Minister Krishna maintained an impressive posture of dignity and good manners. Diplomats negotiating issues that affect the well-being of millions of their countrymen, and sometimes the entire world, must bear in mind that 'Public opinion compels governments, which usually know what would be wiser or more necessary or more expedient, to be too late with too little or too long with too much, too pacifist in peace or too bellicose in war, too appeasing in negotiation or too intransigent,' as Walter Lippmann, the American intellectual, said in 1955. Mass opinion has a growing power, but it has shown itself to be a dangerous master of decisions when the stakes are life and death.

The Mumbai carnage of 26 November 2008 would have been impossible without the active support and incitement of Pakistan's ruling establishment, particularly sections of the army and their poodle, the ISI. The facts of the matter were well known to Foreign Minister Qureshi. Mr S.M. Krishna did not have to inform him about the Headley disclosures nor was it necessary to extract a public apology from the foreign minister of Pakistan. All the energy employed in making Pakistan admit that the Mumbai terrorists are Pakistanis, and in creating elaborate dossiers for the consumption of the world press and foreign governments, is a colossal waste. Instead, Prime Minister Manmohan Singh, who was also the home minister and the home secretary, as well as the external affairs minister, should have sincerely congratulated the people of Pakistan on their return to democracy. Mr Krishna should have told his counterpart that India was most anxious to render all possible assistance to Pakistan in strengthening its democracy and achieving economic prosperity. Mr Krishna should have conveyed to Mr Qureshi something like: 'You should trust your elder brother India; we only want a regime of complete peace and cooperation with you in solving all your major problems.' Only after creating the right atmosphere should Mr Krishna have gently conveyed to him that India realises water will be the biggest problem of the 21st century. India appreciates Pakistan's concern about water shortage. India will not add to Pakistan's difficulties but we will cooperate in finding new sources of water supply and will ensure a fair division of existing supplies. Eventually Mr Krishna should have touched on terrorism, hinting how, by a strange configuration of cosmic forces,

Pakistan itself is a victim and how eliminating terrorism is sure to benefit both India and Pakistan equally. What I am advocating is a Gandhian approach. I am sure it would have evoked a much more helpful response than the one we got by insisting on a confession of crime and culpability from the foreign minister of Pakistan.

However, despite this setback, India and Pakistan have to sort out their problems. The dialogue must resume and an honourable solution found for all pending disputes. Pakistan is not able to forget Kashmir and India cannot forget the imminent threat of terrorism, mainly or almost wholly exported from Pakistan or POK. The history of Indo-Pak relations firmly leads to the conclusion that India has trouble from Pakistan only when Pakistan ceases to be a democracy. It is unfortunate that time and again the Pakistan Army has supplanted the fragile democratic apparatus in Pakistan and established a military dictatorship. It is, therefore, in the interest of India to do everything in its power to strengthen the fragile democracy of Pakistan.

Terrorism is a threat to Pakistan's democracy

Terrorism is a scourge and Pakistan, although befriending terrorists, is not immune to it. Terrorism holds the country to ransom and limits the stands that can be taken to curb this menace. A genuine settlement between India and Pakistan on the issue of Kashmir will make the Pakistan Army retire to the barracks, and its revolving-door democracy stable for a change. Threats of war from India only serve to make Pakistan's democracy wobbly and vulnerable to its old internal enemies. India must try its best to ensure that Pakistan does not turn out to be a failed state. India and the United States are pledged to fight a war against terrorism. For this, our ministers need to focus on clear elimination of terrorism rather than catching a few and punishing them through our judicial process. India and the United States must persuade Pakistan to believe that terrorists are a threat to its fledgling democracy. It is in Pakistan's own interest to cooperate with us in exterminating this lethal virus. The three governments need to act together in order to destroy the terrorist *jihadists*. This action is urgently called for and must be undertaken before any *jihadist* organisation can lay its hands on nuclear weapons.

Although the war against terrorism cannot be fought without neutralising the states that foster, finance and harbour terrorism, I see neither courage nor inclination to pursue this goal. We know the birthplace of both Sunni and Shia terrorist organisations. Responsible nations must persuade the UN Security Council to take decisive action against these cradles of terror. If the Security Council's action is paralysed by the veto of an ally of one or the other nation, we must be prepared to act alone in the exercise of our right of self defence expressly recognised by the Charter of the United Nations.

It is time for the United Nations and the Security Council to intervene more meaningfully and effectively in all matters Pakistani. The US must talk to Pakistan frankly. It is impossible to accept Pakistan's lame defence that it was not aware of Osama living in the garrison city of Abbottabad right under the nose of the Pakistan Army. Washington should make it clear to Pakistan that if the money given to it for fighting terrorism is diverted to other purposes, it will not receive any aid ever again. Anything less than that will be tantamount to American complicity in the practice of terrorism, including the practice of terrorism against the US itself.

The United States is not short of responsible statesmen who have declared in unambiguous terms that Pakistan has proved to be a state sponsoring terror. Congressman Dana Rohrabacher, a senior member of the House Committee on Foreign Affairs and an experienced, influential policymaker is a typical representative of this class. He has introduced a Bill in the House of Representatives to stop all aid to Pakistan. The Congressman has even alluded to the November 2008 carnage in Mumbai. Pakistan's efforts to drive a wedge between the US and Afghanistan, obviously to curry favour with China, should also not go unnoticed. The role of China—though it has a lot to fear from Pakistani terrorists—is to be on the side of Pakistan and so to weaken India's position in the subcontinent.

As the need for sincere joint action increases, its possibility seems to diminish. Pakistan is now in conflict with the Security Council while relations with the USA, its long-standing ally on whose charity Pakistan's economy thrives, are on the verge of breakdown. Meanwhile, *jihadis* continue their rampage, fulfilling the Biblical prophecy of the Armageddon. A nuclear war will cause unbearable damage to India, but Pakistan may well not survive to enjoy it.

Hope for the future

Both Pakistan and India face stupendous problems in a century that is unique. It is a century of extremes, in which we have two options—we can either come together and usher in a new era for both countries, or, we can trigger a new Dark Age for humanity lost. We have to search for strategies to prevent further tragedies that lurk in our path and ensure a better world for ourselves and posterity.

At the beginning of the 21st century impartial economists were advising India and Pakistan that since before Partition we were an integrated economy, Partition of the country need not have drastically disrupted the existing economic arrangements. Unfortunately, the economic policies pursued by both countries since, could well be described as cutting-off one's nose to spite one's face.

An illustration would prove this. At the time of Partition, Pakistan was agriculturally more advanced, while India was industrially more advanced. Pakistan always had an abundance of jute, which the manufacturers in Kolkata absorbed. After Partition, Pakistan began to develop an independent jute industry. Politics based on communal hatred and suspicion took over and systematically tried to undo economic patterns and networks of centuries and generations. It was only after globalization that entrepreneurs in both countries turned towards ending this suicidal economic isolationist trend that had already destroyed millions of livelihoods. The compulsions of economics were inevitably creating a vested interest in each other's prosperity and a climate of peace for which all traders yearn.

Modern democracy has four fundamental commitments: adult franchise, equality of religion, gender equality and economic justice. We should steadfastly focus on these polestars. Let us also realise that governments and bureaucracies are not the only solution; they can be the biggest problem of any democracy. Civil society and its guardians who understand and possess the necessary will and commitment can achieve for our countries what our governments could not. We are facing malevolent monsters: climate change, violent religious extremism, abysmal poverty and war that could end civilisation. Unity, compassion and an embrace of love are the solutions. Governments often take obdurate positions, and it is tragic to see that every time we take a step forward in Indo-Pak relations, it is followed by dissonance and a breakdown of initiatives. Failed overtures have become the hallmark of the India Pakistan relationship. I firmly believe that it is the people of both nations who can make a difference, and must be heard.

Relations with Pakistan require the highest statesmanship. Partition and its horrible aftermath have unfortunately coloured our response to Pakistan. We cannot honestly claim that we have ever gone out of our way to win the hearts and minds of the people of that country. India has always been opposed to the two-nation theory, but we forget that Quaid-e-Azam Jinnah, the founder of Pakistan, had himself repudiated it as soon as he won independence for his state. He had declared that Pakistan would be a democratic, liberal and just state. It would live peaceably with its minority Hindu population and relations with India would be of friendship and cooperation. Unfortunately, Jinnah died soon after Partition and the first prime minister, Liaquat Ali Khan was cruelly assassinated. Its excellent first Constitution of March 1956 was superseded and luckless Pakistanis have had to suffer long and repeated spells of autocratic military rule.

The present is the chance to undo the past. Pakistan has got back its democracy; its warmongers are lying low; the establishment understands the futility of war and the Pak created monster of terrorism has now turned on its creator. War is not the option. A no-war pact with no loopholes and escape routes is the only option to pursue. Everything else will take care of itself.

2
Kashmir—Time to Move on

The Kashmir conundrum is probably one of the most vexatious and solution-resistant disputes in the contemporary world. It has the ingredients of everything portentous and worrisome: Kashmir's borders are international, touching Pakistan, China and Afghanistan. It was the hotbed of international intrigue during Independence and during the process of accession to India. Today, cross-border terrorism is *de rigeur*, and Jammu and Kashmir has become the favourite playground of the ISI. The Kashmir conundrum has divided communities and populations, brought untold miseries into the lives of the local population and created deep divisions in international politics.

Kashmir has always been the master of its own destiny

Jammu and Kashmir has always enjoyed a special status. During the Raj, it was not a part of British India but a semi-independent state affiliated to the British Crown by a special relationship, which came to be described as the 'paramountcy' of the British Crown. The contents of the relationship were never clearly defined, but it was understood that no ruler of any Indian princely state could negotiate with the British Crown or its representative, on a footing of equality. However, within this context, the princely state of Jammu and Kashmir was like an absolute monarchy under the Dogra ruler, Maharaja Hari Singh.

Post the public protests of 1931 the people of Kashmir started demanding democratic rights. In his speeches of defiance Sheikh Abdullah convincingly made two points: first, the Treaty of

Amritsar between the British and Raja Gulab Singh in 1846 was a sale-deed unacceptable to the people of Kashmir and required to be abrogated; second, the Maharaja should quit bag and baggage and leave Kashmiris alone to decide their own future. The Quit Kashmir Movement was started about half a decade after the Quit India Movement was launched. Sheikh Abdullah was arrested and prosecuted. His defence came from an Indian leader and criminal lawyer of outstanding abilities, the late Asaf Ali. Despite his brilliant advocacy Sheikh Sahib was jailed in May 1946.

The National Conference, under the leadership of Sheikh Abdullah, framed a manifesto of what was called 'New Kashmir,' which was unanimously approved on 30 September 1944. The manifesto was presented to Maharaja Hari Singh on his return from the Imperial War Cabinet. It required that all the people in the state of Jammu and Kashmir be guaranteed freedom of conscience and of worship. It further laid down that no citizen should be arrested or detained except by decision of a court of law. All citizens would have the right to receive guaranteed work and the right to rest. All students were to have the right to receive education, and scholarships were to be given to deserving poor students. Women citizens would be accorded equal rights with men in all fields of national life, and law should give special protection to the interests of mother and child.

The manifesto also required that the highest legislature of the state, the National Assembly, be elected by citizens of the state through electoral districts on the basis of one deputy per 40,000 persons for a period of five years. The Council of Ministers of the state should be responsible to the National Assembly. Section 27 of the manifesto required the position of the ruler to be reduced to that of a constitutional head.

This manifesto was clearly a promise of creating a secular democracy with constitutional guarantees of liberty in the state.

On the eve of Indian independence, the British Government made it very clear that paramountcy would lapse and whatever rights and privileges comprised paramountcy would revert to the state simultaneously with the coming into existence of the two dominions of India and Pakistan. In 1947, with independence and the departure of the British from India, the State of Jammu & Kashmir became wholly independent. The state had three alternatives: to join India freely, to join Pakistan freely or to remain independent without joining either of the two. One important issue remained unresolved: whether the rights of paramountcy reverted to the autocratic ruler of the state or to the people of the state. While Indian leaders pleaded that on the departure of the British, sovereignty vested in the King should revert to the people of every state, the Muslim League of India insisted that it should revert to the ruler, however incompetent, corrupt or autocratic. The Muslim League won and on 15 August 1947 the leaders of the National Conference as well as the Muslim Conference were in prison. The Maharaja was determined to remain independent and began negotiating Standstill Agreements with both the new dominions of India and Pakistan. Today, few people in Pakistan even realize that responsible government in Kashmir was postponed by the pleading of the Indian Muslim League and the leaders of Pakistan themselves. They ensured that the Maharaja became the sovereign.

The rest is history—invasion by Pak soldiers disguised as tribals, a panicky Maharaja approaching India for help; the instrument of accession; Indian Army reaching Srinagar when the invading tribals had practically reached the gates of the city; and the armistice agreement when the last invader was to be driven out from Kashmir.

Many of the problems of today's Kashmir are rooted in Pandit Nehru's unforgivable blunder of taking the Indian case to the Security Council. The seemingly naïve, (some called him arrogant), Pandit Nehru had no experience of the intricacies and pitfalls of international politics. Even the United Nations, partial though it was to Pakistan, mandated a plebiscite only on the condition that all Pakistan forces, regular and irregular, withdraw from the entire state and the plebiscite be held under the umbrella of Indian sovereignty. Pakistan knew that its local followers, the Muslim Conference, had no majority or adequate political hold over the people. The Sher-E-Kashmir and his National Conference were the real representatives of the people of the state and power was effectively transferred to them.

This does not, in any way, reduce the fact that it was the tribal invasion of 1947 that compelled the Maharaja to sign the Instrument of Accession. It was an unconditional, voluntary and absolute surrender of the subjects—defence, foreign affairs, communication and currency—to the federal Government of India at the Centre. A Constituent Assembly elected by Kashmiris was installed in 1951 and, in exercise of its independence and sovereignty, Kashmir became a part of the Indian Union. India does not own Kashmir, but its title deeds to sovereignty are legally and morally impeccable. The Constitution of India was not foisted on Kashmir, but was subsequently adopted in material parts by the sovereign Constituent Assembly of Kashmir. It is true that the Government of India had promised a plebiscite to confirm the accession, but the plebiscite was to be for the entire state, it had to be held under Indian sovereignty and Indian flag after every Pakistani soldier and civilian had withdrawn to their own country. Pakistan never fulfilled this condition. Instead it gave away a part of Kashmir to China, changed the demographic character of Pakistani portion of Kashmir and denied freedom and democracy to the area controlled by it. In perfect honesty, the Constitution makers of India added Article 370* to its own Constitution. As the famous Campbell Johnson in his book *Mission with Mountbatten* wrote: 'The legality of the accession is beyond doubt... It should be stressed that the accession has complete validity both in terms of the British Government's and Jinnah's expressed policy statements.'

In 1948 the National Conference formed the interim government in the state. It was expressly declared that as soon as normal conditions were restored, steps would be taken to convene a National Assembly based upon adult suffrage to frame a Constitution for the state. In September 1951, the Jammu and Kashmir Constituent Assembly was established to carry out this great task. This is azadi at its highest as can be seen from the declaration which was made on that historic day:

'Today is our day of destiny. A day which comes only once in the life of a nation ... after centuries we have reached the harbor of our freedom which for the first time in history will enable the people of

---

*Article 370 of the Constitution of India grants special autonomous status to the state of Jammu and Kashmir. Despite repeated and strident calls that it be repealed, the Article remains. Article 370 is part of the original draft Constitution of India and forms an integral part of it. The concurrence of the Constituent Assembly of Jammu and Kashmir, which no longer exists, would be required before any change could be made to the status of this Article. In addition, to repeal this Article would be unconstitutional and therefore illegal as repealing it would be to alter the 'basic structure' of the Constitution of India which, as articulated in Article 368 of the Constitution, is clearly beyond the purview of any Amendment to the Constitution.

Jammu & Kashmir, whose duly elected representatives are gathered here, to shape the future of their country after wise deliberation and mould their future organs of the government. No person and no power can stand between them and the fulfilment of this their historic task...'

The Preamble of the free Constitution of Jammu & Kashmir states:

'We, the people of the State of Jammu and Kashmir, having solemnly resolved, in pursuance of the accession of this State to India which took place on the twenty-sixth day of October, 1947, to further define the existing relationship of the State with the Union of India as an integral part thereof, and to secure to ourselves

'Justice, social, economic and political; Liberty of thought, expression, belief, faith and worship;

'Equality of status and of opportunity; and to promote among us all; Fraternity assuring the dignity of the individual and the unity of the nation.

'In our Constituent Assembly this seventeenth day of November, 1956, we do hereby adopt, enact and give to ourselves this constitution.'

Commentators and sympathizers of the Kashmiri problem would do well to remember that the Constitution of India was not foisted upon the State and that it applies only in those parts that have been voluntarily accepted by the people of Jammu & Kashmir. The state is primarily governed by its own Constitution, unlike any other state in India, and Kashmir has voluntarily become part of a free, progressive, secular republic. That is azaadi, the highest political freedom a citizen can hope for. People who are blessed with genuine democracy, with constitutionally protected rights and duties of individuals, and an independent judiciary to enforce them, have attained true azaadi. Any violent action to secure more of it, or of a different kind or content, is a crime of terrorism or treason or both.

Pakistan and India must be transparent in their dealings with the local populations on both sides of the Line of Control in Kashmir. The international community must be able to certify that there is no colonial-style exploitation of their material resources. The Kashmir problem is not insurmountable and could have been solved long ago, but the political will and adroitness to do so has been lacking. If the president of Pakistan is ready for negotiation, the prime minister of India has to be willing. If parties like the BJP advocate immediate cessation of diplomatic relations, the people of India should, and will, dismiss it as political bankruptcy and electoral insanity.

Pakistan is the enemy of Kashmiriyat

Sindh, where I was born, was the cradle of Sufism. Our greatest poet, Shah Abdul Latif, was a disciple of Hindu mendicants and preached the gospel of love and charity, and the annihilation of the ego. A breathtaking and magnificent synthesis of the two faiths, Hinduism and Islam, had been achieved in Sindhi society. Hindu children got new clothes on Eid, and Muslim children on Deepawali. Quaid-e-Azam Jinnah did not get the partition resolution passed in the Sindh Assembly until its chief minister, Allah Bux Soomro, was shot dead in broad daylight in the town of Shikarpur. I have believed that Sufism is the essence of Islam. My love for Kashmir is based on my belief that Kashmiriyat is just another name for Sufism. Lal Ded, the famous Shaivite yogini and a rebel against the caste system of Hindus, propounded for Kashmir the gentle Sufi version of Islam, very much like Shah Abdul Latif of Sindh.

Shaikh Nuruddin, the scion of the Rishi family of Kashmir regarded Lal Ded as his spiritual mentor and prayed to god that she grant him her spiritual power. I had hoped that Kashmiris would become the philosophical and spiritual gurus of modern India.

Today, Pakistan is exterminating the Sufis. The Sindhi Muslim is angry and would like to secede from Pakistan. It is tragic that hard-line elements in Kashmir are party to a satanic conspiracy to hand over the valley of Kashmir to the enemies of Sufism and Kashmiriyat.

Kashmir Committee—finding solutions based on people's aspirations and dialogue

Constantly drumming the oft repeated argument of the Pakistani establishment and some of its Kashmir supporters, that the Kashmir struggle is the unfinished business of partition, is pointless. To move forward, it must be recognized that even in 1947 the Muslim majority states were not as a whole allowed to seceede from India and join Pakistan. The provinces of Punjab, Bengal and Assam had to be sub-divided. It is more than clear that the inhabitants of Ladakh, a region which is almost two-thirds the area of the whole state, the inhabitants of Jammu and the inhabitants of Baltistan want passionately to remain united with India. They are completely opposed to joining Pakistan and have no desire for independence. The real dispute ultimately boils down to the Kashmir valley, an area approximately 84 miles in length and 84 miles in width, as against Ladakh, which alone is about 33,500 square miles. Although it sounds like a petty dispute on the face of it, the overtones and emotions are so strong that the Kashmir Valley has been the cause of three wars between Pakistan and India during the last 50 years; strains of violence that explode every now and then, recurring cross border terrorism; and incalculable human and economic loss.

Since it is impossible to rewrite history, there is no point revising our mistakes or lost opportunities since 1947. Undoubtedly there have been many, such as the minor one where my friend Inder Gujral lost the opportunity of including Pakistan in the Gujral Doctrine for economic cooperation; or the debacle of the Shimla Agreement between Indira Gandhi and Zulfiqar Ali Bhutto, or Prime Minister H.D. Deve Gowda's declaration that India was prepared to talk to Pakistan, but the talks would cover every issue except Jammu & Kashmir, to mention just a few. The more practical thing to do would be to discard the accumulated baggage of the stated positions of decades that have multiplied and compounded into a complex web, and start afresh on a new slate.

Politically, it is true that some Kashmiris did not want Indian overlordship. Despite this, Pakistan knew that Kashmiris would not automatically plump for Pakistan. A negotiated settlement seemed a viable solution. It was then that BJP Prime Minister Atal Behari Vajpayee decided to negotiate with the Hurriyat Conference led by its new head Abbas Ansari. A Kashmir Committee, of which I was a member, was also formed at this time to assist in finding a solution to the Kashmir conundrum. Around 2002, the Kashmir Committee opened negotiations with the Hurriyat Conference. A serious search for a settlement which left no one disgruntled, defeated or humiliated was on and the Kashmir Committee's confabulations with the Hurriyat sowed the seeds for peace in the form of an agreement reached with five salient features:

1. Terrorism and violence are taboo.
2. A lasting and honourable peaceful resolution must and can be found.

3. The resolution must be acceptable to all political elements and regions of the state.
4. Extremist positions held by all for the previous five decades have to be and will be abandoned.
5. Kashmiri Pandits will be rehabilitated with honour and rights of equality.

A careful understanding of the five points of the agreement show that abrogation of Article 370 of the Constitution of India on the one hand and secession on the other were consciously and finally abandoned. The polestar of the peace process would thereafter be the legitimate interests and rational expectations of all elements and regions in the composite state.

This agreement brought joy to every Indian and to most Kashmiris. The moderate section of the Hurriyat had repudiated the extremists and, at the same time, carried on talking to the Kashmir Committee with the full concurrence of the Pakistan authorities. It is tragic that the usual wooden-headedness of the Government of India blocked a formal solution. At the International Kashmir Peace Conference held in Washington, my friend Ashraf Jehangir Kazi, the distinguished ambassador of Pakistan to the United States argued that the Kashmir Committee had initiated a process of acceptable change. If anyone refuses to accept this, it would only show that he is an enemy of peace, regardless of his pretended postures and rhetorical assertions. Since then, the State of Jammu & Kashmir has held elections, which, unlike the earlier ones, were acclaimed by the entire international community as free and fair following which a democratically elected government has functioned in the state, doubtless causing frustration to the sympathizers of Pakistan, overt and covert. An all-party-parliamentary delegation toured the state and revived the dialogue in 2010. This limited agreement shows that the Kashmir problem is not unsolvable. In fact, it had almost reached a solution on two occasions during its long and tragic tenure—first, when the Australian jurist, Sir Owen Dixon headed the five-member UN Commission for India and Pakistan, and second, when the Tashkent Declaration was signed. The first was frustrated by Pandit Jawaharlal Nehru and the second was set at naught by his daughter, Indira Gandhi, both of whom reached the highest positions in Indian life and politics.

Unfortunately, the exit of the BJP government after the 2004 elections proved a major setback in resolving the Kashmir issue. The new United Progressive Alliance (UPA) government did not want any interference in conducting the Indo-Pak dialogue. The Committee almost suspended the excellent, results-focused work it was doing although we kept appealing to the Hurriyat not to backtrack on the agreements achieved. However, in October 2010, the Government of India appointed a set of interlocutors—Dilip Padgaonkar, Radha Kumar and M.M Ansari—with the mission of taking the peace process further after due consultations with the several stakeholders in Jammu & Kashmir. Mr Dilip Padgaonkar was my colleague in the Kashmir Committee, but I do not have the pleasure of knowing the other two interlocutors personally. This does not detract from their stature or merit. Whispers around Delhi suggested that while the interlocutors were sincerely trying to talk to the people of J&K, they were scarcely talking to one another. This subsequently appears to have blown up into a full scale war, after it was discovered that two of the three interlocutors accepted hospitality from the ISI-funded Ghulam Nabi Fai to attend conferences in plush capitals of Europe and the US. Till date, the interlocutors have made no significant contribution to the peace process.

The formula for a final settlement of the Kashmir problem or the Indo-Pak dispute about Kashmir remains elusive although the problem is not insurmountable. The Kashmir Committee saw hope in the National Conference proposal for additional autonomy, the PDP proposal for self rule and the settlements proposed during President Musharraf's visit to India. Each provided a good starting point for a constructive dialogue and a sincere search for solutions.

Such an opportunity existed when President Pervez Musharraf was in power in Pakistan. In line with the decision of the Supreme Court of Canada in the Quebec Secession Case reported in 1998 (2) SCR 217, the Kashmir Committee proposed a solution on the following lines:

1. India and Pakistan must ensure self-determination on both sides of the LOC; in other words, a secular democracy in which religious, ethnic and linguistic minorities enjoy the full package of civil and political rights. The governments

of both sides must owe their legitimacy to free elections and adult franchise.
2. Governments on both sides must fully protect the basic rights of citizens, which in the final analysis, must be declared and enforced by a wholly independent judiciary.
3. Both governments must have full legislative and executive control over all subjects except that the two central governments will exercise jurisdiction and authority only in respect of those subjects which strictly and directly are related to the subjects of foreign relations, defence, communications and currency.
4. The continued existence of democratic governments and Rule of Law on both sides will be guaranteed by the United Nations as if there is a treaty to that effect between India and Pakistan.
5. A committee, the composition of which will be settled by agreement and which will consist of the representatives of India and Pakistan as well as the two state governments, shall ensure that central authority is not used in the state in a manner directly or indirectly amounting to colonial exploitation of any kind. The suggestion of this prestigious body will be implemented in good faith by the two governments. Any dispute between the two governments will be settled by arbitration, mediation or judicial adjudication, but never by force.
6. For this purpose, the Government of India and the Government of Pakistan will set up consulates in Muzaffarabad and Srinagar respectively, which will be charged specifically with the duty of encouraging free movement of citizens, goods and services.
7. Any attempt, overt or covert, by Government of India or Government of Pakistan to alter this arrangement will be considered aggression as defined in international law and would compulsorily attract intervention by the UN Security Council.
8. It will be the obligation of Government of India and Government of Pakistan to protect the two state governments from external aggression and internal rebellion and disorder. The details of this proposal can be worked out by experts

acting in good faith and commitment to peace and friendship between the two nations.

In substance, these proposals prompted a draft from Gen. Musharraf, which was ultimately published by the Kashmir Committee as its own proposal to Government of India. It is a pity that Government of India remained absolutely indifferent.

And so, we missed the bus a third time.

The People's Democratic Party (PDP) proposals of 2009 on Self Rule can be the starting point of a fruitful dialogue. An all-party conference on Kashmir was held in Delhi, where representatives of every shade of opinion in the state were present. Of course, there were no representatives of what we call the Pakistan occupied Kashmir (POK). The Hurriyat, however, was well represented by Professor Abdul Ghani Bhat. The well known leader, Muzaffar Beg of the PDP, presented a paper entitled *'Jammu & Kashmir: The Self-Rule Framework for Resolution'*. I have read and re-read the document with care and empathy. Although the document is somewhat confusing, it is clearly well intentioned, and its apparent ambiguities and contradictions obviously stem from attempting to reconcile the conflicting interests that have made the problem nearly insurmountable. I sincerely hope I am not wrong in my conclusion that the PDP plan does not stand for secession from India.

The preface declares, 'The essence of this document lies in trying to suggest a creative framework for resolution of the issue without compromising the sovereignty of the two nation states involved.' Wisely, it argues that 'a return to the past is neither possible nor desirable. The past offers no hope. The world has undergone a change and we have to be a part of that changed system.' Its Executive Summary makes it clear that the concept of Self Rule as a political philosophy is being articulated around federalism and confederation that allow for sharing of power between two levels of government. The basic premise of the new strategy is peace through economic reconstruction. This reconstruction of the state's economy has been designed in a manner that supports the transition from conflict to peace through the rebuilding of the economic framework.

Although the paper makes a strong case for the demilitarization of the state, it also recognizes that this must be preceded by demilitarization of the mindset of the people involved. While rejecting plebiscite for carrying a huge baggage of rhetoric and a possibility of arousing of polemical furies, it hopes that the market will override the Line of Control. Finally, it leaves nobody in doubt that the PDP rejects secession from India by declaring that some provisions of the Indian Constitution applicable to the state would be retained, though some may have to be rolled back according to the genuine requirement of both the Union and the State.

Government of India should have welcomed this paper and started a serious dialogue with all political elements involved, but it is too much to expect from a government that is totally bereft of out-of-the-box political acumen. The 79th paragraph of the paper reads: 'PDP believes that the unity of the State reflects the essence of our secular culture, and its preservation is of the utmost critical importance, both on principle and for legitimate strategic reasons.'

This should have gathered all the disparate political elements in the state to commend this paper as the core of the dialogue between India and Pakistan.

To quote my friend Mani Shankar Aiyar's article in Tehelka, 'The dialogue must be uninterrupted and uninterruptible'—a phrase he has been trying to sell to the people for the last 20 years.

In March 2012 prominent members of the Bar Association of India had an occasion to interact with a high-powered delegation of lawyers from Pakistan led by Asma Jahangir, President of the Pakistan Supreme Court Bar Association. The dialogue was constructive and fruitful. Some of the key points on which we achieved unanimous agreement were:

1. The two governments shall forthwith denounce war as an instrument of national policy and enter into a 'no war' treaty, which shall be registered with the United Nations. The obligation shall be absolute without any loopholes or escape routes.
2. All disputes shall be solved by negotiation or agreed mediation.
3. The unsettled ones shall be settled by decision of agreed judicial tribunal and, failing that, by reference to the International Court of Justice if the dispute is of justiciable character, and in other cases by arbitration of agreed arbitrators or by the International Arbitration Tribunal in existence.
4. A permanent advisory body of the two Bar Associations shall be created with equal representatives of the two associations

to educate public opinion and bring democratic pressure to bear on both governments to act on and enforce these resolutions as early as possible.

Some Indian lawyers and I visited Pakistan and our interaction with various elements of Pakistani politics strengthened our belief that a constructive dialogue can produce a solution. It was then that we revived the Kashmir Committee and even secured the services of two new members.

The Committee visited the Kashmir Valley in June 2011. Practically every element of the political and social landscape met us, some at our invitation and many more on their own. The only exceptions were Yasin Malik and Chief Minister Omar Abdullah. Even Syed Ali Shah Geelani spoke of peace and non-violence. Hardly anyone spoke of secession. Everyone wanted a compromise or recognized the need for give and take.

The Committee also visited Jammu in July 2011. Every political party representative complained of neglect. It was the day students had been attacked by the police for peacefully demanding a vice-chancellor for the local university. We visited the police station and found the SHO more sensible than many politicians. The visit pleased almost everyone and media reports of the time were most encouraging. *The Northlines*, a leading newspaper of Jammu and Kashmir carried an article on 25 July 2011 that said, 'The three-member Kashmir Committee, headed by Ram Jethmalani, seems to have outclassed the government appointed three-member interlocutors, led by Dilip Padgaonkar, as far as the range of interaction with the cross section of the society is concerned. Political leaders, Kashmiri displaced people, students, and members from the sector of industry and bar have shown keener interest in their meetings with the team led by Jethmalani during its current visit to Jammu.'

The way the Kashmir Committee has had free and fair discussion with separatists, both moderates and hardliners, in the Kashmir valley last month indicated that it had better acceptability among the separatists than the interlocutors. During their series of visits to the Kashmir valley separatists, both moderates and hardliners, refused to interact with the interlocutors.'

The people of J&K have been open about their problems. They have spoken about the misuse of the Public Safety Act, corruption in the government machinery, poverty and the lack of opportunities for economic and human resource development, lack of infrastructure and power etc. The Kashmir Committee intends to undertake multipronged initiatives to address these issues, particularly public interest litigations regarding illegal detention cases under the Public Safety Act—a practice that is rampant in Omar Abdullah's government.

It will be the endeavour of our Kashmir Committee to facilitate negotiations between all parties to bring about peace in J&K. In the process we will also try and reach the hearts and minds of the people and solve their day-to-day problems that depend so much on the State and Central governments.

AFSPA is not as draconian as it is made out to be

One of the issues of contention for the people of Kashmir is the Armed Forces Special Powers Act (AFSPA). It is true that AFSPA is an inheritance of our colonial past with an Ordinance of the same name promulgated in 1942 to counter the Quit India Movement, and the desertion of British Indian soldiers to join the Indian National Army, conferring vaguely defined special powers to the armed forces to arrest and use force, even kill, civilians on mere suspicion. In 1958, the Ordinance was converted into the present AFSPA and enforced in the northeast while the state of Jammu and Kashmir has been under AFSPA since 1990. The Bill was introduced by Govind Ballabh Pant, then union home minister, who remarked while introducing it, 'This is a very simple measure. It only seeks to protect the steps the armed forces might have to take in the disturbed areas... It will be applied only to such parts as have been declared by the administrations concerned as being disturbed... After such a declaration has been made, then alone the provisions of this Bill will be applicable to that particular area. I do not think it is necessary for me to say more in this connection. It is a simple measure.'

It should be remembered that the Armed Forces (Jammu & Kashmir) Special Powers Act, 1990, of which complaints are now being made by some mischief mongers, was not foisted on Jammu & Kashmir by the Indian Parliament. It was done with the concurrence of the state government. It is open to the state government to withdraw its concurrence and request the repeal of the Act or its suspension. The request will virtually be binding if it is shown that the state is no longer a disturbed area.

Let us look at what the Act does. It confers upon members of the Armed Forces the following powers:

(a) Any commissioned officer, warrant officer, non-commissioned officer or any other person of equivalent rank in the armed forces may open fire if he/she is of the opinion that any person is acting in contravention or breach of any law or order;
(b) He/she may destroy any arms dump or any structure used as training camp for armed volunteers or utilized as a hide-out by armed gangs wanted for any offence;
(c) Arrest, without warrant, any person who has committed a cognizable offence or against whom a reasonable suspicion exists that he/she has committed or is about to commit a cognizable offence;
(d) Enter and search, without warrant, any premises to make any such arrest as aforesaid;
(e) Stop, search and seize any vehicle reasonably suspected to be carrying any person who is a proclaimed offender;
(f) Power of search to include powers to break open locks; etc.

The Act grants immunity to members of the armed forces taking part in these operations.

Let us examine powers (a) and (b).

Power (b) although wide in its scope, does not deserve to be called draconian. In the first place, it does not involve the killing of innocent persons. It may involve the destruction of some property, which may not have been actually used as a training camp for creating terrorists or providing them with hideouts. But if that action is a *bona fide* mistake, it may call for compensation by the government to the owners of the lost property. That is justice enough. It is worth noticing that this power has hardly been used and there have been no serious complaints about the misuse of this power.

It is only power (a) which is somewhat too wide. It justifies the armed forces firing in case of any breach of law or order. This has the potential to result in unjustified firing and loss of life in some situations. It undoubtedly behooves the army personnel, in whom this power is vested, to exercise it with great care and only against imminent terrorist factions. Those who want the withdrawal of this power should be prepared to compose its catalogue of unjustified firing episodes. I do not believe that this power has been misused frequently or on a large scale.

The leaders of our armed forces are patriotic, sober people. They do not go about shooting innocent persons. Though I am willing to concede that there must have been some unfortunate cases of this kind, mercifully, they have been very rare. Besides, the so-called powers of the armed forces are not powers, but duties. They are the duties of ordinary police officers, which the Army is always most reluctant to perform. There will be no need to keep that Army if the people of Jammu & Kashmir take on the responsibility of defending its frontiers from infiltrators and terrorists, imported or indigenous. Kashmir is the master of its own destiny. This is what the interlocutors should explain to the people.

I do not believe that this law must be withdrawn in the present circumstances. However, the state government as well as the central government must appoint a small committee of credible citizens to inquire and report on the misuse of this power and take the steps necessary to control its misuse.

Indian leadership that talks for the separatists

AFSPA can only be removed when there is a conducive environment and terrorists are neither being exported into India nor supported by our neighbours.

Jammu and Kashmir Chief Minister Omar Abdullah made a dramatic announcement on 21 October 2011 at a Police Commemoration Day function, that some parts of the state might do away with AFSPA within days, as the security situation had improved and there was peace in these areas. Perhaps the young chief minister spoke too soon. He did not realize what was happening in Pakistan. The situation there is tragic beyond measure. Our unfortunate neighbour is witnessing the rise and growth of Islamic militant groups that are threatening not only India but also the very society that sustains them.

Despite the Pakistan government's sincere efforts, *jihadi* groups continue to thrive with the tacit support of sections of the military and intelligence establishments. It is no exaggeration to say that

Pakistan is now on the verge of Talibanisation. Pakistan, and indeed the United States, cannot deny that the Taliban, a monster they created, is now out to devour its own creator. The Afghans have complained that the radical Islam of the Taliban has spread from the religious seminaries of Pakistan where Taliban leaders were trained. These seminaries attracted enormous Saudi funds and were accompanied by the dangerous Wahabi creed. Despite long commitments, Pakistan has not yet decided to live in complete peace with India. Young Omar should realize that any talk of wholly or partially withdrawing the AFSPA from some areas is dangerous and subversive to India's security.

Omar Abdullah's dramatic statement evoked a smorgasbord of reactions, touching upon everything except the real issue. The Congress representatives, including Saifuddin Soz, reprimanded the chief minister for announcing important policy measures without consulting them. PDP Chief Mehbooba Mufti said that the 'AFSPA issue is being used to divert attention of the people from the custodial death of the NC (National Conference) worker'. Mirwaiz Umar Farooq, of the Hurriyat Conference stated 'if pro-India political parties in Kashmir are really sincere, they can repeal the Disturbed Areas Act on the floor of the J&K Legislative Assembly to make the AFSPA null and void.' Omar's political friends in Delhi, including the prime minister, Sonia Gandhi, home minister, finance minister and defence minister heard him and gave him a polite cold shoulder, advising him to wait for a few months before rushing into partial revocation of the AFSPA in his state. BJP leaders strongly criticized the move on grounds of national security. The Army's response was predictable—they opposed even partial lifting of AFSPA from the state, saying it would 'hamper the Army's operations against terrorists and their network in the state.' The Ministry of Defence and the Army said it would be a dangerous move as militancy was still rampant, infiltration was on the rise and terror training camps flourished in Pakistan Occupied Kashmir; that once the AFSPA is withdrawn from an area, it would be 'politically' difficult to re-impose the Act if trouble on the terror front arose again. There would be a massive public outcry against any such move and the state government would not be able to handle it. Pakistan's ISI and terror outfits would use the non-AFSPA window to consolidate in these areas. The Army also contended that going by past experience, one peaceful summer cannot be the benchmark for revoking the

Act, and that in the wake of the US withdrawal from Afghanistan, Pakistan is sure to become more adventurous in Kashmir.

While Omar Abdullah was talking to Delhi, there was a series of blasts in and around Srinagar on 25 October 2011, the eve of Diwali. Omar toned down and conceded that more discussions were required, that his effort was to reach the goal of partial withdrawal of the AFSPA and simultaneously allay the apprehensions of the armed forces. He added that 'I am not in the business of playing politics with national security. The effort is to narrow the differences between what we would like to see happening, and what the Army has so far publicly stated...'

One wonders how the chief minister of a state can make such irresponsible and unconsidered statements. View, for example, Omar Abdullah's statements of January 2011 when he objected to the plan to hoist the tricolor at Lal Chowk on the occasion of Repulic Day. Why should a chief minister of one of the states of India object to hoisting the national flag? The flag expresses the external sovereignty of India and, internally, the dedication of all Indians 'to the service of the nation to the end that this ancient land attain her rightful and honourable place in the world and make her full and effective contribution to the promotion of world peace and the welfare of mankind.'

Article 51A in the Chapter on Fundamental Duties and Fundamental Principles of governance makes it the sacred obligation of every citizen of India to respect the national flag. It is a reminder of the ideals and institutions for which the Constitution enjoys the affection and respect of every decent Indian. It is time all Kashmiris understood that they owe a debt of gratitude to India. Their autonomy and prosperity are India's priceless gift to them.

One of the earliest pieces of legislation, The Emblem & Names (Prevention of Improper Use) Act, 1950 makes it a serious criminal offence to trample upon or otherwise bring into contempt the national flag of India. Another emblem enjoying the same protection and dignity is the national anthem. Section 3 of the Act makes it a criminal offence to prevent anyone from singing the Anthem or causing disturbance to any assembly wanting to sing it. To prevent any person from hoisting the national flag at a public place is also an offence under the Act. I find Omar Abdullah's objections unpalatable.

A reported judgement the Supreme Court of India has thus settled the law. The constitutional right of Freedom of Speech and Expression includes the exhibition and planting of the flag by every individual provided it is done in a respectful manner. No government can interfere with this right of an individual or a group of individuals to unfurl the flag and let it fly so long as it does not interfere with the legal rights of somebody else. The action constitutes expression and manifestation of his feelings and sentiments of pride in the nation.

It would have been easy to understand the terrorist element in Kashmir and the said agents of Pakistan objecting to the hosting of the flag in a public place, but it is difficult to forgive Omar Abdullah, the grandson of the Sher-E-Kashmir, temporarily joining that odious class of mischief makers. The only extenuating circumstance for young Omar is that he lost his courage to fight the practitioners of mayhem and murder whose number seems to be increasing in the valley under the influence of Pakistani incitement and money. Some people may well forgive the inexperienced Omar, but it is impossible to condone the despicable action and attitude of the Congress, the entire central government and of course the prime minister and the president of the Congress Party. The opinion of Rahul Gandhi, touted as the heir apparent, is also of interest here. Did he concur with the decision of the government that the flag should not be hoisted at Lal Chowk? If he did, he should have the honesty to proclaim to the people of India why he indulged in such shameful action.

That some hired goons will create disorder is not a justification for destroying the constitutional rights of millions of people who would have been proud if the Tricolour was seen spreading the message of love and loyalty to India and the civilized world from Srinagar's Lal Chowk. The Constitution of India cannot be trampled upon by a few criminals. An offence has been committed by the leaders of the Congress who virtually joined the ranks of terrorists by advising the BJP to desist from hoisting the flag and conniving with the police assault on them when they reached the state.

Such acts call into question the moral integrity of the Congress party and its allies.

The politics of a nay sayer

This brings me to the question of Mr Syed Ali Shah Geelani's motives and motivations. I have attempted to bring him to a reasonable forum of discussion regarding his grouses, wish-list and the undertakings he is willing to give as a leader of the Hurriyat. Unfortunately, Mr Geelani, despite the eminent position he holds in Kashmiri society, has proved to be a road-block in the peace process. The areas of concern are:

1. The basic motivation of the movement appears to be hatred of Hindus as non-believers and infidels. The dynamo of the so-called Kashmir Movement was a counterfeit Islam which had no resemblance to the great Islam of the Holy Quran or the teachings of its Great Prophet.
2. In 1990, the Jammu and Kashmir Liberation Front had declared in unequivocal terms, 'Islam is our soul, our faith. We do not believe in any other ideology. We are dedicated only to the cause of an Islamic republic. We want to bring about Nizam-e-Mustafa in toto.'
3. This is of major concern to India, a secular country which has more Muslims than Pakistan, most of whom want non-Muslims to be wholly secular. India is struggling to maintain its secular convictions and policies. How can we allow a single Indian citizen to be left at the mercy of stone-pelting hooligans who do not understand the sublimity and grandeur of religions, including that of their own? We have spoken to the Hurriyat of the plight of the Kashmiri Pandits who had been driven out of their ancient homes and are living like refugees in their own country. We cannot condemn them to that sorry fate from which they cannot be redeemed, once they lose the protection of India's secular Constitution.
4. My next concern is whether Mr Geelani and his cohorts are prepared to undertake that there will be a wholly democratic and secular dispensation in any territory that is allowed to secede from India. What will be the guarantee that the undertaking will not be broken?

Why is there such a pro-Pakistan sentiment and how will it benefit the people of Jammu and Kashmir? The standard of living in Pakistan Occupied Kashmir or what is called 'Azad Kashmir', or even the Northern Territories is by no means better than on the Indian side of the Line of Control. Pakistan is suffering from constant instability. Its democracy is fragile and one cannot predict for how long the army and the ISI will remain confined to their barracks. No rational argument has been presented for cessation, which should be based on the real interests of the inhabitants of the valley or which would provide them with the blessings of democracy, assuming they are genuinely thirsting for it.

Pakistan had established, particularly after 1962, a very durable and friendly relationship with China. According to every patriotic Indian, India was a victim of unprovoked Chinese aggression, and China is in illegal occupation of vast tracts of Indian territory. Although the Hurriyat and its friends in Pakistan do not care for the feelings of India's citizens, the Hurriyat claims to stand for Kashmiris. How then can it ignore the fact that 42,000 sq miles of Jammu & Kashmir territory have been ceded to the Chinese by the Government of Pakistan? The Hurriyat has never protested against this Pakistani action, nor shown the slightest concern for the Kashmiri inhabitants of the ceded territory. They are China's slaves, with neither azadi nor *jamhooriyat*, nor with any guaranteed human rights enjoyed by citizens. The Hurriyat is supremely indifferent to their fate, which is an inconvenience for those playing mercenary politics and depending on Pakistan for a livelihood.

Mr Geelani clearly does not speak on behalf of all Hurriyat leaders. He has had extreme differences with many who appeared genuinely inclined to arrive at an honourable, durable and peaceful settlement with India, and his obduracy is an attempt to humiliate and frustrate the moderate Hurriyat leaders and the search for an honourable solution.

As the moderates told Mr Geelani, 'We have all lived on Pakistan's finances, but while we have stopped, you are still in their payroll.' A telling statement on the shift in the mainstream of the Hurriyat. As a citizen of India, Syed Ali Shah Geelani must give up his overt and covert anti-state activities that not only bring him disrepute but polarize communities and make aliens of many loyal muslims.

Home-grown terrorism—making criminals of the innocent

In October 2010, I read the following: 'German intelligence officials have the knowledge that 2,000 residents of this wealthy port city (Hamburg) embrace radical Islamic ideology. They have conceded that 45 of them are supporters of Al Qaeda and global jihad and that others have travelled to Pakistan for terrorist training... There is no dispute that we face an intense abstract danger.' Homegrown terrorism exists even in Germany. As the reports said, 'The recruiting, the radicalisation happens right here, not in other countries.'

Ahmed Sidiqui, a German national and an airport employee, who had travelled to Pakistan with 10 others, had told his interrogators that Al Qaeda was planning to stage attacks in cities across Europe that would mimic the terrorist assault on Mumbai. It is to be remembered that one of the 11 September 2001 terrorists, Mohammad Atta, had studied in Hamburg and was meeting his compatriots in a local mosque called Al Quds. The Hamburg administration was, needless to say, extremely anxious. Suddenly, every one of the 130,000 muslim residents of Hamburg became a suspect and object of hate, even those who themselves hate terrorists.

My thoughts immediately turned to Kashmir.

Religion may have brought hope and comfort to some, but it has a terribly negative balance sheet. It is no exaggeration that all the ships of all the navies in the world can float comfortably in the ocean of innocent blood that has been shed in its name. I respect religious freedom, but only subject to public order, health and morality. My religion is to make as many people happy as I can. The secular Constitution of India mandates a life guided by reason and inspired by love.

Kashmir, like Hamburg, is beginning to rear home grown terrorists—indoctrinated to spread hate and violence and make all Muslims suspect in their loyalty to Mother India.

I have been an ardent supporter of the Rule of Law. I have defended Muslims charged with terrorism in the firm belief that if we cannot protect the right to a fair trial of even hated terrorists, the Indian state would become a terrorist itself. But today that faith is becoming shaky. Must we protect one criminal and endanger the lives and security of thousands of innocent, unarmed men, women and children?

The *International Herald Tribune* of 11 October 2010 carried an article by Jack Goldsmith, a Harvard professor and member of Hoover Institute's Task Force on National Security and Law, titled 'Don't Try Terrorists; Lock Them Up'. Is this the writing on the wall for all Muslims accused of terrorist activities? It would indeed be tragic for the free world if fear and suspicion override our natural desire for fair trial and justice for all.

India has with some hesitation got rid of draconian laws of preventive detention like TADA and POTA. Some governments may well resort to the old expedients and justify the action as a measure of absolute necessity. I am in sympathy with the demand that the Army's special powers be taken away, but the Government of India can well argue, 'Deserve before you desire.'

3
China—Counter the Dragon Before It Is too Late

The shadow of the Chinese aggression of 1962 and our abysmal and humiliating defeat, in which we lost 93,000 sq. miles of Indian territory hangs over us till today. Although both Houses of Parliament passed unanimous resolutions accusing China of perfidy and affirming our resolve to drive out the aggressor however long the struggle may be, no prime minister thereafter has even dared to publicly recall the broken promise, much less to make it good. Nor have successive governments in India become any wiser after Chou En-lai successfully conned Pandit Nehru regarding his real intentions. Nehru died a broken man, his credibility badly exposed and his non-alignment in shambles.

Passive Indian leadership and diplomacy—compounding humiliation

Over the years, the initial humiliation wreaked by the Chinese has been compounded by India's passivity, almost tantamount to cowardice, which has been presented to a gullible and uninformed populace as acts of supreme statesmanship. Indira Gandhi's actions in 1976, Atal Behari Vajpayee's visit to China two years later, and the youthful Rajiv Gandhi's uncalled for trip to China in December 1988, obtained nothing useful except for a joint working group of officials to eternally discuss disputes without resolving anything. All this while the Chinese continue to maintain that India was the aggressor in 1962, and have claimed further 99,000 square miles of our territory.

In 1993, Prime Minister Narasimha Rao gratuitously gifted the Chinese a concession that must have pleased them beyond measure. He declared that the McMahon Line was not accurately drawn, thereby justifying the Chinese intrusions into India held territory. The Chinese are using this abdication as a reference point even now.

Rajiv Gandhi's treaty of peace and tranquility in December 1988 was a clear reversal of our national pledge of 1962. It was a boon to the Chinese and a shameless betrayal of Indian interests.

India's diplomatic debacles in its dealings with China are legion. Numerous joint working groups have been set-up and maps exchanged but no progress has been made in influencing the Chinese establishment on our border disputes. We have followed a policy of appeasement, be it Aksai Chin, the McMahon Line, Arunachal and Kashmir, stapled visas, trade, or terrorism. Instead of redeeming our humiliation on stapled visas for visitors from Arunachal through effective and tough diplomacy, we allowed ourselves to be contemptuously slapped with another stapled visa regime for Jammu and Kashmir in August 2010, because according to the Chinese, it is 'disputed territory'. Yet China continues to engage in military transportation, road and infrastructure building in Pakistan Occupied Kashmir, over which India has legal sovereignty. In fact, the Chinese position *vis-à-vis* India and Pakistan is clearly seen in the fact that it has never even expressed diplomatic solidarity with us when acts of terrorism occur in India from across the Pakistan border.

Raison d'etat, or the policy of naked pursuit of power

China, on the other hand, has got its India act well worked out. It is successfully pursuing its objectives with single-minded determination and complete facilitation from its Indian counterparts. At the turn of the century, it concentrated on encircling India over land and establishing a strong presence in all our neighbouring countries. China's military growth during the last decade and indigenous development of state-of-the-art military hardware, including aircraft carriers and ballistic missiles, has been phenomenal. This would certainly impact the balance of power in the region. A Pentagon Report of August 2011 has warned India regarding China's rapid advances and infrastructure build-up near India's borders and says that China's armed forces are developing 'new capabilities' that might extend their reach into the Indian Ocean.

More recently there are clear indications that the Chinese are spreading their wings, and plan to encircle us by sea as well. If the 2011 reports that the Chinese Navy demanded that *INS Airavat* identify itself and explain its presence in the South China Sea are true, then its maritime ambitions stand fully exposed. Chinese harassment of the unarmed US ship 'Impeccable' in international waters off China in 2009 confirms this. International law regarding the high seas is well laid down, and Indian ships have absolute right of passage in international waters of the South China Sea. What stands out starkly in the incident is the bellicose and confrontational attitude of the Chinese towards India. It is clear that China would like to control the entire sea, which is rich in hydrocarbon and has shipping lanes of regional economies. The US has already stated that the South China Sea is of strategic interest to it, and that it would not accept Chinese hegemony, a move that has been welcomed by ASEAN members. As China expands its naval presence in South Asia and the Indian Ocean, India should do the same in East Asia, and build credible strategic partnerships in the interest of its regional security.

Turning the tables on a passive India

Chinese policies follow the philosophy of Sunzi, formerly known as Sun Tzu. 'All war is based on deception. When able to attack, we must pretend to be incapable; when employing forces, we must seem inactive; when we are near, we must make the enemy believe we are far; offer bait to lure him; if he appears humble, make him arrogant; if he is rested, wear him down; if his forces are united, divide them; take action when it is unexpected.'

China is not our friend and has no intention of becoming one. It is engaged in the diabolical strategy of militarily surrounding us and supplying materials for an aggressive war to both Pakistan and Myanmar. It has never accepted the validity of India's title deeds to Jammu and Kashmir. Pakistan has gifted away 4853 square kms of our territory in the Shaksgam Valley of Kashmir to China in 1963, violating the territorial integrity of Jammu and Kashmir. This was used to construct the Karakoram Highway linking China and Pakistan. Receiving Indian territory—even if disputed—from

Pakistan, makes the Chinese receivers of stolen property. The Chinese have made it clear that they recognize no part of Jammu and Kashmir as Indian. Their 'stapled visas' are another instance of active hostility. When one of our bureaucrats tookup the matter with his Chinese counterparts, he got an evasive and ridiculous reply: 'This is an administrative problem and not a political statement.'

During his visit to India in December 2010, the soft-spoken Chinese Premier Wen Jiabao seems to have succeeded in convincing Prime Minister Manmohan Singh that the border dispute between the two countries belongs to the past, won't be easy to resolve, and requires patience. Instead of using whatever diplomatic language was necessary to call this statement pure poppycock, the even more soft-spoken Dr Singh appears to have succumbed completely. When Mr Jiabao was asked whether he would advise Pakistan to stop terrorist activity, he made it clear that he would not. 'That's for the two of you to resolve,' he bluntly said. Our prime minister obviously tried to flatter his guest in the hope of getting some response which he could sell to the Indian people when he declared that 'the world will listen when India and China will speak with one voice'. The response he received to this piece of flattery was, 'Our relationship is greater than the sum of its parts.' To me the statement is an attractive piece of diplomatic craftsmanship meaning nothing. Without any countervailing advantage, the visit yielded a trade pact which will take the bilateral trade to $100 billion by 2015, a complete economic sell-out in a year when the trade deficit was already approximately $20 billion.

Isolating India

While India continues to remain passive, China has made big investments in all our neighbouring countries. It is building deepwater ports in Pakistan and Bangladesh, including a seaport in Gwadar in the tumultuous Balochistan region that will be run by Singapore for the benefit of China, roads in Nepal and oil and gas pipelines in Myanmar. In 2008 it agreed to build two nuclear-power plants for Pakistan. China has become Pakistan's biggest supplier of military hardware, including fighter jets and guided-missile frigates. In the past China has given Pakistan weapons-grade fissile material and tested bomb design as part of its nuclear support. Pakistan, a near failed state today, could certainly be India's friend, but for China fanning the fires of fanatical hostility towards India. What I have written so far is an accurate account of China's record of anti-India hostility and belligerence. But that does not mean that it is a benign friend of Pakistan. Bolstering Pakistan against India serves Chinese foreign policy's two main goals: weaken and humiliate India, and position itself as the sole dominant superpower in Asia and the entire eastern world. Gobbling up Pakistan can wait for a while and will be child's play whenever China chooses to do so.

Also, China has finally acknowledged that it is constructing a hydro-power plant on the Brahmaputra that could affect the quantity of water flowing into lower riparian Indian states and the Northeast. No river water agreement exists between India and China, and we are not aware of any government initiatives in this respect. China opposes World Bank and ADB projects in Arunachal which we do not counter aggressively. Even official visits to Arunachal by the prime minister and the president are protested by them.

Establishing hegemony

China's ambition of economic hegemony is visible throughout the world. Despite the lack of genuine diplomatic or political cooperation between India and China, we have set a new trade target of $100 billion for 2015 and agreed to open branches of four major Chinese banks in India to promote investments. Our markets are flooded with cheap Chinese products to the ruin of our own small scale industries. India-China bilateral trade stood at $51 billion in fiscal 2009, as against $15 billion in 2005, with a trade surplus of $24 billion in China's favour. We watch, unconcerned, as our once-famous silk industry is killed by imported Chinese yarn and are satisfied that 70% of India's exports to China continue to be primary commodities and raw materials such as iron ore, while Chinese exports constitute power and other value added products that create jobs in China. While we allow our local small industry to be crippled by a flood of cheap Chinese goods, we have done nothing to press China to open up its economy for more value added exports from India.

The Chinese assessment of the financial meltdown of 2008 and the ensuing economic difficulties is that both the United States and

Europe have been weakened. The Chinese believe that the US is in a state of economic stagnation and is unlikely to see the 3-4% growth rate of the past while the Euro crisis has left Europe in a state of financial and political paralysis. By contrast, China can gleefully conclude that its steady economy, currency reserves and continuing rate of growth provide a great opportunity to refashion the global financial system in a fashion that it protects and promotes Chinese interests alone. China has already developed a worldwide network of natural resource arrangements: for example, in Africa it has concluded several pacts to feed its insatiable economy with a steady stream of raw materials from food to minerals. When the US-Europe ship is sinking, China will call the shots because it controls the lifeboat. Visions of being a military superpower and a superbanker or financial rescuer appear to be well founded.

On the political front, the Chinese know that America and several other countries of the world need its assistance to denuclearize Iran, and to a lesser extent, North Korea. US President Barack Obama is frantically seeking a positive and open alliance with it on the Iran issue. Beijing is still to be persuaded to prohibit Chinese companies from trading with Iran. Its sale of gasoline to Iran and investments in oil production are sore points with the US. The real danger is that following the Chinese example, competitors who had initially pulled out from Iran might decide to return. So here too China holds the trump card.

American liberals and an overwhelming majority of the US population no longer believe in the once-tried Monroe Doctrine when they withdrew from the affairs and quarrels of other nations in the belief that its two oceans and military power are enough for US security. The rise of China and the threat of terrorism compel them to search for reliable allies abroad.

The makers of American policy have not failed to notice China's mounting arrogance and truculence towards its neighbours, particularly India, because of the perception of its own power. Instances of Chinese abrasiveness abroad are in plenty, and even the US is not immune from it. For instance in July 2010, at the ASEAN Forum, Chinese Foreign Minister Yang Jiechi warned other nations against using Western countries to settle their disputes with China. More recently they warned US and South Korea against conducting naval exercises in the vicinity of China.

Need to create a 'Balance of Power'

Cardinal Richelieu of France and King William III of England are said to be the originators of the theory of 'Balance of Power' in the 17th century, which remained the dominant principle of European diplomacy for nearly 200 years thereafter. When the idea of a single dominant power directing the foreign policy of European states collapsed, two allied concepts were born, which complemented each other. The first gave primacy to the naked pursuit of national interest, in which the end justified the means. The second asserted that no power should be allowed to become dominant, and if it did, it had to be opposed by a coalition of those unable to stand individually.

The Chinese believe in a carefully crafted, semi-paranoid and cleverly assembled agenda for its pursuit of national interest, a camouflage for 'world dominion'. Logically, our policy should be the pursuit of alliances with secular democracies of the world to ensure that we, and other nations, do not become victims of Chinese aggression and double-talk.

For a long time India enforced its security against any hostile combination of states by a mutual defence treaty with the Soviet Union. In today's political scenario, China poses a threat to all democracies of the world. Under Dr Manmohan Singh India took a positive step when it partnered with the US to enlarge the frontiers of democracy, but that initiative has seen no progress in more than half a decade. A powerful democratic axis must be brought into existence—starting in Washington and running through Europe, Israel in the Middle East, Tokyo in the Far East and all the nations of the Commonwealth. This may well disturb the equations of the present United Nations, but it is time we realised that a majority of its members do not have any sincere commitment to the 1948 Declaration of Human Rights and the more detailed Covenants of 1966. A totalitarian China capable of the horrendous Tianannmen Square butchery and armed with a paralyzing Veto power in the UN makes a mockery of it. It is time we fashioned a more credible alternative, and tried to be the conscience of the world as Gandhiji had hoped and promised.

Time to reclaim our national pride

Buddha and Confucius no longer dominate Chinese culture and thought. It is the ideas of Mao and the deviousness of Chou En Lai that shape the Chinese attitude to a seemingly pathetic and passive India. Mao Zedong's statements: 'The world is ours, we should unite for achievements,' and 'responsibility and seriousness can conquer the world and the Chinese Communist Party members represent these qualities' are statements of pride for the Chinese leadership. President Obama, who represents a world power, may dismiss this nonchalantly, but Prime Minister Manmohan Singh and the Indian leadership must know that India is China's next plum waiting to be plucked. India must close ranks and ward off the menace.

If the border issue with China cannot be promptly settled by mutual give-and-take at the negotiating table, the dispute must be taken to the International Court of Justice. Both parties run equal risk of an adverse verdict. India must project itself as a nation willing to do everything reasonably required to maintain genuine friendship with all its neighbours, particularly China. We should extensively advocate the full text and mandate of Article 51 of our Constitution, which is the obligation of every Government to:

(a) Promote international peace and security.
(b) Maintain just and honourable relations between nations.
(c) Foster respect for international law and treaty obligations in the dealings of organized peoples with one another.
(d) Encourage settlement of international disputes by arbitration.

It is time for us to behave like a self-respecting nation instead of encouraging spurious politeness and wasted hospitality. We have had enough of this futility during the last few decades. It is now time for India to reclaim her lost pride

Section 2
The Mechanics of Power

4
Dynastic Democracy—Bravely Evaluate Your Leaders

Democracy flourished in ancient Greece and Rome—pagan societies in today's terminology—that had multitudes of anthropomorphic gods who shared the emotions, problems and weaknesses of ordinary mortals. There was no omnipotent, omniscient god who was master of the universe and dispenser of all gifts and pleasures. Men fashioned their lives through free choice and fought for what they desired or coveted. These free societies, without shackles of dogma or diktat, could easily govern their people through the democratic form of government that recognized certain liberties in basic form—most importantly, the right to equality.

With the birth of Christianity, the idea of an all-powerful god, beyond reproach criticism or even scrutiny, and the divine right of kings took hold of the minds of people, and democracy was bound to dissolve. Society sank into a condition of slavery; denial of god or any questioning of Him as creator of injustice, evil and pain became punishable under the capital offence of blasphemy. The era of intellectual and spiritual servitude was born, nicknamed by historians as the Dark Ages.

The sovereignty that had resided in the people when democracy flourished was now vested in god. This was indeed a social and intellectual tragedy, but what made matters worse was that some clever people managed to convince the vast majority of the populace that they alone were the anointed representatives of the unseen god on this sorry planet.

However, the idea of democracy has had its own powerful energy throughout history. The domain of democracy, notwithstanding its historical setbacks, has incrementally expanded at a furious pace and the recent Arab Spring has been a refreshing experience. But let us not be lulled into a false assurance that all is well with democracy. Humanity will continue to produce evil men who mesmerize others of lesser education and lower understanding by taking away from them their critical faculties of constantly examining and evaluating their political leaders. Democracy is like a swimming pool. If you do not periodically change the water, it will almost certainly turn into a stinking cesspool.

One of the Christian apostles, Saint Augustine, if I remember correctly, preached that men in power are ordained by god, and therefore beyond all human investigation and punishment. This precept should be abhorrent to all those interested in sustaining the health and vigour of democracy. It was precisely this kind of teaching that produced Hitler and other evil dictators.

It is fortunate that our western-educated leaders, some of them superb statesmen and constitutional experts, fashioned the Constitution of free India that gave us a Democratic Republic where every citizen possessed fundamental rights, the people's sanctum sanctorum, which even by unanimous vote of all its members in both Houses, Parliament dare not trespass. No royalty, no aristocracy, but only the freely-elected representatives of the people are to run the country's affairs. We are duly grateful to our first prime minister Jawaharlal Nehru for he laid the foundation of a stable democracy and hitched his vision to the polestar of peace and economic development. He resisted the temptation of founding a dynasty and even his daughter was told that Lal Bahadur Shastri would be his successor if he had the choice. But let it be remembered that Nehru himself was Gandhiji's choice, and this in a significant sense started the process of weakening Indian democracy. For the bright light of Gandhiji and the universal adulation that he commanded blinded the people and succeeding generations to the enormous debits in his political balance sheet, by no means a flattering one. If the people of India are to truly act as 'sovereign' they must be fully equipped, through education and information, to discern the unpardonable misdemeanors of their rulers, including of the great Nehru himself.

I propose to start with him and then proceed to deal with his successors. The only one amongst his successors who had an unblemished tenure, unfortunately cut short by cruel providence, was the late Lal Bahadur Shastri. We have not produced another like him till today. He was a 'gem of purest ray serene', almost written out from India's political history by flatterers and sycophants of the Nehru family.

Nehru—how does the court of history judge him?

The list of Nehru's failings and failures is long and varied. His first was the betrayal of Tibet. Until 1947, the flag of independent Tibet flew alongside the flag of China. Although in 1921, Britain had informed China that it was recognizing Tibet as an autonomous state under the suzerainty of China and would deal with it on that basis, yet Tibet conducted itself as an independent nation and did not join China as an ally in the Second World War, declaring its neutrality instead. In 1947, its trade mission travelled abroad on Tibetan, and not Chinese, passports. There is absolutely no doubt that up to the year 1950, when the Chinese army entered Tibet to conquer Lhasa, there was no trace of any Chinese authority in Tibet. Soon after Mao's Republic of China was established, China announced that it would march into Tibet. India's own interest was at stake. Our trade agents in Tibet had their own military escorts. Crimes committed by Indians were dealt with under Indian law and not the law of Tibet. Postal and telegraph services were under Indian control. India made a mild protest, which Beijing contemptuously rejected.

Nehru lost his nerve which resulted in the enslavement of the unfortunate Tibetans. The Chinese arrogantly warned us that they would not tolerate our interference. In contrast, one must read a letter written in November 1950 by Sardar Patel to Nehru. He warned, 'We can, therefore, safely assume that very soon they (the Chinese) will disown all the stipulations which Tibet has entered into with us in the past... The undefined state of the frontier and the existence on our side of a population with its affinities to Tibetans or Chinese has all the elements of potential trouble between China and ourselves.' Patel wanted the Indian government immediately to set out a definite policy, particularly in regard to the McMahon Line.

Had Patel's advice been followed, we would not have suffered the humiliation of 1962. Despite advice from within the Congress, Nehru continued to champion China's cause at the United Nations.

It is now well known that even President Truman wanted India to commit itself to the defence of Tibetan independence.

Chou En Lai continued to make a fool of the gullible Jawaharlal Nehru. After swallowing Tibet, he assured India that there was no territorial dispute or controversy between India and China. Nehru continued to rely on the McMahon Line, knowing full well that China had not accepted it, except during the settlement with Burma. In April 1954, surprisingly, Nehru formally recognized Tibet as a part of China without even insisting on the Chinese acceptance of the McMahon Line as the border between India and China. In June 1954, when Chou came to India on a state visit, Nehru chanted 'Hindi-Chini Bhai Bhai'. No one in the Congress protested. Both reaffirmed Panchsheel, a doctrine wholly inconsistent with modern international law and our obligations under the UN Charter.

As soon as Chou returned to China, he formally objected to the presence of Indian troops at a place called Barahoti in UP, claiming that it was a part of Tibet China. Nehru believed that Chou, his very intimate friend, could have only acted out of honest ignorance. At the Bandung Conference next year, Nehru, in the fond belief that Chou was his protégé, put him at centre stage. Even so, the very clever Chou let it be known that China had territorial claims against India, but would use only peaceful means to attain them. In March 1956, the Chinese quietly began the construction of 750 miles of motorable road from Yarkand to Gartok, through Aksai Chin, which they managed to complete in less than two years. Nehru pretended not to know anything about it. Several aggressive incidents, extremely humiliating for India, crowded the years of 1957, 1958 and in January 1959, Chou firmly declared that the China-India boundary had never been formally delimited. Nehru finally saw that Chou's whole policy and its presentation to the people of India was an act of deception. It was in that year that the Dalai Lama had to escape from Tibet and seek sanctuary in Tawang.

The negligence and defeatism of Nehru must be considered a great crime against the people of India. There was total failure to arm the country's troops or to make a correct judgment on China's military intentions.

On the eve of his retirement in April 1961, General Thimayya, a sadly disillusioned man, said to the troops, 'I hope that I am not leaving you as cannon fodder for the Chinese. God bless you all.'

This was precisely the fate Nehru had written for them. His dear friend Chou was now busy with an international campaign to paint India as an aggressor. The 1962 war is too painful a memory to recall. Krishna Menon was the sacrifice, but it was Nehru who was responsible for India's abject humiliation. Even his apologetic followers had to admit that he made a grave mistake, but only a good man such as Nehru could have made it. God spare India from *such good men* or their replicas for safeguarding national interest.

Nehru was obsessed with non-alignment, an idea cleverly planted by Chou En Lai to prevent any criticism or scrutiny of the inner workings of the Communist government of China. It was formally enunciated in 1955 at the Bandung Conference, Indonesia, where Asian and African states met to find common ground and agreement for future cooperation, and proclaimed anti-colonialism and neutrality between the two blocs as pillars of their foreign policy. When our senior diplomat Gundevia returned from Burma around August 1948, he brought a message from Burmese Prime Minister Thaki Nu suggesting an India-Burma defence pact or a mutual defence treaty, which would help both countries in any confrontation with China. Nehru ridiculed the idea, and reportedly said, 'He must be crazy, and wants to provoke China. What is China going to do to Burma? It is really nonsense.' If only he had seen the wisdom of the Burmese proposal, India could perhaps have been spared the humiliation of 1962.

Non-alignment was a lofty pretension that became a cruel joke. No non-aligned country came to our help in 1962. The only two countries that promptly provided substantial aid were the US and Israel, both well outside the non-aligned fold. This obsession with non-alignment and with his own image as a unique, world famous leader, got us what Nehru described as a 'stab in the back'. Actually, it wasn't a stab in the back, it was a clear stab from the front. Nehru's daughter showed greater wisdom when years later she entered into a defence pact with the Soviet Union that saved us from the American Seventh Fleet entering the Bay of Bengal during the Bangladesh War. Burma, meanwhile, rebuffed by Nehru, settled its border dispute with China. The settlement was based upon recognition of the validity of the McMahon Line, a recognition which even Nehru had not been able to secure.

In the new unipolar world even the limited rationale for non-alignment has disappeared. Yugoslavia's successor states have expressed little interest in non-alignment, Malta and Cyprus have ceased to be members, having joined the European Union. The movement now confines itself to social and environmental issues, nuclear testing and drug-trafficking, with no influence whatsoever on long-standing disputes like Kashmir or the Middle East conflict. Periodic attacks on Zionism and Israel occupy it at other times that neither amuse nor enthuse the world order. Even during its heyday, with its membership of economically weak and militarily powerless countries, non-alignment could never challenge the might of the two superpowers.

The foreign policy of every nation must reflect its domestic values and ideals. India is constitutionally committed to maintain democratic institutions, to an admirable catalogue of human rights that protect the security and dignity of the individual, and to religious freedom. India is further committed to promotion of international peace and security, the maintenance of just and honourable relations between nations, respect for international law and treaty obligations, and settlement of disputes by arbitration. All nations that accept these values and obligations must pool their economic, military and moral resources to prevent fanatics like Osama bin Laden and lunatics like Hitler from dominating the world. We are and must be aligned with those who want terrorism exorcised and the area of democracy expanded. To speak of non-alignment when the world today is threatened by terrorists, warmongers and destroyers of democracy is to betray our national interest and proclaimed ideals, deaden our national conscience and destroy India's soul. None could have said it better than Dante Alighieri in his famous Inferno: The hottest place in Hell is reserved for those who in time of great moral crisis remain neutral.

India will be well advised not to invest too much time or energy in flogging this dead horse. Politely we must announce its final demise and speak about it no more. The reasons for this are weighty enough.

In addition to our military and diplomatic humiliation, we also lost about 90,000 sq km of Indian territory in the 1962 war. Both Houses of Parliament passed a resolution unanimously after the ignominy, which gave hope that as a nation we shall redeem our self-respect in the future: 'This House notes with deep regret that in spite of the uniform gestures of goodwill and friendship by India towards the People's Republic of China on the basis of recognition of each other's independence, non-aggression and non-interference, and peaceful co-existence, China has betrayed this goodwill and friendship and the principles of Panchsheel which had been agreed to between the two countries and has committed aggression and initiated a massive invasion of India by her armed forces...With hope and faith, this House affirms the firm resolve of the Indian people to drive out the aggressor from the sacred soil of India, however long and hard the struggle may be.'

Pandit Nehru in his bitter last years had neither the nerve nor the spirit to redeem our self-respect. He died a broken man, with his credibility badly shattered, his Chinese policy and Panchsheel in shambles and his life's work gone up in smoke. Not one inch of territory has been recovered, and China continues to claim Arunachal and more.

Nehru the economist was a myth

Now, a word about the myth of Nehru, the great self-proclaimed economist. While giving due credit to him for his strong conviction about democracy and secularism that are embedded as the fundamentals of our Constitution, for his commitment to land reforms and irrigation projects that he initiated, it is necessary to acknowledge that Nehru's economics proved retrogressive and restrictive for India's economic growth in realizing its complete potential.

From an early age, Nehru was attracted to the socialist world, though Gandhiji's influence did keep him at some distance from absolute Marxism. He attended Communist-organised conferences and was extremely excited by the first such conference that he attended at Brussels in 1927. He enjoyed the company of Madame Sun Yat-sen, and lost no opportunity in expounding the merits of Communism. This is what he had to say to the All Bengal Students' Conference in February 1928: 'Socialism frightens some of our friends, but what of Communism? Our elders sitting in their council chambers shake their grey heads and stroke their beards in alarm at the mere mention of the word. I wish to tell you that though personally I do not agree with many of the methods of Communists, and I am by no means sure to what extent Communism can suit present conditions in India, I do believe in Communism as an ideal of society. For essentially it is Socialism, and Socialism, I think, is the only way if the world is to escape its present ills.'*

It is surprising that Nehru had no exposure to the work of Fredrick Hayek, *The Road to Serfdom* published in 1944, which ultimately flowered into his monumental work, *The Fatal Conceit: The Errors of Socialism*, 44 years later. Neither his letters to Priyadarshini nor *The Discovery of India* indicate any familiarity with wider economic thought.

After the untimely and tragic exit of Gandhiji and Sardar Patel, and the elimination of the brilliant conservative, Rajagopalachari, Nehru became the exclusive repository of almost autocratic power, unfettered and unchallenged, while forming the economic policy of India. He did not realize that industrialization in isolation was only a partial solution to India's economic challenge, as it could not, in real terms, raise employment levels or relieve people from poverty. In fact the effect could be quite the reverse—by eliminating the entire segment of traditional craft and artisans from business—if left unprotected. To placate himself, he decided to inject a large dose of socialism into industrialization, thereby killing Indian entrepreneurship for several decades and subjecting it to 'license raj'.

Nehru gave no priority to addressing the population explosion in India. He overlooked the wisdom of Malthusian theory, that unrestricted population growth begets pauperisation. Perhaps population control might prevent birth of unknown geniuses who would deliver the world from its present evils, but it would also have prevented millions of our population from living sub-human lives—malnourished children, pregnant females without adequate calorie intake, starvation, disease, water wars, human beings living in degrading poverty without food, shelter, education and compassion that brutalizes them—resulting in diabolical crime, religious fanaticism and suicide bombers.

The proletariat was not created by exploiting capitalists alone. Though the underprivileged may feel exploited and politicians may manipulate them to gain power, millions in the developing world owe their subsistence to opportunities that successful entrepreneurs have created for them. The hostility towards private business—both Indian and foreign—damaged the climate for private investment

---

*Jawaharlal Nehru: A Biography by Sankar Ghose, p. 50. Allied Publishers, 1993.

in India, and inhibited economic development. It is a paradox of Nehruvian socialism that social inequity is greater in India than in any capitalist country committed to free enterprise. Our leaders, imitating Nehru, kept mouthing socialistic slogans unmindful of the hordes of caste-based workers, servants, scavengers, etc who served them.

Socialism became more a matter of political propaganda than well considered economic policy. The ever widening gap between the rich and poor has become a threat to the nation, the worst consequence being the exponential rise of corruption. What Nehru initiated and created continues to be a major threat to India's survival as a successful democracy even 50 years after him. The miserable rate of growth, called the Hindu Rate of Growth, should appropriately have been called the Nehruvian Rate of Growth. Economic growth revived only when many years later, we returned to Adam Smith's free market economics. Our growth rate would increase even more dramatically had the Congress Party decided to end corruption and purify itself.

But by now, we have created a country where at least 40% of our population lives in sub-human conditions.

Shastri showed leadership and integrity in political office

Political traditions were relatively less corrupt in those years, and the best qualified Indian became our prime minister after nearly 17 years of the Nehru reign. Lal Bahadur Shastri proved to be the best prime minister India has had so far. As minister for railways and transport, he set a great example of political and moral responsibility in India's political culture, by resigning in the wake of a railway accident at Ariyalur in Tamil Nadu that resulted in 144 deaths in 1956. Nehru informed Parliament that he was accepting the resignation because it would set an example in constitutional propriety and not because Shastri was in any way culpable. Shastri frankly stated that corruption was permeating fast into the political systems and was reaching the uppermost echelons of the state. He set about combating it with sincerity and vigour, and in 1961, as Union home minister, was instrumental in appointing the Committee on Prevention of Corruption under the chairmanship of K Santhanam. The Central Vigilance Commission is one of the offshoots of the Santhanam Committee recommendations.

The most glorious contribution of this diminutive and modest man lay in India's victory over Ayub Khan's infiltration warfare in Kashmir, over his army and tanks. Under Shastri's leadership, Pakistan was humiliated and a Kashmir Settlement forced on it by the historic Tashkent Declaration, later destroyed by the folly of his successor, Indira Gandhi. How Indira Gandhi succeeded in becoming the prime minister is not relevant to my main theme. I am more concerned with what she did to India.

Indira as PM was a tragic mistake

Inspite of the formative damage that Pandit Nehru caused to Indian interests—economic, political and international—I have no hesitation in acknowledging that he was a patriot with integrity. Though not corrupt himself, he took no serious steps to combat corruption. He patronised colleagues who were mediocre and sometimes corrupt, a typical example being Pratap Singh Kairon of Punjab. Although Nehru gave the nation a secular, democratic Constitution, he failed to explain to the nation and his compatriots what it meant. Though these faults were the result of credulity and negligence, he was quite aware of his daughter Indira's lack of qualification for becoming a prime minister. Having made her almost homeless in her early life, he was disappointed by her academic non-performance and dropping out of Oxford. He disapproved of Indira's relationship with Feroze, a hanger-on of his wife Kamla, and her secret engagement to him in Paris.

After Shastri's unfortunate and untimely death, Congress leaders, in their anxiety to maintain the Nehru line of succession, inevitably zeroed in on Indira Gandhi. Commonly referred to as 'goongi gudiya', it was widely believed that she would be a dumb and pliant prime minister and all political decisions would be taken by the party machine. How wrong the Congress' elderly, experienced stalwarts were in their judgment of her character. Even during her father's lifetime, while she had temporarily become the Congress president, Indira Gandhi had given enough evidence of her scant regard for democracy. She persuaded her reluctant father to topple the communist government in Kerala and impose President's Rule. This was the first time since Independence that Article 356 was so grossly misused. Indira accused the Kerala communists of complicity with China, even outraging her husband Feroze who died a year later of a heart attack.

To make Indira prime minister without taking cognizance of her anti-democratic predisposition was a tragic mistake of the Congress high command. Once in power, Indira exercised it to the hilt and had no compunction in misusing it. She trounced both her enemies and allies, and drove her party to the break-point. Whatever faint democratic instincts she might have had, if at all, were destroyed by her son Sanjay. Of her two sons, Rajiv was said to be quiet and sensitive and not attracted by politics while extrovert Sanjay, lively, arrogant and prone to violent behavior, was a born politician.

As a boarder at the Doon School Sanjay is said to have bitten off a chunk of the ear of a fellow student. One of his fellow students described him as a 'lumpen element'. In his late teens he was accused of stealing and joyriding in cars around Delhi. Obsessed by speed and fast-moving cars, he was apprenticed to Rolls-Royce in England where his delinquent tendencies alienated his employers. Asked to account for one of a series of mistakes, he is said to have told his supervisor, 'You people mucked up my country for 300 years, so what's the big deal if I muck up Rolls-Royce?' When Sanjay finally quit his job, a Rolls-Royce executive said they were glad to see his back for all that he was interested in was booze and women. This is accurately recorded in Vinod Mehta's *Sanjay Story*.

After becoming prime minister in 1966, the first calamity that Indira Gandhi inflicted upon the nation was her unruly son, Sanjay. The famous writer Khushwant Singh, who was an intimate family friend of the Gandhis, remembers arriving at a meeting with him and witnessing a pair of supplicant businessmen deliver two suitcases full of banknotes to him. 'I found it hard not to like Sanjay,' Singh admitted, 'but I have to say he was a thug, and he was corrupt.'

Indira Gandhi, with full knowledge of the flaws in his character, handed over a large part of the responsibilities of governance to his care and mercy. He treated the Republic of India as if it were his personal fiefdom. Bribery became endemic, as he autocratically set up parallel operations alongside the mechanisms of government, the culmination of which we see today. It must, however, be acknowledged that his one redeeming feature was that, unlike his grandfather, he was greatly troubled by the enormous increase in India's population. Unfortunately, this beneficial concern was maladroitly translated in action—through compulsory sterilisation, without the backing of law and without the consent of the victims of forced vasectomies. His population regulators, who acted as vigilantes, led by supreme commander and good friend Rukhsana Sultana, paraded through the streets of Delhi drumming up recruits and sterilising millions of men across the country. The atrocities of the Sanjay Brigade at Turkman Gate in Delhi's Old City have not yet been forgotten.

Now let us get back to the actions of Mrs Indira Gandhi herself.

One morning in September 1974, the nation woke up to screaming headlines that top smugglers of the country had been arrested and detained. They were humiliated and marched in handcuffs in public streets and roughed up in jails, their faces prominently displayed on television screens with invectives and sarcasm. Akashvani, the national radio station that exclusively ruled the airwaves in those years, did a media blitz on how the government had struck at the root of our economic misery, and the people applauded euphorically. In this sponsored populist frenzy, any sober, long range appraisal of injury to constitutionalism and democracy became well-nigh impossible. Such was the powerful propaganda machine unleashed by the government and its puppets that controlled it.

As chairman of the Bar Council of India during that time, I wrote the Chairman's Page for a legal periodical published by the Council. I recorded my protest and premonitions in it thus: 'Senator Dirksen of the United States was once scheduled to make a speech on the unusual subject, 'Frogs & Freedom'. A puzzled friend asked what in the devil would frogs have to do with freedom? The senator explained that if a frog with his delicate reflexes is dropped in a kettle of boiling water, and the sides are not too high, he will pop right out of the water. But, put that frog in the same kettle and fill it with cold water, then turn on the gas; and that poor unsuspecting frog will be boiled, because he did not have sense enough to climb out of that water before it got too hot.'

I expressed very strongly that the greatest danger to democracy and the rule of law is not from a violent and manifest blow. It is through small but persistent attack, by gradual precipitation and erosion that freedom is usually and finally lost. I suspected that the government was about to strike a heavier blow against national freedom. This initial incident was only intended to create the right atmosphere to acclimatize the people of India to the illegality of detention without trial. When an inherently illegal statute is put into service for an ostensibly beneficial purpose, champions of democracy from every stream of society must raise their alertness levels and nip the threat in the bud, even if the draconian Preventive Detention law was being used against notorious criminals. After acclimatizing people to the 'end justifies the means' preview with the smugglers, Indira Gandhi's government would very soon start using it against any citizen it found undesirable or inconvenient.

Within a few months, the finest individuals, who were the pride of the nation, were behind prison bars under the notorious Maintenance of Internal Security Act, 1971.

Mature democracies do not approve of detention without trial except in times of grave emergencies, such as war. The prestigious International Commission of Jurists, in laying down minimum conditions of political freedom, has condemned the use of this instrument as a peace time measure.

India's darkest hour: declaration of Emergency

My fears proved prophetic. Not much later, it was Mrs Gandhi's own election to Parliament in 1971 that provided the fuse. Socialist leader Raj Narain, represented by my good friend Shanti Bhushan as leading counsel, had challenged the election in the Allahabad High Court on grounds of electoral malpractices and misuse of government machinery. As usual, this litigation had dragged on, and even in the year 1974 the recording of evidence had not been completed. Ultimately Mrs Gandhi's election was set aside on 12 June 1975, after which all hell broke loose and she blatantly manipulated the Constitution to impose the infamous Emergency on 26 June 1975 by prevailing upon President Fakhruddin Ali Ahmed to declare it on account of 'internal disturbances'. Her main advisors in this thoroughly unconstitutional advice given to the president, were Law Minister Hari Babban Gokhle and Attorney General Niren Dey. And not a squeak of protest emerged from any of her Cabinet colleagues at the 6 a.m. Cabinet meeting to ratify the proclamation. An unsuspecting India had gone to sleep on 25 June 1975 as a democracy and awoke the following morning into authoritarianism.

This proclamation of Emergency was loaded on to the prevailing Emergency announced by President Giri in December 1971 on account of threat of external aggression. India now had the unique distinction of being placed under a dual Emergency, with the attendant abrogation of fundamental rights and other legal denials. But the world knew that the real emergency was Indira Gandhi's personal one, in the wake of the Allahabad High Court judgement announced less than a fortnight before.

The political and administrative barbarism during the Emergency is well documented—arrests of almost all Opposition leaders, Jayaprakash Narain, Atal Behari Vajpayee and L.K. Advani, both of the Jan Sangh, and Morarji Desai, once Mrs Gandhi's father's colleague and also her finance minister, but now in the Congress O, the RSS, the communists. Warrants were also issued against Congressmen like Mohan Dharia, who, once part of Mrs Gandhi's Cabinet, had subsequently fallen out with her. In short, anyone who could defy Mrs Gandhi was arrested. The country was presented with a new set of rules for governance. Freedom of speech and freedom of the press were completely throttled through the use of the official machinery for spying, tapping telephones, press censorship and threats of imminent arrest.

These autocratic actions were followed by extensive amendments of The Representation of the People Act and the Indian Penal Code, all with retrospective effect. The election of the president, the vice-president, the prime minister and the Lok Sabha Speaker were made immune from judicial scrutiny by the 39th Constitutional Amendment Act. The 41st Amendment gave the prime minister permanent immunity from criminal and civil proceedings, so that an appeal to the Supreme Court from the Allahabad High Court judgment was made redundant. Since Indira Gandhi was pretty sure that her appeal did not have much strength within the judicial process, in her new dictatorial avatar, she thought it wiser and surer to change the law with retrospective effect.

An arrest warrant had been issued against me for making a speech against the Emergency and Sanjay Gandhi's corruption at the All Kerala Lawyers Association in early 1976. Through bureaucratic bungling and with a little help from my friends, the warrant could not be served. With fundamental rights suspended, redressal from the courts was out of the question. I had no intention of becoming a martyr incarcerated in prison, and was convinced I could achieve much more by being outside rather than within prison. With a lot of luck and support of my family and friends, I sadly left the country for the US in April 1976 in self-exile. I think my objective of making the international community aware of the breakdown of democracy in India was achieved.

Two years later in November 1978, when the legal heat on the mother and son was strong, I agreed to meet Mrs Gandhi one-to-one, through the intervention of her trusted lieutenant A.R. Antulay. I advised her to apologise to the nation for the Emergency and its wrongs, after which we could forget the past and all cases against her would be withdrawn. I drafted the apology for her, but she decided against it.

Indira was both loved and hated

Indira Gandhi was both loved and hated at different times by the people of this country. Loved for her bold and nationalist actions through which India with all her disadvantages could still hold her head high and shine in the international community. And hated for Indira's autocratic and anti-democratic actions within the country that reached its nadir in the Rule by Decree during the years 1975 to 1977.

After her tragic assassination on 31 October 1984, the nation's grief was genuine and heartfelt. But the thinking population could not miss the fatalistic undertone, that she was devoured by the Frankenstein monster she had herself created.

History remembers Indira for her patriotism during the Bangladesh crisis, for standing up fearlessly before the might of the US when they threatened us with the Seventh Fleet, for her statesmanship in signing the Indo-Soviet Treaty of Friendship and Cooperation in August 1971, giving a befitting reply to the American hegemonists.

Bangladesh was her finest hour, but history will judge her harshly for deviating from Lal Bahadur Shastri's Tashkent process of January 1966 to her Simla Agreement of 1972, where inexplicably, she allowed Pakistan Prime Minister Bhutto to outwit her—she who was the victorious prime minister on every count.

Indira Gandhi left behind several legacies—dynastic rule, economic control through populism—such as, bank nationalisation, Garibi Hatao and the 20-point programme—but most importantly, she left behind a centralised institutionalisation of political corruption that has matured into another Frankenstein, devouring the nation and the poor of India.

Through some inexplicable twist in her game plan, whether through conscience or *thanatos*, she ordered a general election in 1977 which she need not have, in her situation of absolute power. That saw her first Waterloo. The second was her last at her residence on 31 October 1984, when her life ebbed away. And the nation mourned inconsolably.

Cementing of dynastic democracy

On 31 October 1984, Indira Gandhi was assassinated at 9.20 a.m. and breathed her last at 10.50 a.m. Rajiv Gandhi was sworn in as prime minister that same night. The omens were foul. Delhi was engulfed in a frenzy of mob violence and communal riots as innocent members of the Sikh community were indiscriminately burnt, butchered, and murdered, with orchestration and with the active participation of Congress Party stalwarts.

I met the home minister, P.V. Narasimha Rao, that very night, urging him to take immediate steps to protect Sikhs from further attacks but was told the situation was not being controlled by him. Neither the president nor the new prime minister was available. With about 50 practicing lawyers from the Supreme Court, including the late Mr Tarkunde, and Mr Kapil Sibal, I ventured into the areas where Sikhs were hiding in sheer terror, to find not a single policeman on duty. My daughter Rani rescued a few injured Sikhs and took them to AIIMS but the doctors refused any medical help, and admission was out of the question. Fortunately, my good friend Dr Jain took charge of them in his private, but not very well equipped, clinic while we went around the disturbed localities. We divided ourselves into groups of three and four to help the victims as much as we could. Mr Tarkunde and I were attacked by a mob. We merely sat down on a large stone and told the attackers that we were ready to be killed. But someone in the crowd recognized us and our lives were spared.

It is a shame that in many cities of India genocide reigned while the guardians of law and public order remained wholly paralyzed by undoubtedly secret instructions of the new dispensation. On 2 November, curfew was announced throughout Delhi, but not enforced. The Army was deployed, but was ineffective because the police did not co-operate and it could not resort to force without the consent of senior police officers and executive magistrates. The mobs continued to rampage.

It is a deplorable failing of Rajiv Gandhi, that having taken over the mantle of prime minister through dynastic compulsions of the Congress party, even if on the night of his mother's death, he forgot that he had also taken over attendant public responsibilities. His sole public reference to the anti-Sikh riots can only be interpreted as remorseless, if not inhuman: 'When a giant tree falls, the mother earth below shakes.' During his tenure as prime minister, he exercised neither his moral authority nor his political power to redress the deep injuries of 1984. As on date, no Congress leaders who perpetrated and led the anti-Sikh riots have been punished, and some continue to enjoy important positions in government today. As I have repeatedly stated, it is only the greatness of the Sikh community that they have forgiven the Congress.

The formal institution of dynastic democracy

The formal institutionalisation of the dynastic democracy model had begun, the first in India, with Rajiv Gandhi bearing its imprimatur. This Nehru-Gandhi dynastic entitlement gradually started getting replicated across the country and spread to other political families of India. Today, it has become a political tradition in our democracy, deriving legitimacy from its originators. Indira Gandhi had made it publicly known that her closest political confidant was her son Sanjay. After Sanjay's death in 1980, she persuaded her unwilling son Rajiv to join politics and fill the void created by Sanjay. He was elected MP from Amethi, Sanjay Gandhi's constituency, in February 1981, and became his mother's close political advisor. He then became president of the Youth Congress, and it was widely perceived that Indira Gandhi was grooming Rajiv for the prime minister's job.

What is it in the Nehru-Gandhi family that compels them to anoint only immediate family members as alter egos or heirs apparent? Obviously, their secrets regarding their political and financial misdeeds are such that there is no substitute for immediate family when it comes to trust and protection. The keys to the treasury must always be held by them, the keys to secret cupboards containing their corruption files must never be lost—be it the Bofors case, foreign bank accounts, or smuggling of antiquities, to name a few. Hence, the need for an inner circle of family confidants, a second circle of trusted coteries, and an outer circle of sycophants and hangers-on, who are given blandishments and retainers to keep the inner circle protected and take the blame; or do a cover-up job whenever the need arises. When not in power, these coteries and sycophants must engineer and activate cover-up networks, to hush up or obfuscate any exposures. Dynasty converts all the resources and tools of democracy towards achieving these ends, and perpetuate its continuance, while fooling the nation through homilies on transparency and zero tolerance to corruption.

Dismal at every home front

Rajiv Gandhi as prime minister was singularly lacklustre and mediocre. In one of his debut speeches made during the Congress Plenary Session in Mumbai, he publicly acknowledged the systems of corruption in governance institutionalized by his mother and brother. 'If the central government releases one rupee for the poor,' he said, 'only 10 paisa reaches them.'

His 64th Amendment Bill for giving Constitutional status to Panchayati Raj was defeated in the Rajya Sabha in 1989, and was carried through only when Narasimha Rao became prime minister in 1993. Though Rajiv's heirs claim much political credit for it and the purported decentralisation, evidence from the field suggests that it has certainly decentralised corruption that now runs through new pipelines from New Delhi to state capitals to the villages of India, creating a new breed of village despots and exploiters of the aam admi. And it is highly likely that the amount of 10 paisa reaching the aam aadmi has reduced further.

Rajiv Gandhi was obviously quick to learn the importance of the vote bank. His pretensions to his dream for India and modernity were completely exposed in his stand on the Shah Bano case, in which the Supreme Court ruled that Shah Bano be given alimony by her divorced husband. Muslim fundamentalists agitated that it was an encroachment to their Personal Law. Under their pressure, in 1986, the Congress, which had an absolute majority in Parliament at the time, passed an Act that nullified the Supreme Court's judgement in the Shah Bano case. This can only be seen as retrogressive obscurantism for short-term minority populism, that betrayed the welfare and protection of Muslim women in India. His colleague Arif Mohammad Khan had made a wonderful speech, befitting a rational intellectual, that he was in favour of the Supreme Court position. Rajiv Gandhi pretended to applaud, but soon succumbed to fundamentalist elements and pushed through the infamous legislation nullifying the Supreme Court judgement.

The death of Mr Clean

I hoped and believed that Rajiv's gentle character and his opening salvo against prevalent corruption would master the foul stars very soon.

As I said to a newspaper reporter in Mauritius, 'Rajiv is not spoilt by politics and the company of venal types. No one has heard even an unsavoury rumour about him. He has taken Mr V.P. Singh in his Cabinet who has an excellent reputation for integrity. He has already condemned the prevalent corruption and declared his resolve to terminate it. I think our nation is safe in his hands.'

Well, as it turned out, I was proved wrong soon. The Lankan misadventure proclaimed the poverty of his politics, and Bofors proclaimed the death of Mr 'Clean'; the image he had assiduously tried to create for almost two years, proved to be a complete hoax.

On 16 April 1987 the Swedish radio aired the Bofors story to the shock of Rajiv and his government, and to the shame of the Indian nation. The news sent shock waves through the world media. The respectable Reuters quoted Swedish Radio as saying that, Bofors, the Swedish arms manufacturer, had won the $1.3 billion contract to provide the Indian army with the 155mm field howitzer by paying bribes to senior Indian politicians and key defence officials through a secret Swiss bank account; four installments totaling 32 million Swedish Kroner were paid into secret Swiss accounts in November and December 1986, that could be traced to senior figures responsible for placing India's military orders.

The Rajiv government almost simultaneously stated that the 'radio story is entirely baseless and mischievous'. This denial did not receive the desired display and impact, but it is of the greatest importance and of probative value to one who understands circumstantial evidence of the conduct of an accused after the accusation is publicly made against him. After a secret discussion in the Political Affairs Committee and the Cabinet, the following addition was made to the earlier cryptic denial: 'During negotiations with Bofors, the government had made it clear that the company should not pay any money to any person in connection with the contract... Government policy was not to promote any clandestine or irregular payments in any contract; any breach of this policy would be most severely dealt with... The report of pay-offs is one more link in the chain of denigration and destabilization of our political system... The government is determined to defeat the sinister design with all its might.'

I read with dismay this shocking and clumsy fabrication of the defence. Just as Lady Macbeth's first words on the discovery of King Duncan's slain body in her castle were a complete giveaway of her guilt, Rajiv Gandhi exposed his guilt by his government's strange and emphatic denial of the Bofors story broadcast by the Swedish radio.

Sweden was, after all, a friendly country, and had very cordial trade relations with India. Rajiv and Olaf Palme, prime minister of Sweden were friends and the Indian Army had formally conveyed its decision to opt for the Swedish gun. Acceptance of this decision by the civil authorities was an absolute certainty. Why would the Swedish Radio invent a lie and why would it want to destabilise a friendly government? Neither the Swedish government nor the radio nor any other Swedish agency had done or said anything to denigrate the Rajiv government. How then was it 'one more' link in the chain of denigration?

My experience in handling circumstantial evidence has taught me that often false denials prove guilt more convincingly than positive evidence of it. Hearing the nature of denials of the Rajiv government, I was convinced that the Swedish radio broadcast carried complete veracity which the denials of Rajiv and his conspirators could not demolish. If a jury were trying the case, I'm quite certain that the incredible denials and their complete unsustainability would have been enough to expose the crime of Rajiv and his conspirators.

My immediate reaction was continually fortified as the long list of incriminating circumstances began surfacing. An honest Rajiv, instead of demonizing the radio story, would have said, 'I deeply regret what the radio has reported. We will make full inquiries and request the Swedish government to do the same. Anyone found guilty will be severely dealt with.'

My opinion of Rajiv's reaction was no secret and I had voiced it publicly. So, when an MP needled Rajiv to respond to what I was saying, his downright uncultured, if not vulgar response was, 'I do not respond to every dog that barks.' The newspapers dutifully reported this insult. I responded with as much politeness and sobriety that I could muster, and replied to Rajiv: 'You are lucky I am only a barking dog and not a bloodhound. But do remember that dogs bark when they see a thief.'

During the next 30 days I asked him 300 questions, not one of which was answered by him. Strangely enough, neither has anyone from the Gandhi family refuted Subramanian Swamy's statement that since 1984 Sonia's Gandhi's mother Paola Predebon Maino, and friend Ottavio Quattrocchi, maintained regular contact with the Tamil Tigers. The mother used the LTTE for money laundering and Quattrocchi for selling weapons to earn commissions. To the best of my knowledge, this information remains unrefuted till today.

Although Indian investigators visited Sweden during the years that followed, not once did they seek the collaboration of Swedish police. They failed to cooperate with the Swedish Audit Bureau or its director general, Ingemar Mundeso, or audit director, Bo Sandberg. Bofors, obviously a partner in crime, refused to produce documents for inspection of the Audit Bureau. But the Bureau nevertheless found that there were agents in the deal and considerable amounts were paid to Bofors' previous agent in India. Obviously, at the instance of the Indian government, the Bureau report was not supplied to India, and the embarrassing parts were concealed by the friendly Swedish government. But even the disclosed parts falsified Rajiv's bogus defence that there were no agents. A new falsehood was invented—these payments were not commissions but winding-up charges, that is compensation or severance allowance, for putting them out of business. If that was the case, then why were large amounts paid to Quattrocchi?

The evidence available and the behaviour of the Congress party, whether in power or out of it, to stall and derail any effective investigation into the Bofors case lead to a clear inference that Quattrocchi was the face of Sonia Gandhi, and that this was her share of the deal. In July 1993, the Swiss courts had permitted official naming of the account operators, including Quattrocchi. Yet, before the CBI could question Quattrocchi and detain him, he bolted from Delhi on the night of July 29-30 1993. It is common knowledge that this was made possible through the direct intervention of Sonia Gandhi and the Congress government.

The spurious and slapstick efforts made thereafter to secure Quattrocchi's extradition, the de-freezing of his accounts, the deliberate errors and gaps in documentation by the CBI that had the least intention of trying to extradite the accused Quattrocchi, only establish the misuse of the entire government machinery and tools to subvert legal processes and fool the people of our country. One must then read the proceedings of the Parliamentary Committee called the Shankaranand Committee, which tried to provide a bare fig leaf cover to an otherwise naked Rajiv. It dutifully found that there were no commissions, no middlemen, and no Indians involved. The tragedy of Rajiv was that he destroyed not only his own image, but also destroyed the credibility and ethics of a parliamentary majority as well as all mechanisms dominated by it. A lone dissenting note by All adi Aruna in the Shankaranand Committee says it all—the Commission's findings were a joke.

And failures abroad

What was no joke was India's Sri Lanka diplomacy under Rajiv Gandhi. Called 'India's Vietnam' by some subcontinental analysts, Sri Lanka was indeed a fatal misadventure and a thoughtless military intervention under the guise of peace keeping that brought great humiliation and loss to our Army, before claiming Rajiv's own life.

It was difficult diplomacy for any country under any circumstances. There were complexities of ethnic ties, strategic interests and geopolitical considerations. India had for decades supported the Tamil movement, trained guerrillas and armed them, particularly in the time of Indira Gandhi. To shift from this position to one of allying with the Sri Lankan government, finding a solution to a chronic ethnic conflict, as well as maintaining covert aid to the Tamil rebels would require immense diplomatic skill and manoeuvres, an exceedingly long-term and lateral vision, and sound, capable advisors—all of which seemed lacking.

The ethnic problem in Sri Lanka started after its independence from Britain in 1948. The independent Sri Lankan government indulged in discriminatory policies against Tamil minorities. In the 1970s, two major Tamil parties united to form the Tamil United

Liberation Front (TULF) that started agitating for a separate state of Tamil Eelam in northern and eastern Sri Lanka, within the federal structure. Violence and a civil war erupted, and the government's response was tough. In 1987 the Sri Lankan army laid siege to Jaffna, an LTTE stronghold, resulting in large-scale civilian casualties and a humanitarian crisis. After diplomacy failed to convince the Sri Lankan government to halt the offensive, and after failure of a naval attempt to provide humanitarian assistance, to the rebels, India took a hard decision to carry out Operation Poomalai, an airdrop of humanitarian supplies commencing on 4 June 1987. Sri Lanka was informed that any opposition 'would be met by force'. The airdrop was the only successful mission.

Meanwhile, pressure grew within India to intervene on behalf of the Tamils and halt the offensive in an attempt to negotiate a political settlement. Prior to signing the Indo-Sri Lanka Peace Accord, Prabhakaran was airlifted to New Delhi for one-on-one discussions with Rajiv Gandhi in July 1987. It is reported to have been a very cordial meeting, which ended with Rajiv Gandhi ironically placing his bullet-proof jacket on the back of his future assassin, Velupillai Prabhakaran, saying, 'take care of yourself.' Later, he fobbed off his advisors' warnings that Prabhakaran was not to be trusted and would not keep his word, particularly on the LTTE disarming, and helping India find a solution through the accord that was to be signed in Colombo.

The late Balasingham, Prabhakaran's aide, who accompanied him, wrote later that Rajiv and Prabhakaran had a 'gentleman's agreement' that the LTTE supremo, even though he had deep reservations about the provisions of the agreement, would not oppose it in public, and that he would make only a token surrender of arms. Rajiv had agreed to compensate LTTE's financial loss if it were to dismantle its tax collection regime in Jaffna.

But the shrewd President Jayewardene was able to change Rajiv's mind and extract from him the Indo-Sri Lanka Peace Accord signed in Colombo on 29 July 1987. The gentleman's agreement with Prabhakaran was placed on the back burner. Colombo agreed to the devolution of power to the provinces, Sri Lankan troops were to be withdrawn to their barracks in the north, and Tamil rebels were to surrender their arms. India agreed to end support for the Tamil separatist movement and recognise the unity of Sri Lanka. The Indo-Sri Lanka Accord also underlined the commitment of Indian military assistance on which the Indian Peace Keeping Force came to be inducted into Sri Lanka. However, the LTTE and other Tamil groups were not made party to the talks. Though they initially agreed to surrender their arms to the IPKF, they later refused to disarm.

The Tamils in Sri Lanka felt completely betrayed by the Accord. A day after signing the Accord, Rajiv Gandhi was assaulted with a rifle by a Sinhalese cadet while receiving the guard of honour. The LTTE started to target the IPKF that now found itself engaged in a bloody police action against the LTTE, instead of brokering peace as it was supposed to.

Finally, in 1990, a humiliated India withdrew the last of its forces from Sri Lanka, and fighting between the LTTE and the government resumed. Rajiv Gandhi was assassinated by an LTTE suicide bomber at Sriperumbudur on 21 May 1991, during an election rally. This was the LTTE's revenge for the gross betrayal. Rajiv's Intelligence Bureau failed him in having no inkling of the assassination plot, though it had taken several months to plan, and he failed himself by showing no acumen or understanding of the deep schism that he had caused. The IPKF was for Rajiv, what Operation Blue Star was for Indira.

The 'Kitchen Cabinet', or, the power behind the throne

It was often said that Sonia Gandhi learnt politics at the dining table of her mother-in-law and husband. And so, when the UPA government came to power in 2004, Nehru-Gandhi loyalists were desperate for 'Madam' to take the helm as prime minister. Madam shrewdly refused, but kept for herself the real power as chairperson of the UPA, and of course, Congress president.

I feel therefore, that my ire is well directed. After what happened in Mumbai on 26 November 2008, I felt crestfallen and humiliated. I was naturally angry with the terrorists and their sympathizers across the border. But what they succeeded in doing to us inspite of their small number, made me angrier with our government and its agencies. I was aghast at their incompetence. I resolved to record my real feelings and not act like a polite flatterer.

My survey of the domestic situation and careful scrutiny of the government's conduct for more than a year have left no doubt in my mind that important sections of the government are busy lining their pockets, totally indifferent to the threats facing this unfortunate nation. I believe it will be wrong to blame the Congress party as a whole. Even today it has some individuals of integrity who are concerned for the national good. Congress President Sonia Gandhi, Prime Minister Dr Manmohan Singh and the prime minister-in-waiting, Rahul Gandhi, are the ones to blame.

On the morning after that tragic day, I shot off an angry epistle to Sonia Gandhi. Here are the relevant parts: 'Today, I am writing this with great anguish because my conscience does not permit me to remain silent. I must at least record what I think. For a long time it is obvious to the meanest intelligence that all your Intelligence Agencies are a complete failure and a fraud on the taxpayers. Reliable sources tell me that the ISI has even infiltrated into the RAW. Bangladesh has become a hotbed of anti-Indian activities. This requires the resignation and removal of some political heads but they are reported to enjoy your support.

'Yesterday's incidents in Bombay are proof of your government's incompetence. The names of your corrupt ministers are freely circulating. Don't think that you are not yourself the target. The country is on fire and it needs consolation and security... Neither you, nor your son whom you are projecting as the future prime minister of India, is the solution or even a ray of hope...

'I know this will annoy you but frankly I do not care since you show no concern for the country... I hope and pray that this evokes the kind of response which the grim situation of the country urgently requires.'

There was no significant change. I watched with dismay as the party of illustrious statesmen who led India into freedom virtually turned into a party of dumb, driven cattle, without courage to call their leaders to account. I was more contemptuous of large sections of the press which had lost its critical faculty and wholly jettisoned the obligation to disseminate the truth, however unpleasant, to keep the political sovereign updated and informed.

Flogging a dead horse

Our great Constitution outlawed kings and aristocrats by making India a democratic republic, but the longing for kingship persists in our subconscious. To be the king is the dream of not only the politicians but also of parents who rule over their children, husbands who keep their wives in servitude, and officials who forget their hemorrhoids by imagining that their shabby chairs are thrones.

Without any qualifications whatsoever, Sonia Gandhi fancies herself as an uncrowned empress of India and has psychologically bulldozed her similarly unqualified son into believing that India's prime ministership is his birthright. For a long time I did not believe that he would succumb to his mother's monarchical passion. It was in November 2008, after the monstrous terrorist attack in Mumbai, that I started having doubts. I wrote to him wanting to know more about the loony delusion that his fond mother and vast army of sycophants surrounding him were foisting upon his tender brain. I did not mince words, and plainly told him that he was just not qualified. He did not answer any of the questions I posed to him. I wish he had.

No one could have failed to notice how much space and exposure was provided to Rahul Gandhi by the media. The press gleefully reported that the 'Baton has passed to Rahul', 'Manmohan is dead and long live Rahul' was even exalted to the level of divine prophecy on the authority of a little known astrologer who claimed to have glanced at the horoscopes of the two men, but had evidently not bothered to see the natal chart of the Congress party.

I expected that some sections of the press would have the temerity to stand up and ask a few simple questions to the Prince Charming, the answers to which would have helped citizens to assess the qualifications of their future ruler. Here are a few pertinent questions that should be asked:

1. We have no objection to your mother's ambition to see you installed as India's prime minister. Obviously she did not entertain this ambition either for herself or any of her children in 1991. Are you prepared to take the nation into confidence and disclose the qualifications you have acquired since then to take into your hands the destiny of this complex, most populous and poverty stricken democracy?
2. Do you agree that the best available statesman in the country should fill that post? If yes, how have you convinced yourself that you are the one?
3. Intellectual assets of a leader should be as well known as his financial assets. So, would you kindly let the nation know

what academic qualifications you have acquired, when, how and from which institutions? It will help if you also tell the curious Indian nation what books you have read during the last five years; have you published any articles or any readable material on politics, economics, terrorism, war and peace? Is there even one speech you have made with a single quotable quote that illumines or inspires and gives us some clue to your intellectual attainments? We know quite a few talented young men in the Congress party and naturally people would like to be satisfied that you are better endowed than they. That your mother is Sonia*ji* or your father was Rajiv*ji* is not enough to qualify you to be the prime minister.
4. There have been oft-repeated charges of financial impropriety and worse against your family, including those made by the president of Janata Party, Subramanian Swamy, some Swiss magazines and, most unusually, in a book on the KGB. Why have you not responded?

If you plead ignorance of all the stuff mentioned in the questions above, you do not deserve to be India's prime minister any way.

UP elections of 2012

The results of the UP elections make me proud of my countrymen. It is a clear verdict against hereditary prime ministership, and has spared us a humiliation hundred times more excruciating than the one we suffered in 1962 at the hands of Rahul's great grandfather. It is unfortunate that the young Rahul Gandhi became a victim of a grand hallucination of dynastic rule and a pawn in *la famiglia's* grand design—abetted by an army of self-serving, deceitful, backstabbing sycophants—to secure what they consider is their Indian inheritance. I hope Rahul has learnt that India is not a monarchic or hereditary democracy and does not recognise birthright to prime ministership merely because s/he is descended from the Nehru-Gandhi family.

The people of UP, impoverished and betrayed continually, provided an apt and befitting reply in the 2012 elections that shocked *la famiglia* in its attempts to dynastically colonise India. I hope Rahul, Sonia and the sycophants have finally understood this.

Or are they yet to realise that their grand illusion of dynastic rule in India is breathing its last?

Their public responses were noteworthy. Rahul, in his dark hour, displayed courage and honour, taking complete responsibility for the UP debacle. This meant a stinging slap on the faces of sycophants like Digvijay Singh and Rita Bahuguna Joshi, silencing their inane and predictable statements—that Rahul created an enormous wave, but the Congress Organisation failed to convert it into votes—that the wave was so great that their candidates simply drowned in it, etc, etc. Just who were they trying to bluff? Did these deceitful managers previously have the guts to inform Rahul that at the grassroots level in UP the Congress did not have any organisation worth the name, and whatever it had was busy brokering votes with other parties? Sycophantic, deceitful advisors have been the death of kings and kingdoms. Leaders of democracies need to come out of their ivory towers and develop real contacts with the people who give them power.

Sonia Gandhi's response was disappointing. Rather tentatively, she seemed to blame the debacle on 'too many leaders' in UP. Surely that is an indirect acknowledgement that her leadership was ineffective. And rather inappropriately, in her blinding passion for securing her son's prime ministerial birthright, she tried to absolve him of all blame, thereby snuffing out every positive essence that his statement regarding moral responsibility had created. Not very flattering for her 42-year-old son, still being bailed out by mama in public, as if the UP election was a minor household issue. This merely confirms my point that in *la famiglia's* perception, ruling India is just another petty household matter.

Sonia Gandhi tried to explain the Congress defeat through her usual uninspiring one-liners. She did not even attempt to explain the two causes she mentioned—wrong selection of candidates and inflation. Neither did she suggest any mechanism for addressing them, specifically inflation, which is eating into the stomach of the *aam aadmi*. Instead, she started talking of the next round of state elections in Karnataka, Gujarat, etc., her most statesmanlike statement being that the Congress would 'pull up its socks'. In no way did she acknowledge that the Congress lost because she and her ring of flatterers did not permit any local leadership to grow in UP except from the bloodline.

Rahul Gandhi's advisors and teachers have made him a prisoner and insulated him from reality. Words of flattery and sycophancy are sweet, but always false. They are addictive and destructive, for they make a person averse to any criticism or further growth, and prevent talent and merit from emerging. When Rahul stated that the UP election was a 'good lesson for him', I hope he was thinking along these lines.

Rahul, and scions of other political dynasties in India, should remember that even Nero, the last emperor of Rome, was considered a good administrator as long as he heeded the advice of Seneca, his eminent tutor. But Nero's behaviour became so incorrigible, and the palace intrigues so unpalatable that Seneca left, and wrote that 'it is a dangerous office to give good advice to intemperate princes'.

Yet, Rahul never appeared as someone hankering for the prime minister's job. This was obviously something forced upon him as *Cosa Nostra*.* No doubt he performed all the fiascos advised by his self-serving tutors, without realising the traps he was falling into—whether it was the farce of Kalavati,# the Lokpal Bill, the Dalit home sharing†, competitive minority populism of the most misdirected kind, or the Bhatta-Parsaul padayatra** follies. Finally,

---

*Cosa Nostra, meaning 'our thing', was the colloquial name by which the American Mafia reffered to their organized crime group.

#Rahul Gandhi's much publicized 2009 visit to Kalavati Bandurkar, the farmer's window from Vidharbha, provides a wonderful example of political expedience as the poor woman served the purpose of providing an emotional example of the young leaders 'common touch' and care for the aam aadmi. But, like the people of India, her hope in the young leader ended in tragic disappointment as nothing was done to improve her lot or genuinely alleviate the distress of the poorest of the poor. Kalavati's husband had committed suicide in 2005 and her daughter, also driven to despair by poverty, committed suicide in 2011.

†In an attempt to woo the Dalit vote bank in UP, Rahul Gandhi visited many Dalit homes 2008 onwards, staying in their homes and sharing meals with them. He even took the visiting British Foreign Secretary to stay in a Dalit home in Amethi in 2009. Unfortunately, the Congress party's dismal showing at the hustings in 2012 shows that the young leader's attempt has not been successful.

**Bhatta and Parsaul are two villages in Greater Noida that were in the centre of bitter protests against Mayawati's land acquisition drive. Rahul Gandhi's visit to these two villages in July 2011 was part of his attempt to gain political mileage as the champion of the downtrodden. Although this visit ended in Rahul's midnight arrest, it does not appear to have achieved much else.

he fell into the trap of leading from the front with an unreliable, sabotaging back-up, and no exit route. This is not the way grand ambitions are executed in a state as complex and fractured as UP.

A word of advice to Rahul: 'Find your life where your heart is, young man. It is not too late. You cannot claim India as your birthright. Forget about ruling this country and the *Cosa Nostra*.'

And to *la famiglia*, I can only think of quoting from Cromwell, 'You have sat too long for any good you have been doing lately... Depart, I say; and let us have done with you. In the name of God, go!'

5
Three Blind Mice and the Politics of the Ruling Party

One day, at a busy airport, passengers on a commercial airliner sat strapped-in, waiting for the cockpit crew to show up. Eventually the pilot and co-pilot appeared at the rear of the plane and began walking up the aisle to the cockpit. Both appeared to be blind. The pilot, using a white cane, bumped into passengers right and left as he stumbled up the aisle, and so too did the co-pilot, who was using a guide dog. Their eyes were covered with huge sunglasses.

At first the passengers did not react, thinking this was some sort of practical joke. However, after a few minutes the engines revved and the airplane moved down the runway. The passengers looked at one another with some uneasiness, whispering among themselves and looking desperately to the flight attendants for reassurance. As the plane accelerated, people began panicking. Some passengers prayed but as the plane got closer to the end of the runway, the voices became more and more hysterical. Finally, when the airplane had less than 20 feet of runway left, there was a sudden change in decibel levels as everyone screamed at once, and at the very last moment the airplane took off and became airborne.

Up in the cockpit, the co-pilot breathed a sigh of relief. He turned to the pilot and said, 'You know, one of these days the passengers aren't going to scream, and we're going to get killed.'

The time has come for the nation to scream loudly and in unison. The state is being steered by the blind, and the screaming must not stop until the blind are relieved from their place at the controls. There is no doubt that on all fronts the government is failing the people of India. India, a country of 1.2 billion with one of the youngest populations in the world stands at 134 in the Human Development Index but has pride of place as the 95th most corrupt nation in the world. Of what account is our impressive GDP growth rate if the wealth of the nation is swallowed up in corruption that flows from the top down to every level of officialdom?

Citizens have the right to security—security of food, of livelihood, life and liberty. India is a proud constitutional democracy. We cannot allow our chosen representatives to become dynastic autocrats, sycophants or plunderers who work only for personal gain rather than for the good of the people. Every Indian citizen must stand up and demand accountability from those entrusted to steer and secure the nation, lest our leaders become our own worst enemies.

If we do not end corruption and eliminate insecurity, there is going to be a massive and imminent crash. The corrupt are more lethal to India than the blind pilots, while those who preside over the nation's insecurity are as dangerous as any threat from outside.

Prime Minister Manmohan Singh

Legend has it that Emperor Nero fiddled while Rome burnt. History may similarly someday apostrophize Prime Minister Manomohan Singh for dithering as India plunged into an abyss of failure under his leadership, not for lack of ability, but surely for lack of will.

In the 1990s Manmohan Singh courageously dethroned the public sector from the commanding heights of the Indian economy, a sensible reversal of the Nehruvian freakonomics, which condemned us to the much ridiculed 'Hindu' rate of growth for years and laid the solid foundation for the pyramid of bureaucratic and ministerial corruption. He immediately evoked my admiration bordering on reverence. After the Congress victory in 2004, Dr Manmohan Singh brought us in close partnership with the Americans, a partnership mandated to expand the democratic frontiers of the world and to confer the blessings of democracy on any people wanting to imbibe them. He reminded me of Gandhiji's promise: 'Independent India will be the conscience of the world.'

Conscience requires firm conviction and courage that short term interests will not trump perennial values, and expediency will not drown truth. The idolized Manmohan Singh vanished leaving behind an ineffective and gratuitous prime minister who betrayed the trust of the nation not once but innumerable times, preferring politicking and narrow party interests to statesmanship.

Symptomatic of the prime minister's gratuitousness and subservience to the Nehru-Gandhi family was the certificate he gave to Rahul Gandhi, declaring to a gullible and meek nation that the inexperienced and inept Rahul was perfectly qualified to be its prime minister. Implicit in this was the idea that Manmohan Singh was only warming the seat for him, ever ready to vacate it when His Royal Highness was ready to take over. This is an act of gross betrayal of national interest. It was Dr Singh's duty to examine Rahul Gandhi's intellectual assets and ability, his ideas—political and economic—his plans to remove callous corruption and degrading poverty, his ability to handle Parliament, and the complex problems of our prolific population. This analysis should have been presented to the nation which could then have decided for itself whether or not it considered Rahul fit to be a future prime minister of India. But sycophancy is not the prime minister's only failing.

Exclusive growth

It is surely the job of the leader of a nation to ensure that his government works efficiently for the welfare of all its citizens. Yet, after almost 64 years of independence, and an average of 8.9% growth in the last 10 years, we have achieved the dubious distinction of almost becoming the malnutrition capital of the world. Our 'child under-nutrition' rate of 48%, which includes 20% wasted children, is an international talking point, while our high infant, child and maternal mortality rates and chronic energy deficiency among at least one-third of adults, are matters of national shame. Added to this, the soaring anaemia rates among women, children and men will ensure that the afflicted, who belong to the lowest economic class, will remain disadvantaged. India has the highest underweight prevalence in the world (47%) among adolescent girls as reported in the UNICEF State of the World's Children Report 2011. As long as the population below the poverty line remains malnourished, the malnourished will remain poor.

Why have we reached this state despite our growth rate? Because the growth figures apply mainly to a mere 10% of the population. This economic growth is non-inclusive, and its returns inequitable. Not that one is against economic growth of the nation. That is essential. But it is incumbent upon the government to translate the returns of growth to ensure public good. This is the government's paramount responsibility.

Let me reproduce the statements made by Manmohan Singh on malnutrition in the last few years. On 15 August 2007 he said: 'The problem of malnutrition is a matter of national shame. We have tried to address it by making the mid-day meal universal and massively expanding the anganwadi system. However, success requires sustained effort at the grassroots. Infants need to be breast-fed, given access to safe drinking water and health care. We need the active involvement of the community and panchayats to see that what we spend reaches our children. I appeal to the nation to resolve and work hard to eradicate malnutrition within five years.'

It is not quite clear in what manner the prime minister wanted the nation to work to eradicate malnutrition in five years. The deception is evident. The responsibility of eradicating malnutrition was conveniently passed on to the nation. No concrete programme for eradicating malnutrition emerged from the government.

On 15 August 2008 he stated, 'The problem of malnutrition is a curse that we must remove. Our efforts to provide every child with access to education and to improved health care services for all citizens will continue...' But there was no response from his ministries in terms of any national programme to remove the 'curse'.

On 15 August 2009, Prime Minister Manmohan Singh announced: 'It is our ardent desire that not even a single citizen of India should ever go hungry. This is the reason why we have promised a Food Security Law under which every family living below the poverty line will get a fixed amount of foodgrain every month at concessional rates. It is also our national resolve to root out malnutrition from our country. In this effort, special care will be taken of the needs of women and children. We will endeavour to extend the benefit of ICDS to every child below the age of six years in the country by March 2012.'

Whoever wrote his speech mixed up hunger, food security and malnutrition, all of which are technically different and require different interventions. Again there was no programmatic response, and wisely, the prime minister omitted the subject in his Independence Day speech of 2010. The finance minister's budget speech of February 2011 did not make any mention of any measure to address India's 'curse' of malnutrition. However, the HUNGaMA

(Hunger and Malnutrition) Report of 2011, which is a survey of 112 districts in India, shows that child malnutrition is widespread across states and districts and starts early in life: 42 per cent of children under five are underweight and 59 per cent are stunted. Of the children suffering from stunting, about half are severely stunted while half of all children are underweight or stunted by the age of 24 months.

Despite this dismal situation, our country does not have any comprehensive national programme for combating malnutrition. Apart from directly negating the quality of our human resources, this also impacts our GDP as it reduces physical and cognitive growth of individuals, reduces their productivity and earning capacity, and results in economic loss to the nation. It breeds illness and adds to the health costs of the country. There is enough research and evidence that establish that at least 4% of GDP is lost through rampant malnutrition and anaemia among our population.

A comment on the much vaunted Food Security Act proposed by the National Advisory Committee, which provides for 35 kg of rice/wheat/millet per family per month at ₹3/2/1 per kg respectively for the priority category—that is the poorest of the poor. Translated into calories for an average family constituting five members, assuming there is an equitable distribution of 7 kg per person, it would amount to 234 gm per day, which equals approximately 650 calories (without protein and micro nutrient content) per person per day as against a Required Dietary Allowance (RDA) of average 1,800 calories. This is assuming that the crumbling Public Distribution System actually delivers, and that these calories actually become an addition and not a substitute. While this may amount to prevention of starvation, it would not amount to food or nutritional security. The Bill was passed in Parliament in August 2013, reducing the food grain entitlement to 5 kg per person. However, the scheme remains without any implementation blueprint, except that the leaking Public Distribution System continues to be the implementation vehicle. Cost sharing and responsibilities of Centre and States are yet to be finalized.

I know that tackling malnutrition can be challenging. Its causes encompass gender inequity, negative social customs, lack of information and awareness, substandard care of children, girls and women, poor nutritional practices, unsatisfactory service delivery of government programmes impacting health and nutrition, water and sanitation, and of course poverty. Addressing all these causes simultaneously would require concerted action by various ministries: health, women and child development, food and agriculture, water and sanitation. Getting so many ministries to work in unison can only be done by a powerful overarching authority such as the prime minister.

A committee under the chairmanship of the prime minister was set up in 1994 to do this, but it never met. On 31 October 2008, the PMO constituted another committee with the following Terms of Reference: a) Provide policy directions to address India's challenges through coordinated inter-sectoral action. b) Review programmes for nutrition on a quarterly basis.

It is curious that the prime minister was not kept informed that it is not policy direction that we lack, but policy implementation of our existing National Nutrition Policy 1993. And still more curious that his principal secretary, T.K.A Nair, a man with no expertise in the subject should choose to be the Member Convener. However, this Committee finally met on 24 January 2011, and came up with a decision wholly inadequate to address the dimension of our country's malnutrition.

It is time the UPA government actually focused on the poor or the aam aadmi and took genuine steps to address malnutrition by not only setting up a High Powered Committee headed by an eminent expert to prepare a blueprint on combating malnutrition, but also seriously implemented its recommendations. This would give the poor a chance to be included in India's growth story. And if money is a concern for implementing such a programme, perhaps the prime minister could bring some focus on preventing scams that drain the nation's wealth instead of silently bearing witness to the plunder of India by his various colleagues?

Silence has to be seen as complicity

Dr Manmohan Singh's silence as scam after scam rocks the nation is heart-wrenching. I can only call it complicity when a person of Dr Singh's stature allows plunder of the Indian state. I have exposed in detail the role of senior members of the Congress party in defrauding the victims and kin of the Bhopal gas tragedy of their rightful compensation and feathering their own nests with these ill-gotten gains. Yet the prime minister in his wisdom took no action against the corrupt.

The mask of ignorance is often useful in shedding responsibility but it is sometimes too thin a mask to be credible. What has come to be called A. Raja's scam of the Communication and Information Technology Ministry of the Government of India, did not happen overnight. Its roots and active operation lasted more than three years before the game ended. How then does the prime minister, himself a shrewd economist with a sound understanding of fiscal affairs, plead ignorance and innocence from complicity?

I had myself appeared in one of the spectrum litigations years ago and argued in open court that terrible mismanagement and fraud were going on in the operations of that ministry. The government read our affidavits. Surely it was impossible that the prime minister did not know what was happening, and anyway, it was his duty to know. In fact, *The Hindu* (23 December 2010) also brought to light a letter of 22 November 2007, where Minister Raja informed Prime Minister Manmohan Singh that as a result of the TRAI recommendations an unprecedented number of applications were being received because no cap had been imposed on the number of licenses to be issued in a service area. As a result of this, a cut-off date of 1 October 2007 was announced and a press release had also been issued containing the information that 575 applications had been received for 22 service areas.

Many alternative procedures were debated for dealing with this situation. The minister of Communication and Information Technology obviously wanted the prime minister to concur in his rejection of the honest and sensible suggestion of the Ministry of Law to refer the 2G spectrum allocation issue to the Empowered Group of Ministers (EGoM). The minister clearly informed the prime minister that his ministry had decided to continue with the existing policy, viz., 'first come first served', for the processing of these applications. The cut-off date was brought forward to 25 September 2007.

The prime minister's response, or rather lack of response, to this letter speaks for itself. If the prime minster wishes the nation to believe that he is not tainted by the spectrum scam why have we not been given evidence of his disapproval of the first come-first served policy or his instruction to the erring minister that the decision be left to the Empowered Group of Ministers?

Instead, the response to this important letter is a clever affirmation of what the minister had decided to do in which, by using ambiguous language, the prime minister left a window to defend himself in case trouble broke out. Instead of coming clean to the nation, silence was the cloak behind which Manmohan Singh hoped to prove his innocence. He is obviously familiar with what most persons accused of crime in the United States do. They plead the Fifth Amendment which provides that no person shall be compelled in any criminal case to be a witness against himself. The Americans borrowed it from the Common Law of England, and our Constitution borrowed it from both. It was incorporated in Article 20(3) which ordains, 'No person accused of any offence shall be compelled to be a witness against himself.'

This is somewhat narrower than the Anglo-American rule, because it is confined to the accused and leaves out the witnesses in an ongoing trial. It is difficult to fathom whether Dr Singh's original long silence was his own voluntary decision or induced by his advisers. His act of exposing himself to a well chosen friendly electronic media was certainly long awaited. People were rightly disgusted that like Kumbhakaran of Ramayana our prime minister managed to sleep while the populace was crying aloud in agony, 'We have long credited you with integrity, but our confidence is fast melting; please speak to us in your own interest. If you don't do it soon, we will conclude that you are no better than the crooks surrounding you.'

Such facetiousness ill becomes the prime minister of a great democracy where citizens have the right to demand answers from those they elect.

S band fraud—Rot at the very top

There are many other scams that have disgraced and blackened the integrity of the prime minister and the UPA government and enumerating each here will be of limited value. However, I will mention one in an area that was directly under the control of the prime minister of India.

On 24 December 2004, Madhavan Nair, chairman of Antrix Corporation, a public sector undertaking under the Department of Space and owned by the Government of India approved a contract with Devas Multimedia at a board meeting, leasing for 12 years, 90% of S-band transponder capacity of two geostationary satellites, GSAT 6 and GSAT 6A, to be produced and launched by ISRO. The board, which took this momentous decision, has among its members the financial officers of the Department of Space. For some curious reasons, they were not asked to participate in the board meeting. The credibility of the board's decision is open to serious challenge and the terms offered to Devas were highly suspect.

On 28 January 2005, the same Madhavan Nair, in his capacity as secretary of Department of Space approved the contract. He then submitted the proposal for production of GSAT 6 to the Space Commission, of which he was chairman. He, thus, had no difficulty in quickly obtaining the approval of the Space Commission on 26 May 2005. This stage discloses a suspicious and almost fraudulent operation. The Space Commission received no information from him that in his capacity as chairman of Antrix he had already concluded a deal with Devas in December 2004 or that Antrix was committed to giving away 90% of the transponder capacity of GSAT 6 to Devas, or that the launch and spectrum costs had not been factored in the financial estimate.

Having the decision of the Space Commission with him, Nair now put on his fourth hat as chairman of ISRO. He commenced the process of production of GSAT 6 at an approved cost of ₹269 cr. So a private player, Devas, walked away with a financially succulent contract, the burden of which has to be borne by the taxpayer. The taxpayer is entitled to ask what role of studious supervision and careful scrutiny of the feasibility of such an expensive project came from the prime minister as minister for the Department of Space.

In his statement to Parliament in February, 2011, the prime minister discussed this transaction, but one looks in vain for any credible explanation and exhibition of the care and honesty that are prerequisites for entering into such deals. He claimed he knew nothing about the deal, but the very fact that it has now been annulled, is a confession that fraud had vitiated the transaction. The people must know who practiced this fraud and why the PM did not detect or prevent it.

It is to the credit of some sections of the media that they exposed this clandestine deal and the stark fact that it would result in a colossal loss of a precious national resource without the guardian of public wealth, in this case the prime minister, having performed his elementary duties of a trustee.

The PM continues to claim that he was ignorant of everything that polluted the deal and led to its cancellation. It was hoped that the cancellation would stop all wagging tongues and the people would soon forget the scandal. A proper name for this default is criminal breach of trust punishable u/s 409 of the Indian Penal Code. The excuse that the deal has been cancelled because the government suddenly realized that the spectrum sold is required for security purposes, does not mitigate the crime.

It has now emerged that Devas is a company comprising several former ISRO employees who had managed to pocket precious S-band spectrum for a song for their company. It is time that the people of India and their elected representatives realized that something is terribly amiss with the Department of Space and the nation should be informed of some more facts about the past of this dubious project. The first negotiation between Antrix and Forge Advisors commenced in March 2003, when Dr Kasturirangan headed the Department of Space. By December 2004 the erstwhile CEO of Forge had registered Devas Multimedia as an Indian company and become its CEO. In the same month the Antrix board cleared the deal. The inference is obvious. Dr Kasturirangan is today a member of the Planning Commission and his connections with the Department of Space continue.

In our system of Constitutional democracy, the cabinet minister in charge of the ministry is responsible for its functioning. The minister heading a government department cannot, like the three proverbial monkeys, tell the nation: 'I see no evil, I hear no evil, I do no evil.' Much less should the PM who heads this department.

The Antrix–Devas deal has strategic and security implications. In a Cabinet form of government one expects the ministers of Finance, Home and Telecommunications not to allow a deal in which sensitive matters fall into the hands of people never tested for their integrity and patriotism. There is no doubt that this scam is much larger than the 2-G spectrum scam. Media exposure saved the nation. A high-level enquiry is a welcome step but it should not be headed or influenced by individuals who had direct or indirect connections with the deal at any stage.

Although we experience a patriotic thrill each time a satellite is fired into space from Sriharikota, the prime minister could also start finding methods of exercising some control over the unjustified delays and cost overruns in ongoing launches. But considering his blindness to all things related to good governance, it is pertinent to ask if he is even aware of these problems. Does he know why GSLV launches are failing and what his scientists should be doing to prevent further failures? How did he not know that Antrix, a PSU under his department, was approving multi-billion-dollar deals and stealthily gifting away national resources without competent approval and by bluffing to the Space Commission and the Cabinet? Does the PM realize that his space secretary provided false information to the Space Commission, a body where the PM is represented by his minister of state, the national security advisor and his principal secretary? Has the PM realized that his officers and advisers let him down either by conniving or remaining silent? Has the PM realized that Space Commission member Dr Kasturirangan, who initiated the deal with Forge Advisors in 2003 (which later floated Devas Multimedia), sat at the Space Commission meeting on 24 June 2005 without uttering a word about it when the subject was discussed and approved? Is it possible that the PM really knew nothing of all this?

The much awaited CAG report on the Antrix–Devas deal was tabled in Parliament, on 15 May 2012, a deal that was estimated to have been bigger than the 2G scam, had it not been aborted by a vigilant media. This contract, executed or not, is significant, because it pertains to the mismanagement of a department coming directly under the supervision of the hallowed prime minister.

The CAG report turned out to be a damp squib. It reiterated facts already exposed and dissected in the public domain, added some technical details, financial data, shareholding information of Devas, but left gaping holes of unanswered questions.

I have repeatedly asked these questions: Why does the CAG report dismiss the B.K. Chaturvedi High Powered Review Committee appointed by the prime minister in February 2011, and provide no clue as to why the second Committee under Pratyush Sinha, with an almost identical mandate, was appointed, and what advantages it held over the Chaturvedi Committee. Did Pratyush Sinha's fallen public credibility after the Supreme Court's observations against him as CVC raise his credentials within government to chair the second mysterious committee and perform a specific mission of protecting the protectors of the scam?

The Sinha Committee, though apparently formal in its mandate, conducted itself in a Gestapo-like manner. The provision of law under which it was operating and its investigation process remains secret. Evidence reveals that it flouted every principle of natural justice. It is a fact that the constitution and terms of reference of the committee were concealed from the respondents, original documents to enable them to file replies were not provided to them, and opportunity for personal hearing before the commission was denied to them despite their requests. Without following any procedures of an enquiry, the Sinha Committee concluded itself in indecent haste, and finalised its report illegally without even a final notice to the respondents. And the most astonishing feature is that notices kept going to the respondents to appear, even after the Committee had submitted its report!

Madhavan Nair and his cronies did not require two high-level committees to establish their guilt in leading the scam. The documents spoke for themselves, and pointed prima facie towards their gross irregularities. But the question is whether they were also made consensual fall guys. What about their supervisors and protectors in the prime minister's office, who allowed the deal almost unto fruition? In his immediate statements, post-blacklist, Madhavan Nair publicly stated that the PMO was aware of the deal at every stage. There is evidence in Devas correspondence to back this, of Devas CEO having meetings with Prithviraj Chavan MoS, PMO in charge of ISRO, with T.K.A. Nair, principal secretary to prime minister, and Radhakrishnan, Chairman ISRO in late 2010, discussing the GSAT 6 launch, well after Space Commission had decided to annul the contract. Why did the Pratyush Sinha Committee or the CAG not go into these issues? And what about the silent lot of scientist conspirators and experts sitting at the Space Commission meetings of May 2005 and October 2009 (including the present and former chairmen of ISRO, and directors of ISRO Satellite Centre) who by their positions, past and present, or their expertise to qualify for Space Commission membership, should have known all the violated technicalities and procedures cited in the CAG report, but quietly sat without asking any questions they were duty bound to ask, and approved the construction of satellites GSAT 6 and GSAT 6A? I wonder why the CAG has spared them in his chapter on governance and conflict of interest or the multiple-hat phenomena. In fact, the report underplays the role and responsibilities of the Space Commission members, without noting that as per Space Department procedures, Space Commission approvals constitute the inviolable text of subsequent Cabinet Notes.

The closest kept secret of the deal still remains shrouded in secrecy, namely, the suspiciously huge delay between July 2010, when the Space Commission decided to annul the deal and February 2011, when the Cabinet Committee on Security annulled it under public pressure. Note that it was in this period that Devas was dialoguing with important Space Commission members of the PMO and Radhakrishnan, regarding prioritising the launch of GSAT 6. Why does the CAG report ignore these vital facts while discussing Space Department governance?

Disappointing again that the CAG did not consider it important to go into the propriety of reasons for annulment of the contract, issues that have direct financial implications well within the scrutiny of the CAG, as they determine Devas' leveraging power for reparation from the public exchequer. Why was the contract annulled on weak grounds of "imminent requirement of vital strategic and societal applications", when it could more strongly be annulled on grounds of false information provided by Devas (that Radhakrishnan was well aware of) that it had the ability to design digital multimedia receivers and commercial information devices, with ownership and intellectual property rights? The CAG report states that Devas has filed a claim before the International Chamber of Commerce in February 2012, seeking either performance of the agreement by Antrix, or a compensation of US$1.6 billion (₹8,240 cr) plus interest, and costs. I ask Dr Radhakrishnan whether this was a deliberate move, blessed by his bosses in the PMO, who finally approved the clauses for cancellation of the contract, to strengthen Devas' case for reparation. This is a well-tested ruse used successfully by Congress governments in the Bhopal and Bofors cases. Sabotage the government's case and make it fail, and then fool and extort the taxpayer.

I am hopeful that the PAC will examine these issues, as well as the processes and legal propriety of Pratyush Sinha's khap panchayat carefully, particularly regarding its tainted chairmanship and tainted membership of Chairman ISRO Dr Radhakrishnan, who not only had silently approved the construction of GSAT 6A in the Space Commission, but also hobnobbed with Devas, even after the Space Commission's decision to annul the deal. Cherry-picking the guilty only substantiates my suspicion that the Pratyush Sinha Committee had clear instructions from its appointers about who should be made the fall guys, and who should be let off. An examination of the Space Commission membership that approved GSAT 6 and GSAT 6A, with their present and past positions will give accurate information of those members who knew about the deal and sat like silent conspirators, committing the same offence of concealing facts from the Space Commission as Madhavan Nair. Why have they been exonerated?

The CAG report talks at length regarding the absence of good governance in the Department of Space. Madhavan Nair's five hats are old hat indeed. The critical question is how these five hats—without checks and balances, and systemic degeneration—were allowed to flourish under the direct supervision of the prime minister, so much so that Chairman ISRO and his scientist cronies had the gumption to lie to him, to the Space Commission and to the Cabinet as well. Didn't the PM have any oversight mechanisms? If he did not, as appears evident, he is as guilty of dereliction of duty and breach of trust.

The Antrix–Devas deal for the first time exposed the murky underbelly of the Department of Space, which was once the pride of India and is directly under the prime minister. Integrity and scientific excellence have been lost with the passage of time. This Department has had the distinction of having been led by brilliant pioneers like Vikram Sarabhai and Satish Dhawan.

It is time the prime minister reintroduces scientific excellence and probity in ISRO to rejuvenate it.

Fiscal management is dead

Economic fraud goes hand-in-hand with economic mismanagement. We enacted the Fiscal Responsibility and Budget Management Act in 2003. It prescribes in detail the contents of the annual budget. The mid-term fiscal policy statement should tell the people how the balance between income and expenditure is going to be maintained and how scarce capital is proposed to be spent for productive purposes only.

A fiscal policy strategy statement must explain the scheme of taxation, expenditure, market borrowing and the strategic priorities of the government and the rationale for any significant or novel changes in fiscal management. A micro-economic framework statement containing the government's honest assessment of the growth prospect of the economy and the assumptions on which the forecast is based, is a further mandatory requirement.

The more important part is Section 4 of the Act, which totally forbids unaffordable expenses. The government is mandated to take appropriate measures to reduce fiscal deficit as well as revenue deficit to zero by March of year 2009. In that year, the government was required to step into a new era of revenue surplus.

Let us now see what the finance minister actually did. Instead of going down to zero, the deficit instead jumped from 2.5% of the GDP to 6.2%. In other words, it more than doubled. The fiscal deficit is an enormous figure of ₹4.5 lakh crore, as against ₹1.33 lakh crore of the earlier year. The framers of the Fiscal Management Act had permitted such a deviation only in case of a threat to national security or natural calamity or some other cause of similar nature.

More frightening was the revenue deficit—from about ₹55,000 cr to a whopping ₹283,000 cr, or 4.8% of the GDP. These enormous sums had to be procured by market borrowing. Lenders, naturally expecting a rise in inflation, refuse to dish out money except at increased rates of interest. Little may remain of the borrowed money to spend on creation of jobs and employment, or relief to victims of economic distress. Even an incurable optimist will not be sure of being able to augment manufactures, exports or domestic demand. The finance minister is thus no longer a prudent manager, but a reckless gambler. The Fiscal Management Act is dead.

No justification is offered for its demise. If the market does not provide funds for the gamble it is certain that money will be raised by printing more paper, a sure way of producing unbearable price rises and public misery.

India's woes are aplenty and they do not seem to have an end.

Turning a blind eye to terrorism

India has been a victim of terrorism since the 1990s. Not once, but repeatedly. We saw extensive terrorism in the states of Jammu and Kashmir and Punjab, which started with indigenous Kashmiri organisations sponsored and supported undoubtedly by our disgruntled neighbours. More recently the nation has been rocked by the shock and humiliation of 26 November 2008 when 10 deranged men stupefied hundreds of policemen and killed innocent, harmless citizens in various parts of Mumbai, far removed from one another. Of course, something much more terrible had happened to New York seven years prior. But the Americans had no warning that terrorists had become so sophisticated that they could carry out such a diabolical conspiracy on their soil.

We have no such excuse. Reluctant but reliable disclosures made since, clearly prove that we had plenty of warnings of the coming disaster, but our blind or otherwise occupied leaders did not notice them. We were alerted by the 1993 bomb blasts in Mumbai, said to be reprisals for the Babri Masjid demolition. Then there was an assault on our Parliament in 2001, and attacks on our trains by armed terrorists in which numerous passengers were killed in 2006. We had warnings that attacks would be mounted from Mumbai Harbour and that marauders would arrive by sea. Yet, our humiliated nation swallowed all this incompetence and returned the Congress party to power in the election of 2009 with increased electoral strength. Indeed, a remarkable act of faith!

Post the Mumbai humiliation we heard great tom-tomming about a change of guard at the centre to effectively combat terrorism. Union Home Minister Shivraj Patil was replaced by the much-lauded P. Chidambaram and the nation held its breath expecting assertive action to make the nation secure from threats—both external and internal. After approximately a year in the saddle, the home minister kindly disclosed the jaw-breaking name which has been selected for his ambitious scheme, the Crime and Criminal Tracking Network System (CCTNS). The job of this impressively-named organization would be 'to facilitate collection, storage, retrieval analysis transfer and sharing of data and information'. A special branch of the police would be added at the district level in every state. P. Chidambaram claims that the scheme involves a bold, thorough and radical 'restructuring of the entire security infrastructure'. To me the plan reeks more of wish-fulfillment than strategic and conscientious planning, although it received plenty of attention from a subservient and paralyzed press that dutifully reported without exercising its critical faculty and exposing the scheme's total bankruptcy.

Let us look at the prominent features of this plan and my statement would become clear.

State governments were to recruit four lakh policemen within two years. Gaping holes were left providing no information on when and where these 'policemen' were to be trained for jobs which they were unaccustomed to; who would provide the training, what effective weapons they would be armed with, what new techniques would be taught to them for self-defense and for the destruction of terrorists, and what would be the unique character of these new recruits that would distinguish them from the incompetent police force with which we have managed our internal defence apparatus so far.

The home minister also proposed a 'Cabinet Committee on Security' involving the Prime Minister's Office, the Ministry of Home Affairs and the Cabinet Secretariat. How these worthies were to combine, cogitate and arrive at conclusions, nobody knows. What their qualifications were for dealing with this highly complex problem, nobody knows.

During this time, it also came to light that India does not have a database of information since records of crimes and criminals were not maintained in an accessible form at an accessible place where policemen could made use of the information. Everybody knows that most police stations keep records of petty thieves, pickpockets, goondas and blackmailers. The list certainly does not include terrorists—actual or potential. The question of why this simple weakness was not discovered decades ago and who is to be punished for long years of criminal incompetence and manifest dereliction of duty, remains unanswered till date.

Our intelligence gathering apparatus is spread over various ministries. The Intelligence Bureau (IB) reports to the Ministry of Home Affairs while the Research & Analysis Wing (RAW) reports to the Cabinet Secretariat. When, if at all, these two branches share information remains a mystery. Then there are other organizations with equally high faluting names—Joint Intelligence Committee (JIC), National Technical Research Organisation (NTRO), Aviation Research Centre (ARC), National Security Adviser (NSA) and his secretariat all of whom appear to function in silos.

The armed forces have three separate intelligence agencies—one for the army, the second for the navy and the third for the air force. They are all under the umbrella of the Defense Intelligence Agency.

While the imperative needs of analysis, effective action and formulation of sensible policies require unification of these organizations and the closing down of a few, the home minister seems to have revived one more, long since thought to be dead: the Multi Agency Centre (MAC) which has been renamed the National

Counter Terrorism Centre (NCTC). It is claimed on behalf of this revived corpse that 'it has been operationalised'.

What does it mean? Who heads it, runs it, to whom does it report, who is politically responsible for its competence or lack of it? These are questions which the nation is entitled to ask and to receive sensible and simple answers.

Even though the home minister is not unmindful of serious turf wars amongst these organizations and their prolific membership, he has left it to the stars and to inscrutable providence to ensure that all organizations function efficiently and resolve the problem of information sharing amongst themselves. This lack of information sharing has been the bane of national security and a boon to miscreants who seek to destabilize India through vicious terrorist attacks.

Address injustices that are the source of Maoist power

Along with terrorism, national security also faces threats from growing internal unrest. The government was practically in a state of denial of the problem till 2008-09. Today approximately 80 districts across nine states are considered to be infected by the Naxals or Maoists and government writ has little currency in these areas.

The Maoist guerrilla army is almost entirely made up of desperately poor tribals living in conditions of chronic hunger that verge on famine of the kind we associate with sub-Saharan Africa.

Home Minister P. Chidambaram, who has more knowledge of Indian stock exchanges than hunger of tribals in the forests, and Prime Minister Dr Manmohan Singh who knows more about GDP figures than about the misery of millions, are not the answer. They just do not know. And they do not care to know either, about tribals who have been exploited for centuries and more so during the 60 years of Independence. Some glimmer of dignity is provided to tribals by Maoists who live amongst them. They do not believe, for instance, that the roads that are being built in Dantewada are meant for them or their children. Their mortal enemy is the National Mineral Development Corporation.

The price of progress

Mining companies are swiftly taking over the bauxite rich, low, flat-topped hills of south Orissa that have been home to the Dongria-

Kondh tribe long before there was a country called India or a state called Orissa. The Kondh worshipped and watched over the hills as living deities; the hills made their life possible. The Niyamgiri hills are covered by cool forests which induce moderate rainfall, and provide water for the rivers and rivulets that flow from them and irrigate the lands below. The hills, ancient and the only home of the Kondh, have been sold to a British company called Vedanta owned by Anil Aggarwal—the Indian billionaire who lives in London in a mansion that once belonged to the Shah of Iran.

Vedanta is after the tribes of Orissa, their hearth and home and their pots and pans. The destruction of ecology, disturbance of environmental harmony and the death and destitution of lakhs of Dongra-Kondh are imminent. Vedanta's response is cruel: Why not? It is only the price of progress. America, Europe and Australia have a history of killing indigenous populations: why not India?

The Niyamgiri hills have been sold for their bauxite while government has announced Operation Green Hunt, a war purportedly against the Maoist terrorists headquartered in the jungles of central India. In reality, it is a cruel, avaricious and corrupt war against the landless, the Dalits, workers, peasants and weavers of the region. These weak, downtrodden, almost-forgotten people are pitted against a juggernaut of injustice by a cruel society and corrupt politicians. I regret that even the Supreme Court, presided over by a Dalit chief justice, has been unwittingly supportive of a policy that involves wholesale corporate takeover of these people's lands and resources.

The war against tribals must stop. It can be stopped, but not by Manmohan Singh and Chidambaram. The common man must speak up. Police arms and uninhibited murder are not substitutes for hospitals, schools and clean water. It is possible the *vox populi* will be drowned out by media barons in the pay of corrupt politicians. But people must not allow mining companies to exterminate the army of passive resisters.

Of course one condemns the violence of the Maoists but they are not terrorists. The recent atrocity which killed more than 70 of our guardians of law and order must be dealt with according to law, but without cruelty or contempt. But let us not forget that in 2004, when the ban on the Peoples' War Group (the earlier incarnation of Maoists) was lifted in Andhra Pradesh, their rally was attended in Warangal by 15 lakh Indian citizens. Maoists draw their power from the atrocities perpetrated on the poor who, decimated by overwhelming force, have been forced to flee into the jungles of Chhattisgarh and join the comrades already working there.

In April 2010, the prime minister said, 'Maoists are the single largest internal security threat to the country.' On 6 January 2009 he thought that Maoists had only 'modest capabilities'. On 18 June 2009, at a meeting of state chief ministers and in Parliament he was more forthright about what he really felt: 'If left wing extremism continues to flourish in parts which have natural resources of minerals, the climate for investment would certainly be affected.' Does it not sound like a sell-out to crony capitalism? To me it does. Corrupt governments are not the solution to the problem. They are the problem. Society has to reform itself and eliminate insane, caste-ridden injustice and cruelty.

Vedanta reached the Supreme Court seeking sanction of its scheme to acquire tribal land and set up vast industries. The following paragraph occurs in the 2007 judgment of the Supreme Court:

'On the other side we have a picture of abject poverty in which the local people are living in Lanjigarh tehsil including the tribal people. There is no proper housing. There are no hospitals. There are no schools and people are living in extremely poor conditions.'

It was no business of the Supreme Court to draw up a list of some improvements in the scheme presented by Vedanta. But in essence, the Supreme Court encouragingly declared, 'come back to us and we will approve your plan.' To say the least, this has been one of the most unusual exercises of judicial power, particularly when it knew that Vedanta had been found guilty in Norway of environmental damage and human rights violations.

The court advised, in essence: 'Make the application in the name of Sterlite, a Vedanta associate.' Vedanta had been described as the subsidiary of Sterlite in the pleadings, but that did not matter to the court. Vedanta was just an associate; maybe a bad one, but its association was good enough for the court.

P.B. Sawant, a distinguished ex-justice of the Supreme Court, now wholly committed to social service, says that the Maoists must be thanked for making known the injustice done to the people of the region. Talk to heroes like Binayak Sen or Shoma Chaudhary of Tehelka, and you will know the horrifying truth. It is not a matter without significance that Home Minister Chidambaram was a non-executive director of Vedanta, drawing an annual salary of US $75,000. Of course, he resigned when he became minister. But it is difficult to get rid of past friendships and loyalties—even for a minister.

An independent People's Tribunal comprising distinguished judges and social workers has found that there has been persistent and gross violation of the rights of the poor and the Fifth Schedule rights of the tribals. The government remedy of Salwa Judum (Peoples' March) is wholly counterproductive and will only lead to slaughter of the innocent. It has already proved a colossal failure. The only sensible solution is to address the injustices that are the primary dynamo of Maoist power. They will respond.

It is true that the Maoists adopted a part of the Communist vocabulary when Muppala Lakshmana Rao formed the Communist Party of India (Maoist) in 2004. But the Maoists have realized that the Indian state is not likely to wither away. It is the biggest folly to treat them like terrorists whom we have encountered in Kashmir, Delhi and Mumbai. A wise and humane government can deal with the Maoist movement by unconditional talks to evolve a programme of redressing the festering grievances of the tribals and ensuring rapid economic growth. Instead it sells tribal land to corporate giants who are rightly seen as predators and agents of an insensitive government.

Vote bank politics obfuscates the truth

Appeasement of the Muslim vote bank by the so called 'secular' parties of our country takes many forms. In this regard, Gujarat provides a valuable lesson. The Gujarat police and the Special Investigation Team, set up by the efforts of the National Human Rights Commission and the consent of numerous organizations, including the Gujarat government, have found that the burning of innocent *karsevaks* in Godhra was a pre-planned attack not very different from macabre terrorist action. Those who planned this horrendous act must have known that it would lead to reprisals and that reprisals would mean great injury to and suffering for the Muslim minority community.

This did happen. So why did the conspirators of Godhra want these horrible reprisals against their co-religionists? The answer is not difficult to find. Common sense tells us that they must have acted as agents of our foreign enemies, who, at that crucial time, wanted to humiliate India in the comity of nations, frustrate the peace process between India and Pakistan, keep the Kashmir insurgency alive and make it a source of finances and other material intrusions in Pakistan's failing resources. At the same time, they wanted to provoke disorder and chaos in India, and hurt our ability to defend ourselves against armed attacks from hostile quarters. To these planners, the death of a thousand or so innocent Muslims would not have been too much of a price to pay to make India grind its nose in the dust.

In an article in January 2003, in the aftermath of the Godhra riots in Gujarat, I wrote that the nation must admit that the grave and sudden provocation provided by the mayhem had seriously blemished the conduct of our law enforcement agencies. I even appeared in the Supreme Court and advised the transfer of the riots cases from Gujarat to courts outside the state. I publicly advised Chief Minister Narendra Modi that he must see to it that Hindus and Muslims were locked in an embrace of love and mutual understanding. I am glad that Modi did not have any different opinion about the role he had to play. He did his best to apply soothing balm to the wounds which both communities inflicted upon each other. It would be well to remember that a large number of Hindus were killed by police actions during the riots in which Muslims were killed.

It is a pity that the central government and even my friend Lalu Prasad Yadav, in their quest of political objectives, decided to create a perversion of the truth. They concocted the story that the Godhra killings were not the action of terrorists but of an innocent kerosene stove; that Godhra was just an accident and the aftermath was planned by the Gujarat government. Our so-called secular central government overlooked what *jihadi* Muslims did to Akshardham temple as well as to some temples in Jammu, including the revered Raghunath temple.

Indian Muslims, by and large, are honest and loyal citizens. They should, in one voice, condemn these actions and pour scorn on the perpetrators of Godhra and the purveyors of lies who keep the two communities in a state of burning anger and revenge. They should also see through the game played by the union government. They should advise the jihadis to change course in the manner that Pakistan's president Pervez Musharraf was compelled to do in the aftermath of the World Trade Center holocaust. He took a 180-degree turn. He advised the Pakistan militants, in the name of Allah and the Holy Quran, to fight against illiteracy, poverty, backwardness and hunger. The days of *Jihad-e-Asgh*ar (the lesser jihad, of war) are over, he argued and 'what is badly needed is *Jihad-e-Akbar*' (the greater jihad, that of cleansing oneself). Terrorism will achieve nothing and Islam will grow and prosper only when there is peace, which is its essence and meaning. The beautiful flower of Islam will have a resplendent look in the larger bouquet of Indian pluralism. There are heartwarming developments which we have failed to notice, or publicize adequately, such as the declaration made by thousands of Muslim clerics who, under the inspiration of Dar-ul-Uloom, confirmed that terrorism is condemned by Islam. There is not one word in the Holy Quran to sanctify the killing of innocent, unarmed children, women and old men. The terrorists are too cowardly to engage military forces and regular combatants. Tackling terrorism will require unapologetic honesty and total moral clarity. Rogue states must be identified, named and tamed. To hobnob with them, for whatever reasons, is treason against the Indian nation.

Appeasement abroad

The Middle East is a dangerously troubled area. In formulating our policy we have to do some fresh thinking, owning past mistakes and striking a bold path guided by international law and impartial justice. We should not subordinate these for short term electoral gains as, shamefully, we have done for many long years. We must give no quarter or hospitality to nations that breed terrorists and sustain armies of criminal murderers, nor to those who cannot exist without destruction of another member state of the United Nations. India is a secular nation although in the evil scripture of some fanatic groups we are classed as infidels who have forfeited their right to live. We cannot and must not allow nuclear weapons to fall into the hands of those who are sworn to destroy us. World peace requires sacrifice from all concerned, but we will not call for any from those whose survival and security is not fully secured. In sum, we will shun warmongers, overt and covert, but build monuments to those who die and have died to make the individual and nation safer. We must raise our voice in solidarity with those who seek freedom from dictatorships or demand legitimate human rights.

Despite this ideal, the great Dr Manmohan Singh was drowned in paralysing silence when the brave citizens of Tunisia, Egypt, Bahrain and Libya took to the streets in what has come to be known as the Arab Spring; not even when Muammar Gaddafi's guns and tanks began to mow down unarmed freedom fighters did we raise our voice. In morbid longing for the Muslim vote our prime minister has allied himself with counterfeit Wahhabi teaching, letting down the pristine pure religion of Islam of the Prophet. The Indian nation feels ashamed when torture and death are rampaging through Brega and Zawiya, or terror and despair loom over Tobruk and Benghazi. We have become accomplices of vicious tyrants by the dumbness of our prime minister. He has simultaneously betrayed our American partners who have finally decided to act in defence of freedom and democracy. But he has kept alive for his party the chimera of the Muslim vote.

Communal Violence Bill will divide society

The Prevention of Communal and Targeted Violence (Access to Justice And Reparations) Bill proposed by Sonia Gandhi's National Advisory Council, consisting of 138 sections and several schedules running into 66 printed pages, is mischievous in its thinly-concealed aims and objectives. The need for a marathon criminal statute arises only when the prohibited conduct has assumed endemic proportions and the statutes already in force are ineffective to eliminate it. In other words, it has turned into a chronic cancer of the national multitude. Yes, occasionally in some isolated corners of the country communally targeted offenses do occur, but our people are far too civilised to indulge in them with regularity and frequency, to cause what the great Bentham in his *Theory of Legislation* called 'alarm'.

Even on those rare occasions when communal violence erupts, it is almost always at the instigation of some evil gang leaders working for ignoble political ends. It is such criminals who occupy the upper decks of our social and political life who have to be identified and eliminated. The current available laws have never been used against them. Will somebody kindly examine the statistics of prosecutions and convictions for such offences? The propsed Bill is not designed to cure alarm, instead it is intended to create false alarm, which the leaders will translate into crimes, more social tensions and divisions of our nationhood and patriotism.

The Communal Violence Bill was drafted by the National Advisory Council headed by Mrs Sonia Gandhi, and put as an agenda item for discussion at the National Integration Council meeting chaired by the prime minister on 10 September 2011. Although of dubious legitimacy and playing leap-frog with prescribed procedures, the eminent government lawyers who had questioned Anna Hazare's audacity in preparing a draft Lokpal Bill remained silent on this Bill. Obviously, a draft from the NAC (a nominated body of activists, social workers and professionals, without any constitutional or parliamentary status), proposing a central law on a state subject, and without consulting the states, was far higher in the government's pecking order than a draft from humble Anna Hazare. And woe betide any minister or MP who dared to question its legitimacy for being included in the National Integration Council agenda without following the prescribed procedures.

It is known that a badly shaken government was anxious to divert the enraged public mind from corruption to something else—from Kalmadi's Commonwealth Games and the 2G scam to non-existent atrocities on minorities that would polarize communities and perpetuate vote banks.

Even a cursory reading of the Bill shows that it is unconstitutional, anti-national and a communal piece of pseudo-legislative work. Unconstitutional, because it violates the federal principle and poaches into the powers of the states as prescribed by the Constitution and the Seventh Schedule.

The Bill is anti-national and communal because it seeks to divide a polity through novel manoeuvres: by the repugnant definition of the term 'group' in Section 3(e) that clearly violates Article 14 of the Constitution. 'Group' means a religious or linguistic minority, in any state in the Union of India, or Scheduled Castes and Scheduled Tribes within the meaning of Clauses (24) and (25) of Article 366 of the Constitution of India. The lack of good faith in the NAC intention becomes abundantly exposed.

Communal violence, regardless of which community perpetrates it, is criminal and anti-national. If the NAC was keen on addressing this issue, it should have established its *bona fides* by viewing it in a secular perspective, and through the prism of a sound analytical framework to identify recurring causative factors and then suggesting the best preventive and punitive measures, after consultation with legal experts and political parties. The draft does not envisage a mere grant in aid or a welfare scheme for minorities; it contains a Bill, the provisions of which have a sinister implication on Constitutional provisions and the prevailing laws of the land, namely, the Indian Penal Code and the Criminal Procedure Code. The NAC's objective to provide a symptomatic framework for 'good communal violence' and 'bad communal violence'—as if communal violence can be equated with cholesterol—comes through clearly by the definition of 'group'. It is trying to achieve the ultimate by communalizing even communal violence, and ensuring that it further destroys community coexistence in our country.

Social scientists, civil society organizations and administrators would broadly agree that communal violence assumes serious proportions only when fanned and encouraged by local political/religious leaders. Sometimes, communal violence is engineered by political leaders to disgrace a government, and effect a leadership change, such as happened in Karnataka in 1990. But mostly it is stray incidents, for example, desecration of places of worship during religious festivals that turn into large communal clashes with the encouragement of local political/religious leaders, who then retreat into the background, leaving innocent, ordinary people to suffer. Police behaviour would differ from person to person. An honest and conscientious police superintendent would act fearlessly and exercise his ample regulatory powers in accordance with law, whereas a corrupt and political policeman would take orders from his political bosses.

The NAC has several eminent members who would be aware of the dynamics of communal violence and also community dynamics at the grassroots. I am informed that following the dynastic model, there is an outstanding tri-generational advisory group consisting of an elderly retired civil servant, his former joint director, and probationer. I do not think this triumvirate has taken into account the sociological impact of their Bill on the minorities who, by and large peacefully, inhabit the villages and towns of India. Nor has there been any agitation for this Bill from the religious and linguistic minorities. In fact, chief ministers of several states, including UPA partner Mamata Banerjee of West Bengal, have criticized the bill as violating the federal structure. Eminent jurists, particularly the former chief justice of India, Justice J.S. Verma and Justice B.N. Srikrishna have argued against it. So why impose a bill, which the BJP rightly termed as 'dangerous for the country', on the minorities?

I would like to make one suggestion to the NAC. Can we stop seeing persons belonging to minority communities as a sheaf of ballot papers with the luckless Hand stamped on them? Can we stop seeing them as a bank of votes and instead give them the respect due to human beings who wish to live with dignity, peace and security; with religious and cultural freedom that is guaranteed to all citizens by our Constitution; with aspirations for themselves and their children for education, employment and opportunity; and do everything possible in state and society to provide such an enabling environment. Wooing them with such laws will only ghettoize and alienate them further. It will neither provide them any long-term, sustainable social and economic benefits, nor strengthen national unity.

Minorities of all shades have produced men of magnificent intellectual attainments coupled with ennobling compassion for fellow citizens and a spirit of sacrifice for the greatness of the Indian nation. We can produce many more by a proper system of liberal education that fosters genuine secularism and rule of reason in place of blind superstition and fanatical faith. This is the need of the hour.

Of rallying points, Hindutva and a vibrant opposition

Democracy has often been somewhat inaccurately equated with government in discussions. There can be no discussions without a powerful Opposition. An opposition party is a medium of communication between lawmakers and the people. People with grievances against the government seek solutions through Opposition parties. Of course this proposition does not exclude the voter's access to politicians belonging to the ruling party, but power makes politicians too arrogant to tolerate criticism or too insensitive to sympathize with grievances. It is not without significance that after the Emergency of the seventies when the Janata Party came to power, it conferred on the leader of the opposition all the perks and privileges of the prime minister.

However, the Opposition is not meant to be a demolition squad. It must learn to give credit to the executive for whatever good it does for the nation. It must appear to the people as an alternative government. Every Opposition party must, therefore, have free play in its joints and must be prepared for course correction if it is on the wrong side of popular opinion, except when it is honestly convinced that the popular mood is only a temporary disorder.

The BJP has to introspect and realise that it has an anti-minority outlook that even the majority does not appreciate. My complaint against the BJP has been that the Hindutva projected by it for its electoral purposes is a counterfeit Hindutva. Its core has no resemblance to the real philosophy. Hindutva, properly understood, is neither the product nor the property of any political party, not even the Jana Sangh of old and the BJP of today. It was not manufactured at the Shiv Sena home in Mumbai or at the RSS offices in Delhi. Hindutva is the core of the Indian Constitution to which all citizens of India swear allegiance and complete loyalty and, as the Supreme Court has said in 1995, 'is a way of life or a state of mind and cannot be equated with or understood as religious Hindu fundamentalism' (paragraph 40 of JT 1995(8) SC 407 p. 637). It is a pity that the BJP has not been able to explain to people that Hindutva and Indian secularism are practically synonyms. Here are two passages from the writing of C. Rajagopalachari, India's first Indian Governor General, and another from Jawaharlal Nehru, the first prime minister of free India.

Rajagopalachari wrote, 'Secularism is an ill-understood word. If a state declares that its government shall be secular, it does not mean that its rulers or Parliament will be agnostics or atheists. It does not mean that it dislikes and discourages religion. It means that persons of various religions will all be treated justly and without any discrimination based on religious differences. Justice to minority groups does not mean injustice to the majority. It does not mean that boys and girls will be deprived of the advantage of the disciplines based on the religions professed by the families to which they belong. Pious people in a secular state, are to be respected, to whatever faith they belong, and encouraged to guide their flocks as before in the path of righteousness and self-restraint. In connection with this matter of secularism rightly understood we have, by accident, if one may say so, a firm doctrine in hinduism, to support non-discrimination and equal respect for all pious people.'

Nehru had this to say: 'How are we to consider the scriptures of various religions, much of it believed by its votaries to be revealed scripture? To analyse it and criticise it and look upon it as a human document is often to offend the true believers. Yet there is no other way to consider. I have always hesitated to read books of religion. The totalitarian claims made on their behalf did not appeal to me.'

The BJPs lack of clarity and vision in explaining Hindutva has it consistently mired in controversy, alienating not only minorities but also many Hindus instead of using it as a rallying point for all Indians. This, as we have seen, impacts at the hustings.

The BJP and its allies suffered an electoral debacle in 2004. They had five years to ponder on that somewhat unexpected political disaster, but did not improve their position in 2009. The factors which worked against the BJP in 2004 became more lethal when compounded with heavy infighting amongst top leaders, lack of effective leadership, inertia, paralysis of the will to change course and persistence of chronic follies. The Congress, on the other hand, grew stronger during that period. But that strength induced in them illusions of invincibility, which in turn bred an insensitivity and nonchalance to the invasion of termites eating away at their foundations. It was sheer good luck for the Congress that the Opposition parties were worse, indulging in what to the normal citizen plainly looked like attempts at self-immolation. They were so busy destroying one another that they had no time or inclination to detect the crimes of the Congress.

Between 2004 and 2009 the opposition parties individually and collectively failed to perform their appointed role in a democracy. They failed to expose the sins of the ruling coalition which, if competently done, would have brought about the end of the UPA, and even incarcerated many of their leaders in jails. The redeeming feature was that some citizens did remember that democracy is like a swimming pool: if you do not periodically change the water, it must inevitably turn into a cesspool. Voters have begun to smell the stink in precisely the same manner they did more than five years ago, when they threw out the BJP-led NDA.

In 2004, I was a Member of Parliament and had the distinction of being an ex-minister of the Vajpayee Government. I had held the portfolios of Urban Development and then Law, Justice and Company Affairs. But during those two years I had tendered my resignation half a dozen times, which was not accepted. My forced and totally undeserved exit from the Council of Ministers came as a welcome relief, and I did not feel any bitterness. But several things had made me very angry—the way journalists from *Tehelka* and their supporters were treated for a sting operation that embarrassed the BJP government; the attempts made for a political compromise with Jayalalitha, who had invited scathing criticism from the Supreme Court; and for ignoring my advice based on the two judgements of the Supreme Court in the case of Bilkis Yakub Rasul and the famous Best Bakery case. My view was that the union government should consent to all riot cases being transferred out of Gujarat to restore the confidence of the muslim minority in the integrity of the judicial process in India.

The people of India routed the BJP government in the 2004 elections, and I stood vindicated. But I was despondent too. The people's verdict also rejected, in the process, Hindutva, which I revere and consider our greatest national asset. After speaking to others and during some serious soul-searching, I arrived at three conclusions: first, the BJP had not been able to project genuine Hindutva, but a counterfeit version of it. Second, the leadership of the BJP had not made any serious effort to understand this concept or make others understand it. Third, Hindutva was too precious to be jettisoned just because of two electoral failures. It is time the BJP and all its allies understood the pure brand and unanimously accept it as the principal agenda of a coherent united Opposition.

I neither liked nor encouraged the BJP move to erect a Ram temple at the site of the Babri mosque in Ayodhya. I had never approved of rathyatras to publicise the plan. Even though I believe that the story of Rama is a product of the fertile Hindu imagination, it is certainly a tribute to the great genius of the hindu race. I would have welcomed the prospect of non-hindus understanding the greatness of Rama's character and adding to the number of Rama's devotees. At the same time, I firmly believe that building one more temple to Rama's memory is by no means the best way of achieving this. On the contrary, it was sure to make large numbers resentful and hostile. If the temple is to be built, it must be only when Muslims, Christians and non-Hindus in large numbers participate in its construction, surcharged with genuine respect and reverence for Rama.

The Babri Masjid, contrary to my wishes and advice, was demolished. The temple has not yet been constructed and there is no chance that it ever will be. The communal gap has only widened and even some Hindus have ceased to be Rambhaktas.

The detractors of Hindutva are partly right, because quite a few who have claimed Hindutva as their creed have neither understood the philosophy nor practiced and propagated it in the way it was intented. It is unfortunate that Hindutva as practised by some has come to mean ill-will and hatred against those who do not subscribe to one or the other sects of hinduism, mainly the muslims and christians. This misuse of Hindutva and its grave distortion must be exterminated from decent political and social discourse. One must also find fault with those who understand the real nature of Hindutva, but who never care to explain its true meaning to its detractors and the minorities. Never is Hindutva explained from any pulpit or religious platform. No Shankaracharya, or mutt-adhipathi, or saint, or teacher has cared to preach to his flock the tolerance, compassion and rationality which together constitute the core of Hindutva.

I would suggest that instead of making the Rama temple a part of its agenda, the BJP and its allies must declare that they will construct a University of Secularism and Religious Harmony at the disputed site in Ayodhya. Both the temple and the mosque can exist in the vicinity, but with everyone's consent.

No effective opposition to dislodge the Congress from power is possible without the BJP being a part of it. All those who are convinced that the Congress must go, must give up calling one another names. The professed secularism of many parties, in any case, is a big joke. It is an empty, cheap election slogan. Hindutva, in its real incarnation, should bind everybody together. For the benefit of those who suffer from an incurable allergy to the word Hindu, we must have an Urdu equivalent: perhaps *Hindustan ki tahzeeb* or *Bharat ki parampara*. Similar phrases could be discovered in all regional languages.

Why the Congress must go remains to be explained to the nation, particularly to the uninformed who do not know that this country is not poor, but is kept poor by corrupt rulers without conscience or compassion. Over the years they have perfected the art of beguiling the starving millions with visions of El Dorado. 'Vote for us and the heaven of prosperity is just round the corner,' is a promise made every five years. It succeeds like magic. In their horrible misery, the poor themselves forget who has been cheating them. Hunger makes even memory fragile.

This must be at the top of the agenda of the whole opposition.

Underming democracy—curtailing freedom of thought and expression

To ban Joseph Lelyveld's biography of Gandhi titled *Great Soul* is to lend invincible credibility to an easily demonstrable lie. I expected at least my friend Veerappa Moily, our law minister not to commit such an incredible folly. Regretfully, he did exactly that. His thoughtless pronouncement, 'history will not forgive us if we allow anybody to draw adverse inferences about historical figures and denigrate them', makes the whole nation look like foolish believers in the veracity of a conclusion not expressed, but only hinted at in the book. I am sure neither Moily, nor the governments who slapped a ban on the publication of the book have read it through, and with a cool head concluded that the author did actually label Gandhiji as a homosexual.

I fully agree with the author that the ban is 'shameful'; it is 'shameful' for any democratic government to act on the advice of people who have not taken the trouble of procuring a copy and diligently scanning its pages and contents. The author has publicly claimed that he has written a responsible and sensitive book. To project it as a sensational potboiler is plain poppycock, if not criminal. The author has unequivocally declared that no offensive words of any kind have been used against Gandhiji and he has specifically denied insinuating that Gandhiji was bisexual or homosexual. There the matter should have been allowed to rest. The Moilys and the likes of him have only pushed up the sales of the book and multiplied unwarranted inferences that the text does not even pretend to raise or support.

The ban does dual damage to the Father of the Indian nation: first that a libel has been uttered by the author, and second, that it cannot be proved false by evidence and reason. If raising of this avoidable controversy did mean a great electoral advantage to someone, the only fair course would have been to institute a civil action for libel or even a criminal case for defamation in a court of competent jurisdiction. It would at least have been a level playing field for both the plaintiff and the defendant.

There would have been the technical difficulty of finding a Gandhi heir with a cause of action, a technical requirement of the law. Already Gandhiji's great-grandson Tushar has publicly condemned the ban, rightly arguing that the great Gandhi does not need the protection of today's political leaders whose actions are grounded in pure self-interest rather than a reverence for Gandhiji. Here are his exact words: 'If the government of Maharashtra bans the book, it will be a greater insult to Bapu than that book or the author might have intended. I will challenge the ban.' He said he was against the culture of banning books and added, 'How does it matter if the Mahatma was straight, gay or bisexual? Every time he would still be the man who led India to freedom.' Some honest people may even add that to say of a person that in his youth he did feel drawn to someone of his own gender is no allegation of immorality, but a plain statement of universal validity; they might well quote the philosopher Rousseau in his famous book *Emile*.

Mr Moily should have thought of India's reputation of being a robust democracy boasting of fundamental human rights, the most important and valuable of which is the freedom of thought and expression. He needs to be reminded of the famous dialogue of Voltaire and Rousseau: 'I don't believe a word of what you say, but I will give my life to defend your right to say it.'

An author's right to publish the truth as he sees it ought to be respected and even admired for the courage and pursuit of truth that precede his conclusions. Assume that he erred in his interpretation of the letters that provided the basic material for his views. Does that make him a malicious rogue out to blacken Gandhiji's image? Does he have a base motive for destroying reverence which millions the world over feel for that greatest of men? Is he a sexual pervert who wants sexual abnormality to spread under cover of Gandhiji's association? These are some questions that supporters of the ban must ask themselves and return honest answers before ruining the nation's reputation for commitment to democratic principles. Bad speech must be neutralised by better speech, and erroneous opinions outlawed by reasoned argument. The best guarantee of truth emerging is for it to collide with error in the free market of ideas. Dissent strengthens democracy and its tolerance fortifies our commitment. Choice, curiosity, questioning, inquiry, deduction, the powers of the questioning mind—in other words, certain freedom—appear to crown the present stage of evolutionary advance; and even those who do not accept the idea of a spiritual order would not deny that if advance is to continue, it is unlikely to take the direction of purely material mutations. Reason, however, holds the key to the future. That is what our secularism means.

This aspect of democracy is an expression of India's ancient culture. No one can doubt the splendour and purity of the summits of Indian thought. No one questions the value of its spirit of tolerance and detachment. I am almost sure that Tushar Gandhi really represents Gandhiji's soul on this issue. Mahatma Gandhi will not want his reputation to be shielded by a Moily. He would rather do without it. Gandhiji was always willing to own his mistakes and failures. He would certainly disapprove of converting any mortal into a god, which we in India tend to do. The weakness of Indian democracy is that our voters, the rich more than the poor, and the educated more than the illiterate, allow their conscience to be benumbed by the sight of power.

Our critical faculties become paralysed when we evaluate our powerful politicians and ponder over their frolics and follies. Gandhiji never claimed to possess absolute truth. His most renowned book is *Experiments with Truth* and not 'Absolute Truth'. He might have shocked us by declaring that Lelyveld's book is free of error, making the book a chosen asset to the nation.

Horse-trading has to stop

Political vocabulary started changing around the end of 2011, reflecting the acute political instability that was fast setting in within the UPA. While returning from his US visit on 27 September 2011, the prime minister used the words 'mid-term elections' for the first time. Of course they were used in the context of accusations against the Opposition for what he called their 'premature restlessness'. But the fact remains that they had never been used before, not even at the height of the spectrum crisis. And we know that our prime minister is never impulsive, always speaks in measured words, even if his government is strangled from within or without. As far as the Opposition is concerned, its duty to the people and to democracy is more than clear at this critical juncture. People are angry with corruption. The Opposition will be betraying the people if it does not oust this government.

The BJP national executive meeting on 2 October 2011 was also in an election mood. Top BJP leaders, for the first time, announced that they were gearing up for midterm polls. What was refreshing was that they were saying all the right things: that they needed to win more allies for the NDA and stay united if the party wanted to make a serious bid for power. They stressed on good governance, combating corruption, addressing price rise and the BPL issue, and reaching out to the grassroots. The BJP needs to select its prime ministerial candidate with care. He must be acceptable to the Opposition parties, have a standing with the people, be known for his impeccable political, moral and fiscal integrity, and must be able to make India proud in the company of world leaders. In consultation with its allies the BJP should project a shadow cabinet. The voters must be assured that they are not falling from the frying pan to the fire.

India's political canvas generally defies any logic, pattern or prediction. But what I can say with certainty is that 2011 will go down in history as the Year of Scams. Logically, ethically and circumstantially, any other elected government in the world would have resigned long ago. But the UPA government and all its heavyweights against whom there is documentary evidence of criminal connivance, continue unabashed. The prime minister appears to be outwitting his detractors within the party, who regularly sound a weekly Rahul alert—routinely crying wolf. The coalition government is now focusing only on numbers. At any given time there must be an adequate stock of numbers, with carefully calculated permutations and combinations to provide for anticipated or unforeseen exigencies and redundancies. And like any other commodity, numbers can be bought, sold, traded, given IOUs or promissory notes.

Good governance is the need of the hour

Cobbled numbers have come to the rescue oft times, but how much longer can these numbers sustain the government? Sooner or later, the election test must be faced. The BJP must have a national, contemporary, secular, inclusive and people-oriented agenda to win more allies to form the next government. As rightly pointed out at the BJP national executive meeting of 30 September—01 October 2011, they must learn from the mistakes of the Congress whose primary concern was to secure 8% growth and provide stimulus packages, while ensuring that the growth dividend never reached the people, but was parked in foreign banks. Is it any wonder that the poverty lines and hunger indices in this country have remained more or less static over the past decade, while the billions in black money in foreign banks have multiplied manifold?

The Planning Commission chief seemed to have a death wish to join the Bourbons of France when he swore that ₹32 per day was adequate to ensure release from poverty. It is a pity that India is not France of 1789. The poor were given the NREGA, a repackaged and better-funded conglomeration of previous employment generation programmes. Unique identification numbers are being used in lieu of service delivery towards subsistence living in order to distract the aam aadmi with false illusions.

The BJP must rectify all this, and give guarantees to the poor that it will address their basic needs. Good development programmes have existed for decades. But it is indifference, politician-bureaucrat nexus, and lack of effective monitoring and accountability that result in corruption and siphoning off funds meant for the poor.

As is well stated by the BJP, the common man's urgent needs can be met only through 'good governance'. However, this much-used, weary term needs to be defined precisely. What is good governance and how do we bring it about? The present archaic administrative and financial systems inherited from colonial days continue to operate with minor modifications, even though the exercise of state power has altered. Today, both administrative and financial powers are exercised by the elected representatives and permanent bureaucracy at five different levels: Central, state, zilla panchayat, block panchayat and village panchayat. However, there is complete asymmetry between the rules governing the conduct of business, and this present system of administration. The Service Rules, Disciplinary Rules, Financial Accountability Statutes, Rules of Business have not been adjusted to the present system of administration and in this asymmetry, corruption rules. There are no financial or administrative codes for elected representatives exercising such powers, no accountability or disciplinary rules governing them, even though they are the final authorities to authorize the expenditure of public money. Financial malfeasance by political custodians of public money can only be punished by the usual IPC provisions applicable to all citizens, and the Prevention of Corruption Act, the operation of which is optional in state governments.

It is this lacuna that gives phenomenal opportunity to the politician-bureaucrat nexus to flourish, and prevents development funds from reaching target groups. Long years of working with archaic financial procedures have given the bureaucracy a unique specialization in circumventing regulatory provisions, and providing perfect paperwork to satisfy their requirements. Behind every corrupt bureaucrat will be a protective politician, and behind every corrupt politician will be a bevy of carefully selected, supporting bureaucrats.

The BJP should break this noxious partnership to provide good governance. A think-tank comprising a few honest, committed and experienced persons, who can think out of the box and innovate, will provide a framework for the governance we need.

The BJP must win allies by aggressively countering the false propaganda being leveled against it about communalism and obscurantism. It should articulate a modern, contemporary and secular agenda in national and public interest, overarching all security, economic, social, developmental and cultural issues. Additionally, the BJP must assure the minorities of its secularism—that all minorities are guaranteed equality, religious and cultural rights under the Constitution, and are intrinsic to India's great composite culture of Hindutva. Their inclusion in India's economic progress is of priority, and they should be reassured of this. This is essential to counter the propaganda. To take a case in point, Digvijay Singh accused Anna Hazare of being communal, just because the RSS supported his movement against corruption. Is fighting corruption communal? The RSS has every right to support anyone fighting against corruption, whether civil society, the jamayat, or the Roman Catholic Church. Would it be more ethical in Congress' eyes for the RSS to oppose the campaign against corruption?

It is this sort of false propaganda that must be aggressively countered.

Vibrant nationalism, national unity and security are paramount in any nation state. Let the BJP reiterate the Constitutional separation of religion and government, that religion is a personal matter between man and god, and that religious faith does not colour governance.

Finally, there is no substitute for enlightened, committed and honest leadership; governance through setting a good example; zero tolerance for corruption; and placing national development at the top of the agenda. I live in the hope that the Messiah will appear.

6
Public Service—for Man, Mammon or Master?

No person is closer to the role of god than a judge. He holds the key to life, liberty and happiness of plaintiffs and defendants through the powers vested in his office. He is the conscience of the people and the watch-dog of society ensuring fair play whether between state and citizens or between independent nation states. The character of the judge, like Caesar's wife, must therefore be above suspicion—incorruptible and free of fear or favour. Yet, the current situation in India is tragically different. That a litigant can gain admittance to a judge's residence and say in substance, 'I have fixed up the other fellow on the bench, you name your price',* reveals the kind of esteem the public has for the judiciary. Nobody thought of having the culprit arrested. The chief justice of the High Court took no steps. Even the story of a lakh and a half in the loft of a judge's chamber did not disturb the somnolence and serenity of the chief justice of the High Court or any other judge of the court. If this be true, something revolutionary is needed to reinvigorate the judicial system, a priceless legacy of British rule with its emphasis on absolute integrity and technical competence, and prompt and inexpensive justice. Every citizen today knows that our judicial machinery has totally crumbled. It should be the primary duty of the government and the Parliament to restore the system to its former pristine glory.

---

*In the 2008 Cash-at-Door scam it was claimed that ₹15 lakh intended as a bribe for Punjab and Haryana High Court judge Nirmal Yadav, was erroneously delivered to the residence of Justice Nirmaljit Kaur.

Ability, transparency and accountability—the bedrock of selection

The present method of recruitment and dealing with judicial delinquents is outdated and impracticable. In 1993 a credible and foolproof impeachment motion against V. Ramaswami, a Supreme Court judge failed* because the ruling party did not vote and the required two-thirds majority could not be collected. Parliament's corruption sustained its companion, judicial corruption. A National Judicial Commission with powers to hire, fire and relocate judges is the only solution.

I cannot emphasize enough that the appointment of a judge is serious business, requiring the highest degrees of vigour and diligence in the process of screening and selection. We saw an illuminating example of how a judge should be grilled when President Barack Obama nominated his solicitor general, Elena Kagan, to be a judge of the US Supreme Court in May 2010. As part of the prescribed confirmation proceedings she was required to appear before the Judiciary Committee of the senate and for more than two full days she sat before her interlocutors who asked penetrating questions to discern her real attitude, inclinations and fixed convictions on all issues waiting for possible adjudication before the country's courts. Kagan is known to be an unorthodox thinker who defies ideological categories, so it was difficult for senators—both Democrats and Republicans—to discover the real Elena Kagan. She was questioned about her published articles, her lectures to her students as Harvard law dean, and briefs she signed while acting as solicitor general for the Bill Clinton and Obama administrations. Kagan showed considerable dignity, poise and a disarming sense of humour. It was brought out, however, that she had also signed an unfortunate government brief supporting a statute that made it a crime to provide any form of expert advice, even legal briefs, to terrorist groups. Many defended her action as being part of her duty as a lawyer for the government.

---

*V Ramaswami's ostentatious expenditure during his tenure as chief justice of Punjab and Haryana caused the Supreme Court Bar Association to call for his impeachment. Although BJP and Left parties sought his removal from office, and the investigating committee comprising eminent judges, both serving and retired, found him guilty of 11 out of 14 charges, the impeachment vote failed as Congress MPs abstained from voting. Kapil Sibal was V. Ramaswami's defence lawyer.

Kagan is a woman of absolute integrity and her public career of more than two decades is spotlessly clean. Yet the decision on her appointment as associate justice of the Supreme Court of the United States of America was not unanimous. In an editorial, *The New York Times*, advised the senators of both parties to cast aside their political differences and try to explore the mind of the distinguished nominee. Her televised interview in front of about 80 senators was impressive by any standards. She made it clear that she respected precedents and would not depart from them except in very unusual circumstances. Her judicial modesty included respect for Congressional legislation.

I was deeply interested in the details of the proceedings because for years I have advocated the creation of a National Judicial Commission with power to appoint, transfer and dismiss our superior court judges. The present method followed in India is secretive, wholly non-transparent and undemocratic, with gaping holes in its filtering mechanism, which allow incompetent and corrupt judges to pass through. This is not to denigrate every judge appointed to our High Courts and Supreme Courts. I am aware of distinguished judges of total moral integrity and intellectual competence who have deserved all reverence and have lent lustre to the judicial office. For obvious reasons, I can neither identify them nor their exact opposites. But one thing is certain: the present method of appointment and removal has been a conspicuous failure and must be displaced by a Constitutional amendment. My revered friend Krishna Iyer has rightly characterised it as 'incestuous.'

The major defect of the present system is that it totally ignores the role of the Indian Bar. In the United States, despite the immense power of the senate, that august body itself has not hesitated to seek advice of the American Bar Association (ABA) on judicial appointments. In 1952, President Dwight D. Eisenhower began the practice of sending nearly every federal judicial nominee to the ABA's Standing Committee on the federal judiciary. In England, judges are appointed by, or on the advice of the Lord Chancellor, who, for decades also happened to be a member of the executive. At a lunch meeting of the Bar, he was asked a flattering question: 'How do you always make such good appointments?' His answer was: 'If I don't, can I sit at this table and look straight in your eye?' This shows how the reputation of the appointing authority itself depends upon the opinion of the practicing Bar. Members of the

Bar know the character and judicial competence of both aspiring and sitting judges much more than anybody else.

It is also worth remembering that judges are required to sit on benches before which all sorts of matters turn up. Some matters may arise out of areas of law of which one, some, or all the judges on the bench do not have the faintest idea. Litigants have had the misfortune in serious criminal cases of facing a bench where not even one of the judges could claim any familiarity with criminal law. Counsels even find it difficult to decide how much enunciation of the relevant law they must attempt, or when to stop in the belief that their arguments have been understood by the bench. It is easy to deal with a loquacious judge, but it is difficult to fathom a silent one, and the ignorant usually adopt a sphinx-like posture.

Only perceptive practitioners, sitting in court, notice the frequent miscarriage of justice taking place before their eyes. Correction does not require legislation; setting up traditions binding on the Chief Justice of the court is enough.

Foreign investors in India and India's lucrative international trade depend upon swiftness and competence with which cases are decided. It is a scandal that 30 million cases are pending in the subordinate courts. Prestigious law commissions have time and again reported that we need to multiply our courts five times.

By reason of its unpardonable dilatoriness, criminal justice has, by and large, lost its deterrent punch. Crime and criminals continue to grow and threaten the stability and security of Indian society.

During the seventies, the Bar of this country had resolved that it must be consulted in the matter of judicial appointments. This is its professional right and duty, which must be exercised with restraint and responsibility. While I do not recommend the wholesale adoption of the American method, its transparency must be extrapolated into any future method which we devise for ourselves.

Law Day oath: forever renounce violence, corruption

The Supreme Court celebrated Law Day on its lawns on 26 November 2010. The Hon'ble Chief Justice of India, his companion judges in the Supreme Court, the chief justice of the High Court of Delhi and his brother judges, the Attorney General and Solicitor General of India and other high ranking law officers were present. Members of the Bar had collected in large numbers. The marquee was full and about 250 lawyers patiently stood on the sides from the beginning to the end. The guest of honour was our minister of law and justice, the hon'ble Veerappa Moily, who has quite endeared himself to the Bar by his unflinching cooperation and support.

The Hon'ble Chief Justice, in his eloquent and impassioned speech pointed out that the problem of arrears in our courts, which makes many citizens angry with the judiciary and despairing of the judicial process, is not attributable to any remissness on the part of the judges. The judges are doing a heroic job under the unfortunate constraints that are the creation of others. He was obviously referring to the executive of the country, but extremely polite as he is, his complaints were couched in pleasing and diplomatic language. Legating the audience with facts and figures, he almost won a complete acquittal of the judiciary on this long pending charge. The representatives of the Association thanked him in appreciation.

The hon'ble law minister delivered a scholarly address on the concept of Rule of Law and details of our Constitutional system, which has created a polity based on that overriding and sacred principle. Attorney General Goolam Vahanvati impressed the lawyers' fraternity with his scholarly analysis of the Supreme Court judgments on the Rule of Law.

As president of the Supreme Court Bar Association, I administered to the audience an oath which reflects the earlier practice of reading out a charter. It was said that the sanctity of our renewed commitment to the Rule of Law does call for the admission of an oath as a moral sanction. The context of the oath had the concurrence of the law minister, the attorney general and the Chief Justice of India. The context of the oath is reproduced below:

'*I take oath and hereby pledge that I shall, at all times, abide by the Constitution, respect its ideals and institutions and uphold the human rights of all my fellow beings.*

'*Recognising that Rule of Law is the foundation of our constitutional system, I shall, forever, renounce the use of violence, bribery and corruption, appeal to religious passions and promotion of religious and ethnic hatred.*

'*I shall ceaselessly promote harmony and the spirit of brotherhood, uphold the dignity and equality of men and women and to the limit of my economic capacity, provide help to the disabled and deprived.*

'I have resolved that as an individual, either citizen or resident, I shall not compromise with terrorism and bravely fight it with all my resources until it is wholly exterminated and world order and peace are fully restored. My contempt for terrorists extends to their collaborators and groups or governments that finance them, harbour them or in any manner abet their evil designs.

'I shall fearlessly expose wreckers of the Constitution and breakers of the law, refuse to lend them respectability or prestige, insist on vigorous and impartial enforcement of law against even the high and mighty and strive to promote justice—social, economic and political.

'So Help Me God.'

It is well to remember that in the United States of America, the celebration of Law Day was proclaimed as a national duty by a proclamation signed by President Dwight Eisenhower on 3 February 1958. The annual celebration day was fixed as 1 May. The president was seeking to formally recognise a two-century old tradition fondly remembered and nourished by the citizens of the United States. President Eisenhower's proclamation described it as a tradition of adherence to the Rule of Law as the only safe and stable foundation for a free and just society. Our Constitution too is based on the same fundamental principle. The president especially urged the legal profession along with press, radio, television and motion picture industries to promote and participate in the observance of Law Day. It is a matter of great satisfaction that the celebration of Law Day has been adopted in most democratic countries. Our Supreme Court has not fallen behind.

Honesty required that in the presence of the members of the Bar it should clearly be stated that the Rule of Law abhors the Rule of Scams. More than 37% of India's population lives below the poverty line, despite the miserable and humiliating definition of poverty line. Honesty requires that the people of this country must be clearly told that we are a rich country but have been condemned to misery and almost sub-human existence by the dacoits who have over the years stolen enormous wealth which actually belongs to the nation. That wealth should rightly be used for addressing poverty, and the development needs of the poor. An estimate of the quantum stolen is about $1,500 billion—an amount which, if distributed in India, will provide about ₹2 lakh to every Indian family. The association did not flinch from declaring this sordid truth.

The entire legal family of judges, law officers and other members of the legal fraternity must be resolved to recover this booty and get the thieves into prison, where they deserve to be lodged. One hopes that the legal family will rise to the occasion. The law officers of the government are advocates of the people, and not the minions of a minister or the Cabinet. They must help to let the people of this country know the horrible details of the loot that has taken place. The integrity and impartiality of officers of the law is the pivot on which democratic rights hinge.

Of venal sin and judicial misconduct

In recent years, widely reported allegations of judicial misconduct have revealed the extent to which the integrity and impartiality of the higher judiciary has been compromised in our country. These disclosures of suspected venality in some judges of the higher courts have shattered the ineffable image of the judiciary as a vigilant and ultimate protector of the values of a free society governed by law. This grave damage to the judiciary's image has been caused by none other than some Indian judges, courtesy their tendency to hover around the seats of political power.

Contempt proceedings are pending against prominent advocate Prashant Bhushan for having spoken of corruption in earlier Chief Justices of the Supreme Court. Serious exposures were also made by a sitting Chief Justice of the Gujarat High Court. These complaints of corruption in the sacred portals of higher judiciary serve to focus attention on the problem that there is practically no mechanism to examine charges against the judges.

In 1990, the National Front Government, in a rare act of self-effacement, introduced the Constitution 67th Amendment Bill in the Lok Sabha. This Bill sought to transfer the power of judicial appointments from the executive to a National Judicial Commission. However, the constitution of the proposed Commission called for many changes.

For instance, if the government has a voice, the leader of the Opposition must also be heard, lest the ruling party should manage to sneak in its loyal supporters to the prejudice of other deserving contenders. The Bar and the academic community must have a say and so also the Lok Pal who attends to corruption charges against the high and mighty.

The other major problem is the weeding out of judges who are corrupt, or, at any rate, not believed to be totally honest. The threat of possible impeachment has proved worse than useless. The procedure is extraordinarily cumbersome and the initiative lies in the hands of politicians. No wonder that judges had much better character when they held office at the pleasure of the Crown under the old Government of India Act 1935. The privy council, and later the federal court, could investigate and decide complaints of judicial misconduct, as well as mental or physical incapacity. Impeachment, a purely political remedy, must be scrapped and the powers of the federal court conferred on the National Judicial Commission. Instead of having two different commissions for appointments to the Supreme Court and High Courts, there should be one. Only the state government and the leader of the opposition in the state legislature must be consulted for High Court appointments. There is need for intensive debate amongst lawyers, academicians, and all concerned sections of society. A remedy must be speedily found for what is doubtless a grave malady.

Judges are the fulcrum of our Constitution

India is not a mere democracy. It is something much more. It is a Constitutional democracy, and the Preamble to our Constitution calls the nation a Democratic Republic. There is a vast difference between the two, which many laymen as well as legislators and bureaucrats do not understand. In a mere democracy, the majority of the elected representatives of the people constitute the sovereign. In a republic, the power of the majority to lay down policies and promulgate laws is subject to severe restrictions, and these restrictions are the parameters of the sovereignty of the individual citizen. The Constitution of India confers upon the citizens certain fundamental rights that create for him a *sanctum sanctorum*, which all the members of both Houses of Parliament, even acting unanimously, cannot occupy or trespass upon. Parliament has only limited power in this field. It can impose some restrictions on the exercise of fundamental rights, but these have to be in pith and substance for carrying out certain specified purposes. Moreover, the restrictions have to be reasonable, commensurate with the object to be achieved. It cannot use a sledgehammer to kill a fly.

Every citizen has a right of what is popularly called Freedom of Speech and Expression. This right of free speech is the right to freely circulate one's opinion on any issue, not merely opinions which the ministers or other people like, but even those which they do not approve of, or even hate. The restriction of this fundamental right has to be reasonable. Whether it is reasonable or not, is not for the lawmaker to decide, but that vital question can only be decided by our independent judges. Judicial review of legislative action is a basic feature of our Constitution upheld in the Keshavanand Bharati sense.* So far as judicial review of executive action is concerned, it is much more extensive. The courts have the power to mandate the performance of neglected legal and Constitutional duties of the government and every other public functionary. The court also has the power to annul any executive act not justified by law or taken for some oblique purpose, which has nothing to do with the purpose for which the power was actually created.

Both the branches, the executive and legislative, must at all times recognize the controlling power of the judiciary. This, however, does not always happen. Politicians in power and bureaucrats, big and small, find judges a nuisance. They get red in the face when the judges legitimately expose their non-performance or bad performance. Inevitably, it creates tension in the relationship of the judicial with the remaining two branches. Aharon Barak, an eminent judge of the Supreme Court of Israel, in his scholarly book *The Judge in a Democracy* tells us: 'Tension between the courts and other branches is natural and, in my opinion, also desirable. If the court's rulings were always satisfactory to the other branches, it would raise suspicion that the court was not properly fulfilling its role in the democracy.'

I have a slightly different approach to this problem. If a litigant were to decide how judges should act, he would be interfering with the administration of justice and committing contempt. A litigant cannot decide what views the court in which he appears must hold on the issues in the case before it. The judge will form his opinion after hearing patiently, thinking soberly and deciding

---

*The Supreme Court's ruling in the 1973 judgement of the Keshavananda Bharati case upheld the principle of the 'basic structure' of the Constitution of India and ruled the Parliament did not have the power to pass an amendment that in any way altered the basic structure of the Constitution.

impartially. Government is generally the biggest litigant. Hence, there is constant tension and conflict between the honest citizen and the corrupt, indifferent or even honest bureaucrats, who according to their rules of business must remain loyal to their ministries, or other such corrupt or indifferent agencies. The judges must stand on the side of the honest citizens and share their anxieties, concerns and sufferings. It would be a sad day for our democracy if a cozy relationship of co-operation and harmony comes to exist between the two branches. Tension is a democratic necessity.

In February 2011 a conference of lawyers from the Commonwealth was held in Hyderabad. Surprisingly, no member of the Executive Committee of the Supreme Court Bar Association was invited to attend, but it has been reported that during the conference, the prime minister complained against judicial interference with the workings of the government which, in its arrogance, considers itself to be omniscient and omnipotent. He apparently forgot that a litigant must argue his case in court and not in a public meeting.

It is true that of late criticism of judges is also becoming a somewhat embarrassing affair. If someone asks, 'is there corruption in the judiciary?', the honest answer is, 'yes, there is'. Even so, a tribute to the judiciary is justified and called for. With all its faults and lapses, small and big, the judges are by and large angels compared to the members of the political class. If politicians produced a Mahatma Gandhi, B.R. Ambedkar, Sardar Patel, Lal Bahadur Shastri, a Jayprakash Narayan and Ram Manohar Lohia, the judiciary has produced stalwarts like Harilal J Kanya, Vivian Bose, S Murtaza Fazal Ali, Mehar Chand Mahajan, MB Shah, PB Gajendragadkar, M Hidayatullah, MC Chagla, O Chinappa Reddy, VR Krishna Iyer, MN Venkatachaliah and JS Verma. We have chief justice S.H. Kapadia, a refreshing addition to the long line of judges of the highest integrity and competence. Brave judges like justices AK Ganguly, GS Singhvi and RM Lodha hold the judicial torch aloft and are an honour to the nation. One must not forget the late Mr Justice Khanna, the lone dissenter in the Additional District Magistrate, Jabalpur Emergency case* in whose memory

---

*In the ADM Jabalpur vs. Shivakant Shukla case, also popularly known as the *Habeas Corpus* case of 1976, the Supreme Court decided to uphold Indira Gandhi's government's right to suspend all fundamental rights during the Emergency. Justice HR Khanna was the lone dissenter on the 5 member bench that deliberated the matter.

the *New York Times* of 1976 advised the Indian nation to build a monument out of sheer gratitude.

The function of the judge is to see that law is enforced and the lawbreaker punished. Today the Rule of Law is unfortunately displaced by the rule of successive scams. The soul of Law is in torment. Good lawyers and all good men can see that law enforcement is suffering from lack of oxygen. It needs fresh air to fuel the combustion hidden in its heart.

Thomas as CVC—an error of judgement?

On 3 March 2011, the Supreme Court of India pronounced a judgment quashing the appointment of P.J. Thomas as the chief vigilance commissioner. It declared the recommendation of the High Powered Committee dated 3 September 2010 as *non-est** in law.

The court said, 'The empanelling authority, while forwarding the names of the empanelled officers/persons, shall enclose complete information, material and data of the concerned officer/person, whether favourable or adverse. Nothing relevant or material should be withheld from the Selection Committee. It will not only be useful but would also serve larger public interest and enhance public confidence if the contemporaneous service record and acts of outstanding performance of the officer under consideration, even with adverse remarks, are specifically brought to the notice of the Selection Committee.'

While the Supreme Court order has laid down the guidelines and directions for selection within the panel prepared by the government, which in this case is the Department of Personnel and Training, (DOPT)—also coming under the prime minister—it would be worthwhile for the people to know exactly how DOPT prepares panels for CVC selection or any other statutory appointments. The process is simple. Panels are normally prepared after the Secretary DOPT has ascertained from the highest approving authorities who is to be appointed. Thereafter, selection guidelines are sometimes tweaked to suit the CV of this candidate, so that his selection is smooth. Normally, a panel of three names is prepared to include the intended choice and two dummy candidates. The farce of

---

*Non-est Factum is a defendant's plea to nullify a contract because it was signed without fully understanding its nature and implication.

paperwork commences from the lowest section of the department upwards, and the file moves smoothly without any dissent, until the selection committee approves it.

In this case, the panel contained three names—that of P.J. Thomas, Bijoy Chatterjee and S. Krishnan. It is now in the public domain that correspondence pertaining to Thomas' chargesheet and sanction for prosecution between the Kerala government and the DOPT, headed by the prime minister, was going on since 2006. However, the DOPT suppressed these facts in the bio data of Thomas that was prepared for the Selection Committee.

The decision to use the entire machinery of the government to conceal Thomas's taint appears to have been taken by the UPA government a long time ago. On 25 June 2007, the then central vigilance commissioner, Prityush Sinha, gave Thomas a clean chit, without giving any reasons, and facilitated his entry to the Government of India, in spite of the chargesheet.

One can easily imagine the sequence of events that would have taken place regarding this appointment. Secretary DOPT would have been instructed by the decision makers of the nation, that Thomas must be appointed as CVC.

It is possible that Secretary DOPT may have mentioned something about the chargesheet. A strategy would then have been formulated to use the CVC's closure of the vigilance case against him as an excuse to hide the chargesheet and the sanction for prosecution. Messages from apex offices are rarely lost on secretaries. Anyhow, the fact of the matter is that information regarding Thomas' criminal case was successfully screened out by the DOPT from the Committee.

Had it not been for the Public Interest Litigations (PIL) filed, these facts would not have surfaced in the public domain. The government persisted in its defence of Thomas in the Supreme Court. It was only after the Supreme Court order of 3 March 2011 that the prime minister publicly confessed in Jammu, 'There has been an error of judgment in CVC appointment and I take full responsibility.' This was reiterated on 7 March 2011 in the Lok Sabha, and on 8 March in the Rajya Sabha, with a curious addition: 'Until I went to the meeting of the Committee, I was not aware there was any such case of Palmolein and that it would involve corruption.' He added that he became aware of the case only when Sushma Swaraj raised the issue in the meeting. He also informed the House that the notes for such committees are prepared 'under the guidance of minister of state in charge of the DOPT.' The honest answer should have been that the note which was prepared by the DOPT did not contain this conclusive information.

Minister of State DOPT, Prithviraj Chavan, at a press conference in Pune on 8 March 2011, casually passed on the blame to the Kerala government, saying it was the latter that gave vigilance clearance for Thomas. This was strongly refuted on 9 March 2011 by V.S. Achuthanandan, the Kerala CM who accused Chavan of lying. Copies of official communication sent by Kerala to Delhi regarding Thomas' corruption were being waved around by TV anchors. Chavan then said he was misquoted. But by whom? His own sound box in the live interview in Pune?

So what was so special about Thomas that the government wanted him to be CVC? Neither was he the senior-most, nor did he have experience in the field of vigilance and investigation as required under the CVC Act. What other outstanding or spectacular achievements put him above the other two officers in the panel?

We may not know all these answers but what we do know is, that apart from being chargesheeted in the case, he also worked as secretary of telecommunication, from October 2009 to September 2010, with A. Raja, and had a smooth working relationship with him.

The prime minister and home minister appeared to be in a hurry to appoint PJ Thomas as CVC and so disregarded objections from the leader of the Opposition, refusing to defer the matter even for a day when she asked them to verify PJ Thomas' credentials. In fact, even when there was public outcry at the decision and cases filed in the Supreme Court, the government defended him tenaciously, with the prime minister stating on 6 September 2010, 'I think what we have done is the right thing. Of all the three persons whose names were under consideration, we have chosen the best possible person.'

Obviously, Thomas as CVC would have been invaluable to the UPA. He had already revealed his predilections as secretary of telecommunication by challenging the CVC and the CAG's powers to examine policy decisions taken by the government, laying the foundation to ensure that Raja cannot be brought to book for the manner in which he dispensed 2G spectrum. And yes, it does appear a little strange that *all officers in the panel were those who had worked with DMK ministers.*

Despite the honourable prime minister's excuses, PJ Thomas' selection appeared to be a deliberate decision compelled by a hidden hand rather than an error of judgment.

A spoils system within the Civil Service

The Indian Civil Service was a priceless gift given by the British empire to India—a small battalion of bureaucrats, the best products of British educational institutions, tested by stringent examination, written and oral, supervised by superiors and finally the secretary of state in London. In addition the bureaucrat was a person of high moral character.

When the British left, Sardar Patel, our wisest administrator and statesman did not pack them off. Instead, he retained anyone who wanted to stay and serve India. A tribute to their integrity is in order. They swore allegiance to their new masters and walked the path of absolute rectitude and loyalty. The nation must cherish their memory and applaud their contribution in building the new India.

With decline of character and integrity at the top, sheer osmosis has produced the inevitable degradation and decline. With honourable exceptions who sustain our survival, many bureaucrats have formed self-serving cliques.

What some bureaucrats and politicians could say obliquely, in muffled voices ever since the UPA came to power in 2004, was said bluntly and with remarkable prescience by the former American ambassador to India, David Mulford in his confidential report of 2005, that now in the public domain through WikiLeaks. This is what Mulford has to say: 'Along with Principal Secretary TKA Nair, Narayanan constitutes what is now a Keralite "Mafia" in the PMO. In a bureaucratic culture dominated by North Indian Hindi speakers, this Keralite lock on the PM's inner bureaucratic circle represents something of an anomaly, which could in the long term create new faultlines around the prime minister.' How right he was. He has not gone back on anything he said more than half a decade ago.

Indeed, during the UPA years, the civil services have witnessed a steady, swift and almost complete descent from the Westminster model to a spoils systems within India's permanent civil service, making it a unique sort of permanent spoils civil services.

India's most eminent civil service is the Indian Administrative Service (IAS), which derives its existence and conditions of service from Article 312 of the Constitution. With these guarantees and its permanence of tenure, it was not very difficult for them to use these advantages and convert the civil service into a powerful and captive instrument to control the administrative machinery and achieve its self serving and often anti-national objectives.

An examination of the deployment pattern of officers of the permanent civil service in the last five years confirms Mulford's 'Keralite mafia' hypothesis. The PMO manipulated the system of appointments, empanelments, promotions and extensions to create a perfect nexus between politicians and bureaucrats for personal aggrandizement through government decision. How else can one explain the selection of the tainted Thomas as Secretary Telecommunications, and thereafter abortively as CVC, a matter which brought the government humiliation and disgrace, or the ability of Madhavan Nair to take the fraudulent Antrix–Devas deal almost to fruition? How else does one explain the existence of a cabinet secretary from the same region who receives extension year after year, getting all the relevant rules changed? Obviously, his bosses found him extremely valuable.

Promotions and appointments are controlled by a rite of passage in the civil service called empanelment, which decides whether civil servants, predominantly officers of the IAS, can serve in Government of India as joint secretaries, additional secretaries and secretaries. Though officially the selection is done by a committee chaired by the cabinet secretary and comprising the home secretary, secretary personnel, and principal secretary to prime minister, and then approved by the Appointments Committee of the Cabinet, no one really knows how it is actually done. The rules are changed whenever required to assist a political favourite as files apparently fly between South Block and 10 Janpath. Pencil entries are made deleting and adding candidates as per the dictates of the powerful, and the minutes of the original selection committee are signed only after agreements between the political masters, business houses and captive or powerful bureaucrats are reached. These proceedings are then smoothly approved by the Appointments Committee of the Cabinet comprising the home minister and prime minister. The same controlling clique proceeds to appoint the convenient bureaucrat to high profile, lucrative ministries such as defence, home, finance, civil aviation, telecommunication, petroleum, urban development, steel etc. while officers without clout are consigned to residual ministries, normally the social sector ones. Potential for commissions and kickbacks determine which ministries must have captive bureaucrats, and these are the ministries that the DMK has traditionally claimed.

The UPA added another dimension that cemented the politician-bureaucrat nexus by decreeing informally and formally that ministers have the right of choice of their secretaries. This meant that the empanelled secretary had to do the rounds of ministries where vacancies were imminent, and solicit his case for selection, unless some higher politician or business house had already spoken for him. And it would be naive to think that such an appointment would be *pro bono publico*. An honest bureaucrat has nowhere to turn for redressal as the relevant fora were also clearly controlled by the same mafia. With a sense of resignation all they could do is attempt a joke, 'the Nair you are, the higher you are'!

Thus the 'Keralite Mafia' in the PMO was able to capture the commanding heights of bureaucracy. At one point, the cabinet secretary, the principal secretary to the prime minister, the national security advisor, the home secretary, the foreign secretary, urban development secretary, food and agriculture secretary, civil aviation secretary, textile secretary were not just Keralites, but Keralite Nairs. This was the inner first circle, the critical one. The next circle accommodated spouses of the Keralite Nairs and other communities of Kerala and then come Kerala cadre officers belonging to other states. One look at the GOI directory from 2005-2010 will give all the details.

No one came in their way, not the prime minister nor the UPA chairperson. Mulford could obviously see this nefarious and sinister exercise of power, and hence used an extreme term like 'Keralite Mafia' in his report, instead of 'coterie' or 'caucus'. The Oxford Dictionary meaning of mafia is a 'secret organization of criminals that is active especially in Sicily, Italy and the United States.'

Or was it also a Freudian slip?

And such is the fate of India, to be caught in a death kiss between the corrupt, the corrupting and the cliques—mammon and master, whose interests the public office must serve.

7

Political Life

Against all Odds—the unprecedented rise of Narendra Modi

I have always condemned communal violence as the greatest crime against our precious creed of secularism, its equivalent of genuine Hindutva, and the goal of complete national integration, which is almost within our grasp. Both the Godhra train massacre and the retaliatory riots, apart from taking the lives of several innocent citizens, were a blot on the nation's secular Hindutva values, and a negative reflection on the quality of Gujarat governance. From here onwards, they provided a handle for a combination of forces determined to destroy Narendra Modi. Vested interests from civil society and the media, and of course the Congress, pronounced Narendra Modi guilty of a range of crimes including murder and genocide; called him 'maut ka saudagar', and tried their best to ostracise him from mainstream India.

It all began when the Sabarmati Express carrying non-violent, harmless karsewaks was set on fire and nearly 60 persons were burnt to death on 27 February 2002. Understandably, but regrettably, this provoked retaliation and mayhem resulting in many innocent members of the minority community losing their lives and suffering other indignities. It is equally true that the desire for revenge paralyzed the will of some law enforcement agencies, including some prosecutors and judges. Serious steps had to be taken to restore the confidence of the victims of revenge in the legal and judicial system of the state.

The Congress government at the centre played a diabolical role. A bogus commission was appointed to whitewash the Godhra tragedy and establish that the attack on the train was not the result of a conspiracy of some Muslims, but an accidental stove fire. This canard was fully exposed when a Special Investigation Team appointed by the Supreme Court made their own independent investigation and reiterated that the burning of the pilgrims was a concerted plan by those who must have known that it will inevitably lead to retaliation and atrocities against the minorities—a finding fortified by recent court judgments. These evil calculations had proved to be right. Obviously, the planners wanted India to get a bad name, its national unity and integrity shaken and its defence against scheming neighbours enfeebled.

As the hate campaign against him reached a crescendo, Modi resigned as chief minister in July 2002. The unfortunate riots were followed by state elections, the results of which made the psephologists run for cover. One is reminded of a story, which may well be apocryphal, but is fairly apposite and bears repetition. The Viceroy of India, Lord Linlithgow, wanted to hold an open air reception in Simla and sought, and received, the assurance of the weather bureau that there wouldn't be any showers on that day. But while strolling on the mall, he encountered a farmer and his donkey. Proletarian as he pretended to be, he struck up a conversation with the man and made the same enquiry. The farmer looked at his donkey and said, 'Whenever my mate's ears shake the way they are doing now, it just pours.' The Viceroy made light of the donkey's signal, but his evening party was a wash out. In anger, he had the weather station removed to far away Pune as punishment.

Despite media predictions, Modi won a landslide victory, which astounded even his followers. I congratulated him for his brilliant victory, but I sincerely advised him to wear a look of absolute humility; publicly own that something had seriously gone wrong and loudly proclaim that India could never go forward or retain its independence and sovereignty unless Hindus and Muslims were locked in an embrace of love and mutual understanding. It was important to declare his firm resolve to bring back to the minorities a feeling of absolute security and assure them of every kind of protection by the powers of the state. This has been Modi's strategy, and since then his stature has risen manifold to heights rarely attained earlier.

Modi's Godhra experience changed him completely. He rose from the ashes, and thereafter focused his entire energy on building

Gujarat on able administration and good governance, development and economic growth, and social inclusion. Modi has made Gujarat a land of opportunity and the aam aadmi across the country has grown to iconize him to such an extent that vast sections of civil society see in him the next prime minister of India.

A victim of circumstance

No politician in independent India has been demonized in such a relentless, Goebbelsian manner as Narendra Modi, and no politician has withstood it with as much resilience and courage as he, who has stood firm despite the entire central government, influential sections of the media machinery and sections of civil society arraigned against him.

The policies and conduct of Narendra Modi should be compared with those of the late Rajiv Gandhi. The tragic assassination of his mother led to what may accurately be described as a virtual genocide of the Sikhs. Armed bands of hooligans and murderers went around the streets and colonies of Delhi in search of innocent Sikhs, sought them out and slaughtered them mercilessly. We saw some Sikhs being burnt alive on public roads while crowds watched the heartrending scenes. Although a Sikh president held office, he could not move a finger to help the unfortunate followers of Guru Nanak. I cannot forget those shameful days even now. All that the new prime minister Rajiv Gandhi had to say was a defiant, 'When a big tree falls the earth must shake'. Never did the Congress leadership apologise for the atrocities and the murders. It is the greatness of the Sikh community that they have forgiven the Congress.

Till date, not one Congress leader involved in the 1984 riots has been brought to book* nor has any serious attempt been made to do so. Rajiv Gandhi became, for a while, the media's darling and even his heirs, who themselves aspire to lead this country, have not made any real attempts to reach out to the Sikhs. Modi and his government, on the other hand, have ensured that due process of law is carried out and the guilty convicted. Yet Narendra Modi remains one of the most demonized figures in Indian politics,

---

*Although over 400 people have been convicted for their role in the 1984 riots, no Congress leader implicated has been brought to book.

accused of every crime from providing state sponsorship to the riots to protecting those responsible.

Gujarat minorities have made peace with Modi

The minorities in Gujarat have made their peace with him and acknowledged his contribution and leadership in providing the right kind of development and infrastructure to give them the opportunity to grow. The minorities are important stakeholders and Gujarat has not seen communal violence since 2002. Ahmedabad, which was continuously under curfew in the 1990s, is now aspiring to be a world class city. Modi has overseen heavy investments in roads and power infrastructure, housing and the IT sector. The state has seen an annual growth of more than 11% in recent years, attracting investments from large corporations such as, General Motors and Mitsubishi. There is already widespread recognition that 'Vibrant Gujarat' is the most dynamic state in India and the most secure place to invest.

After Mamata Banerjee's shenanigans regarding the Tata Nano project in Singur, Ratan Tata shifted operations to Gujarat, and in record time the Nano hit the road. Maruti Suzuki, the Congress party's pocket enterprise, is also moving to Gujarat only because of the enabling industrial environment. Maruti is the third car manufacturer, after Ford India and PSA Peugeot, to have announced plans of setting up car manufacturing plants in Gujarat. The Americans, remembered for their denial of US visa to Modi, have in a report by US Congressional Research Service released in September 2011, showered praises on him by stating that Gujarat was India's best example of effective governance, and Modi was among BJP's likely candidates for prime ministership in future elections.

Of smear campaigns and downright perjury

A news report in the *New Indian Express* dated 30 November 2011 provides an unequivocal insight into the manner in which the CBI has been conducting itself in Gujarat related cases. I quote: 'The Supreme Court on Tuesday rapped the CBI for making insinuations saying that the trial courts in Gujarat and its judges were biased and in favour of the state's ex-home minister, Amit Shah, in the

Sohrabuddin Sheikh fake encounter case.' It is 'complete nonsense' and 'contemptuous,' the Bench remarked in the same breath. The CBI's statement that the accused in the case have 'presence of their kith and kin in the subordinate judiciary in various capacities as prosecutors, magistrates as well as judges' was termed as 'highly irresponsible' by a Bench comprising Justice Aftab Alam and Justice Ranjana Prakash Desai. The CBI Counsel floundered in his reply when the Bench asked him whether he wanted the allegations retained or deleted, pleading that he was a late entrant to the case, and would make an application for deletion of the offending paragraphs from the petition.

The Bench was also hearing a petition seeking shifting of the trial of the case outside Gujarat, and remarked, 'At this stage when trial has not commenced, it is premature for the CBI to seek transfer of the case as there is no instance for the CBI to show that the witnesses are turning hostile or there has been tampering of the evidence.' However, the Supreme Court, in its September 2012 verdict, upheld the bail of Amit Shah, although it allowed the case to be transferred to Mumbai.

All one can say is that the UPA, all its investigating agencies and some of their media friends continue to be obsessively fixated with demonizing Gujarat and Modi. This brigade has also become a haven for disgruntled sections of the bureaucracy, who believe that becoming anti-Modi zealots would help them enter some paradise in the UPA government. They take their cue from the case of a Gujarat cadre IPS officer Kuldeep Sharma, who faced criminal charges and caught the fancy of the Central government on account of his anti-Modi utterances, and was appointed as DG-Bureau of Police Research and Development without the mandatory vigilance clearance from the state government.

The Strange Case of Sanjiv Bhatt

A new adversary entered the fray in the form of Sanjiv Bhatt, an IPS officer whose service record reeks of insubordination and indiscipline. Dogged by a Jamnagar custodial death case of the early 1990s, which is *sub judice* in the Supreme Court, he chose to run to the media with his grievances against the chief minister rather than seek redressal through any of the legitimate mechanisms available to him. This is surprising since, as a member of the All India Services, Sanjiv Bhatt is bound by a well-codified set of conduct rules. If Mr Bhatt was apprehensive that he would not obtain justice in Gujarat, he could submit a 'memorial' to the president under Rule 25 of the All India Service (Discipline and Appeal) Rules, 1969. To the best of my knowledge, he has not sought any relief from the statutory remedies available to him. This action of his is a serious violation of Conduct Rules, punishable with a major penalty, including dismissal from service. Added to that, it is reported that he has not filed his property returns, something mandatory for All India Service officers under Rule 16 of the Conduct Rules. Such a track record may perhaps be the reason why the Congress is keeping him at an arm's length, despite his desperate entreaties to use his services more substantially.

A police officer's most valuable professional assets are his weapon and his information, and any carelessness with either can cost him dearly, especially if the information he is careless about is conspiratorial and subversive. This is exactly what Sanjiv Bhatt seems to have done. He handed over charge and his official computer leaving all his emails in an unprotected mode for all to read. The state government forwarded them to the SIT with a request to place them for consideration of the *Amicus Curiae* and the Special Bench hearing the riot cases to see the real motive behind Bhatt's prayer for transfer of the investigation of KD Panth's complaint against Bhatt to the CBI.

What emerges from his emails is a sinister harvest of communication between him and the anti-Modi brigade that appears like a conspiracy against the chief minister and the state, spearheaded by Sanjiv Bhatt, even while enjoying the constitutional protection that he as an IPS officer derives from Article 311 of the Constitution. The mails establish without doubt that Sanjiv Bhatt violated every rule in the book, and behaved like a law unto himself, having the audacity to assume charge in Ahmedabad while posted to Junagarh. He continuously leaked his correspondence with government, including an affidavit to be submitted to the Supreme Court, to the media and other cohorts. The correspondance also reveals a continuous and determined campaign against the Gujarat government, virtually imploring the media to highlight his false affidavit, brazenly trying to mobilize the anti-Modi brigade and 'pressure-groups' to use the 'media card' and influence judicial proceedings before the Supreme Court and *Amicus Curiae*, as well as instigating various activist organisations directly to pressurise the *Amicus Curiae* with a flood of letters.

The mails provide conclusive evidence of Sanjeev Bhatt hobnobbing with the Opposition Congress party in a thoroughly illegal and almost seditious manner to concoct evidence against the chief minister regarding his claimed presence at the chief minister's meeting on 27 February 2002. Top Congress leaders such as Arjunbhai Modhwadiya, Shaktisinh Gohil, Krishnakant Vakharia and Nasir Chhipa, were in constant touch with him, giving him 'packages' and 'materials', and guiding him. Curiously, Bhatt almost seemed to beg Shaktisinh Gohil to provide him with a BlackBerry, something he could well afford himself. Or is Blackberry a code for something else?

As the dots get connected we see an ominous picture of a systematic and larger conspiracy involving Sanjiv Bhatt, top leaders of the Congress in Gujarat and vested interest groups determined to concoct facts and create false evidence to keep the Godhra riot issue alive, almost ten years after the completion of judicial proceedings. Sanjiv Bhatt leaves no stone unturned, continuously contacting third parties and persuading them to swear affidavits to support the false stand taken by him in his affidavit in the Supreme Court, and send them to the *Amicus Curiae* and the Supreme Court.

A true snapshot of the character of Sanjeev Bhatt is seen in his criminal offence of hacking the mail account of the Additional Advocate General and sharing the ID and password with others. He exchanged emails with journalist Rajdeep Sardesai requesting him, 'Please make someone go through the mailbox of Tushar Mehta... If need be, I can sit with someone from your channel and point out the significance of certain mail exchanges.' The silver lining is that Sardesai, a responsible journalist, seems to have given the offer short shrift. The same emails were shared with another journalist, Rajiv Pathak, whose response was identical in refusing to use the unauthorized details supplied by Bhatt, at which Bhatt gives some pious advice: 'Please ensure that the password of TM mail account is neither changed nor shared with anyone else.' Rajiv Pathak very maturely replies, 'Don't worry sir, since it came from you, I have no right on changing or sharing it with anyone. Since my office is not willing to use this, this becomes entirely your property on which I have no claim.'

Well, the journalists showed greater ethics than the cop.

The month of May 2011 kept Sanjiv Bhatt busy trying to get his cronies to influence P Chidambaram and cook up false evidence and cobble together pressure groups. On 18 May he sent a mail to Nasir Chhipa, who is supposed to be close to the Congress party, telling him, 'I was told by Ms Shabnam Hashmi that Home Minister P. Chidambaram can be influenced by pressure groups in the US. All appeals for the safety of witnesses, including myself, have not received the desired response from PC. You may have to work a little on this aspect....'

On 19 May Nasir Chhipa replies, 'We have wrote (sic) letters yesterday to Sonia, IAMC wrote letters and many other organizations. I will email you later.' (IAMC stands for Indo-American Muslim Council.) On 28 May Sanjiv Bhatt wrote, 'Dear Nasirbhai, Any progress on the front of *Amicus Curiae*? Time is running out. We need to act quickly...'

Bhatt, a serving police officer, crosses all bounds when he prepares the affidavit of Subhranshu Chaudhary, former BBC correspondent, and uses it to substantiate his false stand of having attended the meeting at Gujarat Chief Minister Narendra Modi's residence on 27 February 2002. On 15 May, the telephonic coordinates of Shubhranshu Chaudhary are used by Bhatt to file an affidavit in the Supreme Court to collaborate his false statement that he was present in the meeting of the chief minister. Shockingly, the said details are also sent simultaneously to Teesta Setalvad on 16 May for drafting the affidavit to be filed by Shubhranshu Chaudhary. In one of the pre-affidavit mails to Chaudhary, Bhatt tutors him by writing, 'Maybe you can mention that I had met him (Sanjiv Bhatt) on 27th when he was about to go to the 'disputed' meeting.' Does one require any further evidence of the perjury in Bhatt's affidavit?

When Shubhranshu Chaudhary shows reluctance to give media hype to his affidavit, the petitioner writes to him advising use of the media, and asks whether Chaudhary is more comfortable with Arnab Goswami or Rajdeep Sardesai. When Chaudhary's reluctance still persists, Bhatt writes to him, 'My feeling is that we could let the press sniff it out and contact you. It will not only make a good story for them, but also make the print media take notice of your affidavit and finally force the hand of *Amicus* and Supreme Court to take notice and subsequent affirmative action.'

Bhatt openly pandered to the media, telling Shubhranshu Chaudhary, 'I think we should play the media card and make it difficult for the other side. If you fear that *Amicus* and Supreme Court will not take it seriously then media trick can be tried. I will be speaking with Rajdeep Sardesai tomorrow. I will drop a line to him and let him follow up the lead.' On 19 May 2011 Bhatt emails Rajdeep Sardesai of CNN-IBN, telling him that he has information that a senior journalist has 'filed an affidavit in the Supreme Court on 16th May, saying that he was with me when I had to leave for CM's meeting on 27-02-2002... Kindly confirm through your sources in Supreme Court...'

Bhatt also interacted constantly with the prize anti-Modi brand ambassador Teesta Setalvad, whose *raison d'etre* would have been considerably threatened by the fact that the Supreme Court on 1 May 2009, finally disposed of the Godhra riot cases, except for the monitoring of nine major cases. Her Interim Application making baseless allegations against the Special Investigation Team (SIT) and seeking its reconstitution having proved unsuccessful, she found one more opportunity through Bhatt to achieve her nefarious objectives.

The same Bhatt, who claimed that he could not divulge anything before the SIT since 'he is under the oath of secrecy', sent copies of all applications made to the Enquiry Commission and the state government to Teesta Setalvad, and also his affidavit, which was prepared with her help.

Many mails indicate that Setalvad was tutoring Bhatt for his deposition before the Justice GT Nanavati and Justice AH Mehta Commission of Inquiry. Bhatt constantly lamented what he calls the 'pathetic' performance of the Congress advocate during his deposition before the Commission, stating that he felt 'under-exploited', meaning, thereby, that the Congress advocate's cross examination did not exploit his full potential to accuse the government further with lies.

Home Minister P. Chidambaram is reported to have stated to the media that 'he is 'glad' that senior Indian Police Service (IPS) officer Sanjiv Rajendra Bhatt had the guts to file an affidavit in the Supreme Court accusing Gujarat Chief Minister Narendra Modi of complicity in the 2002 Godhra case.' Mr Chidambaram as home minister should realize that even his acute Modi hatred should not be made a handle to irretrievably destroy the discipline and work ethic of the Indian Police Service.

An interpretation of maladies

In sharp contrast to the courage and integrity of Narendra Modi, is the character of Mr Digvijay Singh. I have been studying his public persona for the last decade, particularly since the UPA regime came to power, and his genius had maximum opportunity to flower and realise itself. I invariably awaited his periodic public utterances with much anticipation, to take a peek at his resilient and innovative mind, and the contribution it made to the UPA governance model of chaos.

Digvijay Singh has had a particularly hard life for the last decade since he lost power as chief minister and has had to face the anguish and trauma of the BJP ruling over what was once his great empire. This must have taken an awful psychological toll on him, and his behaviour which appears to be getting somewhat pathological, extreme and often unintelligible, suggests that he has still not come to terms with this reality.

It is reported that Digvijay Singh sought solace in a vow to remain out of active politics for 10 years. Commendable, at a time when Liquorgate was chasing him, the Lokayukta was registering FIRs against him in urban land ceiling and land scam cases, and the Madhya Pradesh Bureau of Investigation for Economic Offences was investigating his Treasure Island Mall scam, for which I believe an FIR was filed. It is hard indeed, having to take painful decisions of self-abnegation in the prime of his life.

I believe Digvijay Singh is a fascinating subject for an in-depth psychological study. What extra-ordinary methods he has devised to fight deprivation, frustration and FIRs! I wish I knew more about his childhood. I know he comes from a princely Rajput family where he would have lacked nothing, but I often wonder whether he was prone to tantrums or indulged in other attention-seeking behaviour as a child, or sucked his thumb beyond the acceptable age in order to gain comfort or a sense of security (a common interpretation by psychologists). Perhaps all these have evolved into the traits he displays for getting comfort and security.

Digvijay Singh's desire to seek attention, either from the general public or the special targeted few, seems to be accelerating at such a rapid pace that I am a little worried about his state of mind. It is getting just a little too repetitive and predictable. In psychology, repetitive speech disorder is considered a serious form of thought disorder, which ranges from delusion, obsessive-compulsive disorder, to something called schizophasia and palilalia, where I believe some chromosome or other is involved.

Digvijay Singh's thought disorder, repetitive speech disorder and obsessive-compulsive syndromes seem stuck on just three subjects: making Rahul Gandhi the prime minister, allying with Jihadi terrorist groups (remember his Freudian slip 'Osamaji'?) and using every opportunity to accuse the RSS whenever an unfortunate act of terrorism happens in India. Obviously, his thought disorder syndrome is so acute, that even our policemen killed in terrorist attacks do not shake it—he calls the Batla House shootout a fake encounter, where two of our policemen died. Even the martyrs are not spared: Hemant Karkare's tragic death in the 26/11 blasts sets Digvijay off on a delusionary mode where he hears voices in an imaginary telephone call from Karkare fearing an attack upon himself from Hindu organisations. The Maharashtra government put the record straight and said that no such thing had happened. This disorder is clinically termed as the full-blown phase of delusion.

The condition of Mr Digvijay Singh seems to have palpably worsened. Even while the investigation into the Mumbai blasts was going on and the country was trying to speak in one voice against the heinous acts of terrorism that claimed more than 200 innocent lives, he predictably stated that he did not rule out the involvement of the Sangh in the bombings. Surely such disordered statements reflect poorly on Mr Singh and his party, both nationally and internationally. Indeed, the WikiLeaks (in ignorance, I'm sure, of his various disorders) calls his behaviour 'crass political opportunism' while Israel snubbed him royally when, during some particularly bad delusionary spell, he tried to compare the RSS with the Nazis.

My sincere advice to Digvijay, as an elder, is he should focus his intelligence and vast experience to reflect upon critical issues of contemporary India—for example, how to remove poverty, how to provide safe drinking water and sanitation to every village in India, how to improve the health status and infant mortality situation in the country, how to increase female literacy—areas in which the state that he led for 10 years is among the worst in India.

But, perhaps, I have got it all wrong. Perhaps he only pretends to have all these disorders so as to gain monopoly of being the Gandhi family mouthpiece, particularly for making Rahul Gandhi the next prime minister. Perhaps he does this so that he can play vote-bank politics of the worst kind, even at the cost of national unity, by creating fissures where none exists. He could claim to be the main architect of making Rahul Gandhi the hero of the UP elections had Congress succeeded in improving its presence.

Perhaps, I have got even that wrong. Digvijay must know, I'm sure, that there is some speculation in the media that he is doing all of this for Rahul Gandhi only in name, while actually working towards his own future as prime minister. Since his ten-year vow will also be ending shortly, to borrow Digvijay's own words, I suppose this possibility cannot be ruled out.

The secret malady of Sonia Gandhi

In 2011, Shrimati Sonia Gandhi disappeared from public life due to an undisclosed indisposition. There were precisely three official statements regarding her unfortunate indisposition. The first was to Parliament on 4 August 2011 by Congress General Secretary Janardan Dwivedi stating that she was diagnosed with a medical condition and advised surgery, and that on the advice of her doctors, she travelled abroad and would be away for two-three weeks. The second statement on 5 August informed that the surgery was over, the surgeon had indicated that the operation was successful, and Sonia Gandhi was recovering in an intensive care unit. He added that 'as this is a personal matter that pertains to her health and medical treatment, her family requests that her privacy be respected.' The last public statement was made on 8 September, by Rashid Alvi: 'Sonia Gandhi is back and in good health' adding that he could not say anything more on this matter.

Other than this, there was a blackout regarding her location, the nature of her ailment and the stability and prognosis of her health condition. Sonia Gandhi was last seen in public during her visit to Bangladesh on 25 July 2011. The nation was naturally concerned and expected more information regarding her ailment, its nature and gravity.

There was also discomfiture across all sections, including reportedly from within the Congress, at this opacity. The aam aadmi found it reminiscent of the old feudal regimes when clear communication between rulers and subjects was unthinkable. The general population remained muted in their reaction, but felt a sense of alienation instead of bonding with her in her difficult hour, as if they were not worthy of being taken into confidence.

This was an occasion to put the privacy of public persons in proper perspective. The freedom movement and the sacrifices of our heroic leaders gave us the gift of Constitutional democracy. The humblest citizen got his freedom of speech, the chief component of human liberty. The Greeks and the Romans had enjoyed democracy, an imperfect one though, both in its content and duration. But with the semitic religions that posited a supreme, all powerful Ruler of the Universe, democracy died a natural death.

Thomas Paine proclaimed the Rights of Man, and the American Constitution explained to the world that the right to criticise holders of public office is the vital building block of a Republican edifice. Then came the role of the eminent judges of the US Supreme Court. In 1964, citizen Sullivan made a vicious attack on the head of the state police, who sued and obtained a decree of damages. Sullivan appealed and the Supreme Court reversed the verdict in a celebrated judgement which holds the field even today. Fortunately, India too found a great judge in Justice Jeevan Reddy who made the Sullivan pronouncement a part of Indian law.

Briefly, the rule is that the people have the right to know practically everything about a person aspiring for political power. It does not matter whether it is for himself or herself, or a relative, or friend. Even if the criticism turns out to be factually erroneous or false and also hurtful to the plaintiff, the latter cannot succeed unless he proves that it is deliberately or recklessly false. Truth must collide with error in the free market place of ideas and win in fair combat. Law will not peremptorily suppress error.

The privacy debate has been going on in some sections in the media and over the internet. But to what extent does firewall privacy apply in this case? Mrs Sonia Gandhi was not on holiday, nor is she a private person like Greta Garbo, who went to neurotic lengths to hide herself from the public. We are talking about an extremely important public figure of India who chairs the UPA which runs the Government of India, a person who heads the ruling Congress that appoints the prime minister, and the chairperson of the National Advisory Council, where she holds cabinet minister status, and tries to play an Eva Peron role by initiating laws for public good and to benefit the poor and marginalised. Does that make her sound like a private citizen of India?

It is ironic that in this day and age, such legitimate information was withheld from the public, and that too concerning the chairperson of the NAC, who was said to have been the chief promoter of the Right to Information Act. The media, normally hungry for breaking news, seemed either unconcerned, or under instructions from invisible powers to lay off. No panel discussions on the subject or political analyses, not even basic information of where she was. Rather unusual. Neither did we see spontaneous public gatherings at her residence, or mass prayer meetings for her health and long life. Was everyone gagged and all spontaneity crushed, or does it mean that the public gatherings and spontaneous adulation of the past can only happen when allowed?

Respect for privacy during a political leader's difficult hour is basic to civilised democratic behaviour. Our people know that. But who has directed this information blackout? Is it she herself and the 'Family', or is it the Congress? Whoever it was should have realised its negative fallout. Shrouding Sonia Gandhi in such secrecy is not really in her or her party's interest. Nor does it demonstrate a healthy relationship between the government and the people in a democracy. A better strategy would have been to recognise the distinction between privacy and secrecy and respect that intersection where privacy must give way to democratic obligation and ethics. This obligation was completely obliterated by secrecy. The health of the person who heads the ruling UPA as chairperson, is a virtual prime minister, is the chairperson of the NAC and president of the Congress is legitimately the concern of the people (without prying into intimate details) and should not be kept under total wraps. There is no doubt that Sonia Gandhi's presence and capacity to function optimally have a direct impact on the future of our polity, and a direct bearing on the way our country is run. So why was there this medieval secrecy? Or are we metamorphosing into some dictatorship of the old Communist variety or a totalitarian regime of Latin America?

My road to the Rajya Sabha

As soon as my candidature for a Rajya Sabha seat from Rajasthan became known, much of my time was wasted in warding off inane and silly questions from the media. Of the many questions asked, this is my response to one legitimate question, even as I ignore its barely disguised malice: 'Why are you hankering for a seat at the age of 86, and don't you think you have abandoned your principles by joining the BJP?' My age is for the party to consider. It obviously thinks I am more useful to the nation than the young cad who raised this question. I challenged him to a game of badminton anytime. That put an end to his childish smirk.

One does not belong to a political party because one agrees with everything the party decides to stand for. One joins a party with which he has fewer disagreements than with others; and because one accepts the party line on vital national issues. However, one voluntarily accepts limitations on freedom of speech and action; you can ignore a whip only if you are ready to resign.

I have been a founder-member of the BJP and its first all-India vice president along with the late, revered Rajmata Scindia. I left the party when some seniors disapproved of my defending Balbir Singh, who had been sentenced to death for conspiring to kill Mrs Indira Gandhi. (Incidentally, the Supreme Court held the case against him to be false.) I was right in upholding the *dharma* of a lawyer against party prejudices. For 22 years I was outside the BJP, but my relations with it were always cordial. Atalji (Vajpayee), whom I have respected as a wise and eloquent statesman, invited me to join his Cabinet twice during the late '90s, without insisting on my joining the BJP. The party has always been mature enough to leave space for dissent and diversity. To make a point on some issues, like the Tehelka-sting, I even had a friendly fight with the BJP in Lucknow in 2004.

In 2010 when I accepted the BJP nomination to the Rajya Sabha, I needed the party and the party needed me. This needs an explanation.

I was a member of the Rajya Sabha from April 1988 to August 2009, my last term being of three and half years as a nominated member. I was always fearlessly outspoken and wrote on every important issue of national concern. I have been a severe critic of the Congress on issues such as the Emergency in 1975, the genocide of Sikhs in 1984, Bofors in 1988 and the LTTE in the 1990s. I have applauded the BJP on its anti-terrorism campaign and partnership with the US, a conviction which led me to support Dr Manmohan Singh's nuclear deal.

In 2007, Dr Singh released my book *Conscience of a Maverick*, a selected collection of my essays and speeches, where he described me as a 'rare national treasure' and generously applauded my courage in speaking my mind. I have always pleaded that democracies of the world must unite, pool their moral and material resources and learn to swim or sink together. Dr Singh shared this view. We also agreed on the urgent need for friendship with Pakistan. Then came India's humiliation on 26 November 2008. A bunch of ten indoctrinated terrorists held Mumbai to ransom, exposing the incompetence of our current rulers. In my intense anguish I wrote an angry epistle to Mrs Sonia Gandhi, which I reproduce:

Date: 27-11-2008
My dear Soniaji,
For one year people around you have prevented me from seeing you. I do not know whether this is intentional or just negligence. I do not know whether it has been authorized by you. The object of my meeting you is not to seek anything from you but to inform you that the country is in a bad shape and your party will face the consequences in the ensuing elections. Today, I am writing this with great anguish because my conscience does not permit me to remain silent. I must at least record what I think.

For a long time it is obvious to the meanest intelligence that all your intelligence agencies are a complete failure and a fraud on the taxpayers. Reliable sources tell me that the ISI has infiltrated even into the RAW. Bangladesh has become a hot bed of anti-Indian activities. This requires the resignation and removal of some political heads but they are reported to enjoy your support.

The 26/11 incidents in Bombay are proof of your government's incompetence. The names of your corrupt ministers are freely circulating. Don't think that you are not yourself the target. The country is on fire and it needs consolation and security.

The terrorists are serving international goals too. I wonder if you know that the Nariman Point building under siege is occupied by Jew families. Residents are being held as hostages. Your ministers in Maharashtra have lost public confidence. They could not even handle a nitwit like Raj Thackeray.

I cannot write in greater detail but I am warning you that the Congress is on its way out. Neither you nor your son whom you are projecting as the future prime minister of India are the solution or even a ray of hope.

I know this will annoy you but frankly I do not care since you show no concern for the country. I have respect for the prime minister and his integrity. But that is not enough. I know his limitations of which you are the main source and cause.

I hope and pray that this evokes the kind of response which the grim situation of the country urgently requires.

Thanking you and with regards

My letter fell on deaf ears. The Empress of India was not amused. Things did not improve and as I am not getting younger, I am a man in a hurry; hence my letter to the BJP president which too I fully reproduce:

Date: 30-5-2010
My dear Nitin,
I write this when my mind is terribly agitated about the future of Indian democracy. When the ruling party is totally immersed in corruption, when the enormous wealth of this country is known to have been stolen away by dacoits, some of whose identity is also known, when the prime minister is anxious to remain one, as long as he can, not being able to extricate himself from the filthy mud of corruption, when key Constitutional positions are occupied by undeserving family loyalists and when poverty and misery stalk this unfortunate land, when religious fanatics armed as terrorists threaten the life and security of citizens and when climate change threatens to destroy the whole planet, this nation needs a strong aggressive and vibrant opposition. Unfortunately the state of the fragmented opposition only adds to the depression of perceptive and caring citizens.

You are doubtless aware of the marginal integrity of the news media. I am convinced that large sections of it have ceased to be the fourth estate and, therefore, practically useless for the health of our polity. A strong newspaper is an imperative necessity to keep the people's 'right to know' alive and effective.

My major concern today is to unify the opposition groups and elements within the UPA which have the conscience and the courage to clean up the filthy mess and with a strong voice to expose the misdeeds of our rulers.

It is with this obsession of mine that I am seeking a seat in the Rajya Sabha to be able to share my thoughts with other legislators on major national concerns of today.

I have been an independent member for a long, long time. It seems to me that I can be more effective if I join the main opposition party. Unfortunately the BJP also requires a new look and change of course—if it has to be an effective leader of the masses and a ruling party in waiting. I have discussed these changes with your major leaders and everyone assures me that once I join the party it will seriously address itself to my concerns. I have been assured that the party shares my anxiety about the future of Indian democracy.

While I affirm my willingness to join, you and your party have to decide the appropriate mode and time.

Kindly acknowledge and confirm.

With all my good wishes and regards.

The party decided that my presence in Parliament was needed for the good of the nation and they decided to make me a candidate, perhaps to control the maverick in me. For the sake of the nation, I did not mind.

Section 3
When Conscience Flees

8
Transparency, RTI and the Lokpal Bill

Demands for access to government information are not a recent phenomenon. In 1946, the General Assembly of the United Nations passed a resolution which stated, 'Freedom of information is a fundamental human right and is the touchstone for all the freedoms to which the United Nations is consecrated.' This was followed in 1948 by the Universal Declaration of Human Rights, which included Article 19 that states that: 'Everyone has the right to freedom of opinion and expression; this right includes freedom to hold opinions without interference and to seek, receive and impart information and ideas through any media regardless of frontiers.'

One of the important lessons of the Second World War was the misuse of information in totalitarian regimes, as exemplified by the notorious role played by Joseph Goebbels and the National Socialist propaganda. In 1971, the British appointed a committee presided over by Lord Franks to examine Section 2 of the British Official Secrets Act of 1911. The Franks Committee found that Section 2 was obscurely drafted and so recommended its repeal. It also recommended the passing of a new statute called the Official Information Act. The Franks report was debated in the House of Commons in June 1973, but because of change of government in 1974, no action could be taken. There is a popular belief in Britain that the government has not yet conducted its affairs with complete openness, and a campaign for freedom of information is persistently on.

In India, similar demands were first made in the 1920s, during the freedom struggle. Throughout our freedom struggle, we rightly attacked our colonial master for keeping the people of our country ignorant of major government policies and the detailed working of its machinery. This undemocratic trait manifested itself in the Official Secrets Act of 1923. Leaders of the freedom movement repeatedly and convincingly argued that the nation was being exploited and robbed of its wealth and material resources by secretly planned policies and projects of the colonial government. The people believed their leaders, rather than the Raj, despite the latter's propaganda machinery and its loyal comprador class.

So, when the British left and India became a democratic republic promising justice to every citizen, people naturally expected that they would acquire full access to details of governmental operations, its motivations, mechanics and consequences. These expectations were misplaced. Our indigenous masters never thought of repealing the colonial Official Secrets Act. Our Indian Evidence Act of 1872 ordained that no court would receive any evidence derived from unpublished official records relating to affairs of state except with the permission of the bureaucratic head of the department concerned, who could give or deny the permission as he deemed fit.

If the criminal activity of rulers is concealed in a government file, or recorded as classified and therefore 'not for publication', the evidence becomes inaccessible to people and unavailable to courts of justice. No public officer can be compelled to disclose information in his official capacity if he decides that public interest would suffer on account of the disclosure.

Though public demand for transparency has arisen from time to time, political parties, of both the government and the opposition, have not been greatly concerned about the people's fundamental right of access to information regarding the government's acts of commission and omission, something without which there can be no real democratic accountability. For a long while the proclaimed sovereignty of the people remained a myth, until the judiciary stirred. Wise judgments from some of our great judges opened the way to transparency in government.

The late Raj Narain, a maverick socialist leader, fought his electoral battles with Indira Gandhi both through the ballot box and in the courts. In the 1975 case of *State of UP vs Raj Narain*, the Supreme Court had to deal with Raj Narain's demand for production in court of a government document called the Blue Book which is supposed to contain the rules and instructions for the protection of the prime minister when on tour. He demanded information hidden in several circulars of the Home Ministry and Defence Ministry regarding the security and tour arrangements of Indira Gandhi, in his effort to prove a malpractice committed by the then prime minister's election managers. He applied for summons to various government officials to produce the relevant evidence. A secretary of the government claimed privilege, arguing that the documents called for related to the affairs of the state and their production was against public interest. The trial judge rejected this claim, holding that it was not an unpublished official record that Raj Narain was seeking. Relying on English precedents, the judge rightly concluded that the claim of privilege on the ground of public interest was a matter for judicial decision and not an autocratic executive right. These authorities clearly establish that even the view of a minister of the government could be overruled by the court. Relying on Indian authorities and the powers conferred on the court by Section 165 of the Evidence Act, the court had no difficulty in holding that it had the jurisdiction and power to rule on the validity of the government's claim.

The Supreme Court directed the High Court thus: 'Look at the document and decide whether the whole document or any part of the document could be made public after resolving the conflict between the two opposing kinds of public interest.' The matter ended up in the Supreme Court where the majority overruled the High Court on technical grounds, and ordered a rehearing.

Right to Information is not a gift

Mathew J, one of the greatest judges that India has produced, delivered a very learned concurring judgement. This is how he dealt with the issue:

'Those who are responsible for national security must be the sole judges of what national security requires. As the Executive is solely responsible for national security including foreign relations, no other organ could judge so well of such matters. Therefore, documents in relation to these matters might fall into a class which *per se* might require protection. But the Executive is not the organ solely responsible for public interest. It represents only an important element in it; but there are other elements. One such element is the administration of justice. The claim of the Executive to have exclusive and conclusive power to determine what is in public interest is a claim based on the assumption that the Executive alone knows what is best for the citizen. The claim of the Executive to exclude evidence is more likely to operate to subserve a partial interest, viewed exclusively from a narrow department angle. It is impossible for it to see or give equal weight to another matter, namely, that justice should be done and seen to be done. When there are more aspects of public interest to be considered, the court will, with reference to the pending litigation, be in a better position to decide where the weight of public interest predominates.'

In a later paragraph he elaborated on this in words that occupy an immortal place in the jurisprudence of democracy:

'In a government of responsibility like ours, where all the agents of the public must be responsible for their conduct, there can be but few secrets. The people of this country have a right to know every public act, everything that is done in a public way, by their public functionaries. They are entitled to know the particulars of every public transaction in all its bearing. The right to know, which is derived from the concept of freedom of speech, though not absolute, is a factor which should make one wary when secrecy is claimed for transactions which can, at any rate, have no repercussion on public security. To cover with a veil of secrecy the common routine business is not in the interest of the public. Such secrecy can seldom be legitimately desired. It is generally desired for the purpose of parties and politics or personal self-interest or bureaucratic routine. The responsibility of officials to explain and to justify their acts is the chief safeguard against oppression and corruption.'

Justice Mathew laid the seeds of a new and liberal jurisprudence. He drew a sharp distinction between two aspects of public interest to which the court had to apply its mind; the first being the harm which may be done to the nation, and the second being public interest, which requires that administration of justice shall not be frustrated by withholding documents that must be produced if justice has to be done. A judge must weigh these two aspects of public interest and if he leans in favour of the second, he has the duty and power to order production of the documents. If the injury to the public is minimal, or certainly less than the injury to the administration of justice, the latter will prevail. The power of the Executive to determine what is in public interest is neither absolute nor conclusive. Outside the field of security there are few matters of public interest that cannot be safely discussed in public. The importance of the above passage lies in the fact that the great judge deduced the people's right to know from the right of free speech guaranteed by Article 19 of the Constitution. How can a citizen speak freely if he lacks full knowledge of the subject on which he is speaking? The logic is compelling and unimpeachable.

When Justice Mathew laid the foundation of democratic transparency, his brother judges were still under the influence of Congress culture, which regarded government constructed barriers to free information as impenetrable. After the Emergency imposed by Indira Gandhi in 1975 came to an end in 1977, the Supreme Court breathed more freely and, in the famous SV Gupta judgment of 1982, delivered an incisive and defining exposition of people's sovereignty and their concomitant right to know. The majority judgment declared in no unmistakable terms:

'The concept of an open government is the direct emanation from the right to know which seems to be implicit in the right of free speech and expression guaranteed under Article 19 (1)(a). Therefore, disclosure of information in regard to the functioning of government must be the rule, and secrecy an exception justified only where the strictest requirement of public interest so demands. The approach of the court must be to attenuate the area of secrecy as much as possible consistently with the requirement of public interest, bearing in mind all the time that disclosure also serves an important aspect of public interest.'

People's untrammelled right of access to knowledge of bureaucratic activities only admits extremely narrow limitations. Any attempt to enlarge the scope of limitations is a betrayal of the Constitution and completely void. This great Constitutional doctrine has to be understood by those who are now beginning to turn the clock back, and reduce the parameters of the right to know.

The Congress did its best to hide its dismay at these majestic pronouncements of the Supreme Court. But the people understood the message, and began to turn to the Supreme Court in search of information. The government, however, remained committed to colonial secrecy. It should have been clear to bureaucrats that the Official Secrets Act was anathema to the Constitution.

The UPA government's doublespeak on Information

The nation had to wait for the NDA Government led by the BJP to frame the Right to Information Act. It was only in 2002, when the BJP government was in power that the Freedom of Information Act was introduced in Parliament and passed. It became the Freedom of Information Act, 2002 (5 of 2003). Two years later when the UPA government came to power, it churlishly decided to deprive the BJP of any credit, which was, in all honesty, due to it. They repealed the Freedom of Information Act and substituted it with the Right to Information Act which became fully operational on 13 October 2005. The repeal of the earlier Act was effected by Section 31 of the new Act. It was by no means an improvement on the earlier one. If the Congress government, led by Dr Manmohan Singh, wanted a better drafted law, they could have got it by amending the law, which is the usual behaviour expected of any successor government. Instead they took credit for this legislation, neither acknowledging the foundation of the Act in the judgments of Justice Mathew and other learned judges of the Supreme Court, nor the sincere efforts of the NDA government to bring it about. The new Act remains in substance a replica, word for word, of the BJP's version. An innocuous group of about eight sections has been added dealing with the office of the Central Information Commission and its state counterparts.

However, the mischievous part was an added clause in the Preamble:

'And whereas revelation of information in actual practice is likely to conflict with other public interests including efficient operations of the government, optimum use of limited fiscal resources and the preservation of confidentiality of sensitive information;

'And whereas it is necessary to harmonise these conflicting interests while preserving the paramountcy of the democratic ideal;

'Now therefore it is expedient to provide for furnishing certain information to citizens who desire to have it.'

It is ridiculous to tell the people of India that giving them information about how their servants and representatives are discharging their fiduciary duties can, in turn, make a government inefficient or significantly deplete its treasury or create gaping holes in the armour of desirable secrecy. The earlier Act had itself put seven kinds of information out of the reach of citizens. The UPA version raised it to ten, a dramatic increase of prohibited information by 40%. One of the additional prohibitions is in Section 8(e): 'Information available to a person in his fiduciary relationship, unless the competent authority is satisfied that the larger public interest warrants the disclosure of such information...'

Every transferee of property for a corrupt or criminal purpose, every executor, partner, agent, director of a company, legal advisor or guardian, stands in a fiduciary relationship. See the list in Sections 84 and 88 of the Indian Trusts Act, 1882. Limiting such information would mean that no scam of the kind for which the UPA government has become notorious will ever be discovered by any investigative journalist.

The Freedom of Information Act, 2002, was described by Parliament as, 'An Act to provide for freedom to every citizen to secure access to information under the control of public authorities, consistent with public interest, in order to promote openness, transparency and accountability in administration and in relation to matters connected therewith or incidental thereto.' By the 14th Section, the Act is to prevail over any inconsistent provision in the Official Secrets Act, 1923 or any other similar law. It must, however, be remembered that the Official Secrets Act has not yet been fully repealed although it should have been, at least to honour a pre-Independence promise. Its useful parts could have been inserted in the new Act.

The preamble to the Freedom of Information Act, 2002 recognizes the rights and duties of the public in a democracy to hold the government fully accountable for its actions, and to assess the propriety and validity of all actions taken by it. 'Open government' is a fashionable expression whose general intention is reasonably clear, but whose practical meaning awaits clear understanding by those who govern.

The Supreme Court has pronounced the law and emphatically declared that, outside the field of security, there is little—which means practically nothing—which can be hidden from the people. This would, naturally, be an uncomfortable position for any tainted government that is hand-in-glove with fraudsters, money launderers and owners of thousands of crores of rupees of black money. In fact, the ministry of personnel has recently confessed that it is considering amending the legislation to curtail the citizens' right to know. The government seems to be no better than the medieval-style khap panchayats of Haryana who are out to defy the Constitution, only to keep intact their murderous traditions.

Corruption thrives when transparency blacks out

Misuse of power opens up another set of questions that the government may find uncomfortable to answer. Take for instance the disconcerting news that Hasan Gafoor, who was the commissioner of police, Mumbai, on the disastrous day of 26 November 2008—when the whole nation was dishonoured by fanatic criminals mowing down innocent men, women and children—was appointed, apparently with the concurrence of money launderer Hasan Ali of Pune, and with the blessings of Ahmed Patel, the political advisor to Mrs Sonia Gandhi, UPA chairperson. A CD containing such disclosure, by Hasan Ali himself, has been produced before the Maharashtra legislature and Hasan Ali has clearly made a statement implicating people high up in authority in Delhi. Questions pertaining to the veracity of Hasan Ali's claim would of course be *de rigue*r as a means of deflecting the public from questions like how Hasan Ali acquired wealth to the tune of $8 billion, was able to stash this money out of sight, to whom this money actually belonged and, last but not least, the names of the powerful people with whom Hasan Ali had a close nexus.

Amendment of the Right to Information Act would go a long way in protecting the identities and true stories of corruption in the highest places. The judiciary and the people of this country must not only mount a powerful movement to compel the government to disclose the truth, but remain vigilant to ensure that the matter is not forgotten.

Prime Minister Manmohan Singh's arguments that the RTI Act 'should not affect the deliberative processes in the government' and 'should not discourage well-meaning public servants from giving full expression to their views' were rejected by the British House of Lords as early as 1968. In the *Conway v. Rimmer*, case Lord Reid said:

'The business of government is difficult enough as it is and no government could contemplate with equanimity the inner workings of the government machine being exposed to the gaze of those ready to criticise without adequate knowledge of the background and perhaps with some axe to grind. But this reason does not commend itself to us.'

The prime minister's argument fortunately does not appear to have convinced even his own ministers. Veerappa Moily, minister of corporate affairs, was obviously unimpressed with the prime minister's reasoning and stated there was a 'need for capacity building within the bureaucracy'. Fortunately he also added that bureaucrats should know how to act against the challenges of RTI while confessing, 'I think in this respect there is deficiency in governance. If that is addressed and also the capacity building is done, things will be all right.'

Every honest officer should have the courage of his convictions. Soon after I assumed charge of the union ministry of urban development in the late 1990s, I made a public announcement that any member of the public can pay ₹10 and inspect any file in my department in which he is interested. This set a cat amongst the pigeons. The secretary to the prime minister wrote to me in panic that I couldn't do this until the Freedom of Information Act was passed. I wrote to him, which meant to my prime minister, that the peoples' 'right to know' had already been declared by the Supreme Court as a constitutional right. The passing of the Act would only provide the mandatory machinery for enforcing the already declared right. I pointed out that my act of allowing people access to information stemmed from my respect for the Constitution, which is a voluntary respect and not only a show that is put on when the law compels respect. No one dared contest this, but I was soon shifted to the ministry of law.

The UPA government, on the other hand, has done its best to keep under wraps information that would reveal to the people of India the depths to which government corruption has sunk. Despite this desire, the years 2010 and 2011 witnessed a hard rain of corruption, with a plethora of skeletons tumbling out of the government's closets. Multiple disclosures of scams in high places bombarded us, but not on account of any government vigilance or commitment to probity, but because of proactive intervention by the aam aadmi and whistleblowers, superb fact-finding by media agencies, and supervision by a responsible, result-demanding and independent judiciary.

In India, the ultimate power lies with the people. It is essential for the rulers of our country to understand that the citizen's right to know what the government is doing, to ask questions about government's fiduciary probity, regardless of how uncomfortable these questions may be, is a constitutional right and not a gift that the ruling party can revoke at will to whitewash known scams and hide those that have not as yet come to light. Indians are tired of corruption and the government's slick cover-up jobs. Should the UPA government in its wisdom decide to tinker with the Right to Information Act, the nation should take action and vote the government out of power on this ground alone.

The Lokpal Bill and the French proverb

Concomitant to the Right to Information is the ability of the state to prevent or punish corrupt and illegal actions by those holding public office. This is a legitimate expectation of a free and democratic people. Hence the demand for a strong Lokpal, or citizen's ombudsman against corruption spanning almost five decades. The history of the Lokpal in India validates the French proverb: 'The more things change, the more they stay the same.' I have always been struck by this proverb, its philosophic, temporal and literary overtones. But to find its perfect validation in the real world was always a quest. Finally, I think I have found it in our great Lokpal conundrum.

Decades have passed since 1968 when the first Lokpal Bill was introduced in Parliament by Shanti Bhushan. Governments have changed, India has changed, corruption has become India's logo and unprecedented popular agitations have taken place, citizens' groups demanding eradication of corruption have crystallized, most notably the public campaign led by Anna Hazare—India Against Corruption. Yet after four decades of failed attempts, we're back to 1968. Rightly, as far as the Lokpal Bill is concerned, the more things have changed, the more they have remained the same.

Law Minister Ashoke Kumar Sen first proposed the concept of a Constitutional ombudsman in Parliament in the early 1960s. Shanti Bhushan in 1968 proposed the first Jan Lokpal Bill, which was passed in the Lok Sabha in 1969, but before it could be passed by the Rajya Sabha, the Lok Sabha was dissolved and the Bill lapsed. Lokpal Bills were introduced eight times from 1971 to 2008, but were never passed. Forty-four years after its first introduction, the Lokpal Bill is still pending in India.

In the absence of serious government action and credible political leadership, the anti-corruption wave of 2011 threw up unexpected leaders. To begin with, Anna Hazare, who started an anti-corruption fast unto death on 5 April 2011, became the rallying point for galvanising the long suppressed rage of the people of India against ubiquitous government corruption at all levels—from high powered 2G spectrum allocations to the little scams that plague their day-to-day lives. The main focus of Anna's fast was the establishment of an independent Lokpal. The public pressure built up by Anna Hazare's campaign against corruption drew swelling crowds each passing day. Eventually the unanimous public expression of extreme disgust against the government's chronic corruption shook the government out of its apathy. After a determined stand was made by Anna Hazare, which was countered by prevarication, obfuscation and confusion on the part of the government, an assurance was given that the government would incorporate the concerns of civil society in the Lokpal Bill. There is no doubt that the anti-corruption wave confounded the UPA government and left it in complete disarray. In a placatory move, the government constituted a joint drafting committee with Team Anna members but the differences between them were too great to be bridged.

When thieves beat up those they have robbed

On 4 June 2011, Baba Ramdev started an anti-corruption fast with the specific objective of recovering black money stashed in foreign banks by Indian politicians, businessmen and bureaucrats, and declaring the money a national asset. The world knows how Ramdev's fast ended a day later, with government repression and a police crackdown at 1 a.m. on a sleeping crowd that included women and children. This was in blatant violation of the provisions of the Constitution, the Criminal Procedure Code and the Delhi Police Act. It would not be an exaggeration to describe it as state aggression against a peaceful gathering. Opinion leaders across the board compared it with Jallianwala Bagh and the Emergency.

The government tried to stifle the Ramdev movement through panic response and intimidation—enquiring into the Swami and his followers' assets, businesses and licenses, and spreading canards that it was RSS sponsored. This begs the question, does the RSS have no right to protest against corruption? Many Congress supporters also claimed that Baba Ramdev was a yogi who became a politician and misused the technique of 'fast unto death' to achieve a political objective, forgetting, perhaps, the number of fasts Gandhiji undertook to get the British out of India. Baba Ramdev and his followers made excellent use of their constitutional rights. It was ironic to see the government first smarming over the Swamiji, and then calling him a thug after he showed his defiance and mettle.

On 8 June 2011, Anna Hazare undertook another fast at Raj Ghat to protest against the brutal suppression of the people's voice at Baba Ramdev's agitation and to support Baba Ramdev's cause of retrieving India's black money. This unwittingly united the two streams of protest: the first comprising the more middle class, urban and semi urban population, and the other comprising the more rural and heartland sections. The fast drew a massive response and Anna Hazare gave the government three months to pass the Lokpal Bill, failing which he promised another fast would commence from 16 August 2011. The government's obdurate stand and refusal to recognize the overwhelming popular support for the anti Corruption movement showed in stark relief the disconnect between the rulers and the popular sentiment.

That the people are no longer willing to be puppets in the hands of political masters, and that their legitimate demands must be met, has unfortunately not been recognized by the UPA government. So August 2011 witnessed what can be called a Grotian moment in the relations between Parliament and the people. Anna Hazare started his second fast against corruption on 16 August 2011, demanding a strong Lokpal Bill to be tabled during the Monsoon Session of Parliament. The government's response, despite the long notice, appeared maladroit and self-destructive, smacking of arrogance and a delusion of infallibility. Threatened with a situation of popular outcry, they found that they had no option but to retract their obdurate stand, listen, and concede at least in some measure.

I call it a Grotian moment as Anna's fast is a sort of marker in the evolution of democracy in our country, when a new paradigm between the people, the elected representatives, Parliament and government suddenly expressed itself. This paradigm change will have permanent and far-reaching consequence on the future of parliamentary and electorate dynamics in the country. The exclusive monopoly of elected representatives over law making was broken, and the people found a mechanism and platform through which they used their democratic power to demand from Parliament laws for their common good. To a large extent they were successful.

Anna Hazare, a simple man whose bona fides are beyond question, succeeded in uniting a crowd of more than 50,000 people participating in peaceful agitation from all parts of the country at Ramlila Maidan. This was possible because of his intuitive leadership and clarity of purpose. The rally had greater intensity and support than Anna Hazare's fast of April 2011. Yet the blundering stewards of government—the prime minister, the home minister, the heir apparent, and the anointed AK Antony—basking in denial and delusion, appeared overtaken by shock, remaining speechless and deafeningly silent. The hogtied government gave several assurances to Anna Hazare regarding introduction of the Lokpal Bill in the Monsoon Session of Parliament, and setting up of a Drafting Committee comprising government representatives and Team Anna, but excluding other political parties.

Anna Hazare, meanwhile, acquired the stature of a people's leader leading a crusade against corruption in a people's movement that was long overdue. No doubt, the cause was of great significance and the result of the people's victory, historic. Meanwhile the government's flip flop and blundering was shameful, demonstrating a complete absence of conscientious ethics, fiduciary probity, democratic management or judicious firmness. Arbitrariness, arrogance, absence of leadership and directionless chaos in governance were exemplified, serving to confirm the whispers of a fractured and headless government fraught with internal saboteurs and coteries.

Initially the government imposed innumerable conditions and refused permission for a peaceful protest at Jantar Mantar. Then on 16 August 2011, they arrested Anna Hazare. After seeing the people's response, they decided to release him, which he politely refused. They permitted him to fast in Ramlila Ground from 19 August and in the process, almost became the sponsors of his fast. But in all this lay the betrayal. The government tried every misuse of the rulebook and the law to derail and defeat the movement, intimidate and arrest Anna and his team, and wait-out for the movement to lose steam.

After the arrest fiasco, the misguided lawyer-ministers of the government, particularly Kapil Sibal, took over as custodians of the establishment, contemptuous of the people's support. They foolishly accused Anna of breaching the Constitution by daring to usurp the functions of Parliament. While watering down strong provisions of the Lokpal Bill, the lawyers resorted to legalistic and divisive arguments to back their stand including that laws could only be passed by the sovereign Parliament, which by majority and whip they completely controlled; that civil society was exceeding its bound, and the Anna Hazare movement had no legal *locus standi* and was acting unconstitutionally in imposing laws etc.

The thesis of the learned lawyers suffered from dreadful democratic perversity. What they seemed to have forgotten was that elected representatives must conduct their actions while in office for the common good of their constituents. And if the electorate strongly feels that certain legislation is necessary for their common good, such as curbing corruption through a strong Lokpal, they have every right to demand the same from Parliament.

Let us not forget here, that our Parliament was preparing to legislate on the very issue through a watered down Lokpal Bill. They also spearheaded a smear campaign against the members of Team Anna. Manish Tiwari, the Congress Spokesman, did a hatchet job on Anna although he later had to retract and apologize for his irresponsible statements. An unintended consequence of the government's attack on civil society and its right to pressure Parliament was a lively debate about how and why the civil society of the National Advisory Council was superior to the *aam* civil society. There is no doubt that some of the credit for the people's victory must go to the government whose shenanigans and exquisite blundering from beginning to end succeeded in infuriating the people and strengthening their resolve to take their fight to the finish.

The intimidatory tactics failed and Anna called for gheraoing MPs' houses and Parliament. A gherao contingent, evading the police barricade by using the Metro, actually reached the prime minister's house on 25 August 2011. It was only then that the prime minister, who appeared either marginalized or deliberately detached, seemed to wake up. The seasoned firefighter Pranab Mukherjee took over, and some semblance of sanity was brought into the discourse. The arrogant brigade peopled by Kapil Sibal and Manish Tiwari was silenced, and the prime minister in his usual self-effacing style became conciliatory, stating that 'our government was prepared to request the Speaker of the Lok Sabha to formally refer the Jan Lokpal Bill also to the Standing Committee.' As confusion continued in the government camp, so did negotiations between government and Team Anna. Pranab Mukherjee successfully drew the discussions towards a consensus on most points, including the three sticky issues of including the lower bureaucracy, appointing

Lokayuktas in states and having a Citizens' Charter, which for long had been a bone of contention. Finally, a compromise was reached.

Rahul Gandhi, the shining star of the Congress party, proposed some 'game changing ideas.' He read out a sheet of paper, the sum and substance of which was that this was not the time to talk about the Lokpal, as it was important to address the systemic, structural, sociological and psychological aspects of corruption. The Lokpal, he argued, must be a constitutional body like the Election Commission, implying thereby that the Lokpal Bill should be kept in the cold storage. His proposal required amendment of the Constitution by a two-thirds majority in both Houses which, I am sure he hoped, would take years to muster. There would be no Lokpal till then. In his 'innocence' he assumed no one would see through his childish ploy. Interestingly, he had no takers even in his own party and effaced himself from Parliament for some time after! Not surprising, this, as he and his family have most to fear from a strong Lokpal. Rahul's cousin, Varun Gandhi, fared much better in Parliament on 27 August, showing greater sensitivity and stating that it was in the nation's interest to have a strong Lokpal.

Sleight of hand

Thereafter, the UPA government had to employ a well orchestrated, subversive legislative strategy—one that could kill two birds with one stone. It had to impress the people of India, albeit through deception and chicanery, that it was serious about fighting corruption, and was fulfilling its commitment to Parliament by introducing the Bill. And simultaneously, it had to ensure that the Bill was legislatively so deficient with errors that it would not pass muster, and so weak and inadequate, that it was sure to be unacceptable to the Opposition and civil society. On 27 August, after a robust debate in both Houses of Parliament a resolution was passed conveying the sense of the House on the Lokpal Bill: 'This House agrees 'in principle' on the following issues—(i) citizen charter, (ii) lower bureaucracy under Lokpal through an appropriate mechanism, and (iii) establishment of Lokayukta in the states; And further resolves to forward the proceedings of the House to the Standing Committee on Law and Justice while finalizing its report.'

Apart from the Congressmen who absented themselves from the Lok Sabha, the UPA constituents themselves opposed the bill.

Naturally, as the mere mention of the word Lokpal strikes terror in their hearts. Furthermore, the government made it very clear that the Bill had no intention of releasing the CBI from government clutches and bringing it under the Lokpal, thereby making a categorical statement that it would continue to hold the final controls regarding which corruption cases can be investigated and prosecuted, and which can be hushed up and allowed to flourish.

This is what the Lokpal Bill offered. The Lokpal will have no power to initiate *suo moto* action or receive complaints of corruption from the general public. It can only probe complaints forwarded by the Speaker of the Lok Sabha or the chairman of the Rajya Sabha. Lokpal will only be an advisory body with a role limited to forwarding reports to a 'Competent Authority'. Lokpal will have no police powers and no ability to register an FIR or proceed with criminal investigations. The CBI will not be under the control of the Lokpal, and the anti-corruption wing of the CBI will not be merged into the Lokpal. The prime minister can be investigated by the Lokpal after she/he vacates office. Judiciary is exempt and will be covered by a separate 'Judicial Accountability Bill'. MPs can be investigated, but their conduct within Parliament, such as voting, cannot be investigated. Only senior officers (Group A) will be covered. All state anti-corruption agencies would be closed and responsibilities taken over by centralised Lokpal. The Lokpal can only refer matters to the courts and not take any direct punitive actions. Penalties would remain equivalent to those in current laws. No protection was provided for whistleblowers.

Lalu Yadav proved himself an able 'supari', using every absurdity possible to attack the Lokpal, while betraying his own terror of the Bill. 'We are sitting here to sign the death warrant of all MPs, MLAs, MLCs and government employees', he said. His final expected and ludicrous allegation against the Bill was that it was anti-minority, since no reservations for minorities were made in the Lokpal. As if to say that practice of corruption and its stoppage, must follow the quota system too.

The malafides of the government were also completely exposed when the Bill was discussed and passed by a voice vote on 27 December 2011. The Congress plunged the House into chaos and with the illegitimate assistance of the Chair, avoided an adverse vote of virtual No Confidence.

Part III of the Bill consisting of Sections 63 to 97, that deals with Lokayuktas in the states, was intentionally and clearly *ultra vires*, so as to ensure that the Bill could not pass unless the Constitution was amended as provided in the 116th Amendment Bill which was simultaneously presented to the Lok Sabha. With that, the fate of the Lokpal Bill was sealed. It was a deliberately confused legislation, with two ministers declaring that the Lokpal Bill was legislation under Entry One of the Concurrent List, even though the recitals in the Preamble to the Bill seemed to rely on Entry Thirteen in the Union List—that it 'is expedient to enact a law, for more effective implementation of the said Convention (United Nations Convention Against Corruption), and to provide for prompt and fair investigation and prosecution in cases of corruption.' This was deliberate obfuscation—the Bill was not implementing any binding decision taken at any international convention.

It was a win-win situation for the government which managed to shackle the Lokpal while making it appear that they had bowed to the voice of the people. As Pranab Mukherjee sagaciously conceded, Parliament 'does not necessarily follow the conventional' way of lawmaking, Anna rightly said that this was but half a victory. Fortunately for the government, Anna Hazare's health slowed down his pursuit of a corruption-free society.

The journey of the Lokpal Bill in the Rajya Sabha was no less turbulent, and matched the subversive and contrived histrionics of the Lok Sabha. The Bill was introduced in the Rajya Sabha on 29 December 2011, the last day of its sitting. Amendments were piling up that mostly dealt with control of the investigative agency, appointment and removal of Lokpal chairman and its members, the public functionaries coming under the purview of the Lokpal, and whether Lokayuktas should be part of the central legislation.

The government was jittery. There was an acrimonious 12-hour debate that ended abruptly at the stroke of midnight, without the House taking a vote on the Bill. The House was adjourned *sine die* by chairman Hamid Ansari after pandemonium persisted. Indeed, the pandemonium strategy was well choreographed, of course with the assistance of the Chair, to duck the crucial vote on the Bill, as the UPA government did not have the majority needed to pass it.

The Bill came up again before the Rajya Sabha on 21 May 2012, with some amendments regarding requirement of two-third instead of three-fourth members of the Lokpal to approve inquiry against the prime minister, exclusion of the armed forces from under the purview of the Lokpal, and omitting notification of the Lokayukta without the state government's consent. However, the position of the CBI remained the same—safe under the clutches of the government.

The UPA government devised another exit strategy in the Rajya Sabha. It procured the assistance of a friendly Opposition ally, the Samajwadi Party, to propose that it be referred to a select committee of the Rajya Sabha, further delaying the setting up of the anti-graft ombudsman which had been hanging fire for four decades. And that is where it rests.

Choice of Lokpal must be transparent

The Lokpal and Lokayuktas should be persons who command total respect and credibility among the public. Hence, the selection process has to be extremely transparent and pass microscopic scrutiny. Corruption has no concessions for sex, religion, caste or community. Reservations and quotas, in their proper spirit are meant to be affirmative action to provide opportunity for development to the less privileged but when it comes to prevention of corruption under what logic can they apply?

As and when the Lokpal Bill is enacted, in whatever form, how will the most suitable persons be selected for Lokpal by the Selection Committee prescribed in the Bill? One would expect that in the first stage, a Search Committee stipulated under Section 4(3) of the draft Bill would be constituted to recommend suitable names to the Selection Committee. This circles around the vital question of who should be the members of this Search Committee, and how the selection process can be made most transparent. It may also be noted that the draft clearly states in the same section that the Selection Committee, in addition to the recommendations of the Search Committee, 'may also consider any person other than the persons recommended by the Search Committee'. Hence, the scope for arbitrary selection by the government remains embedded in the Bill.

Evidence from the past reveals that the selection process of the ombudsmen, be it the central vigilance commissioner at the centre or the vigilance commissioners in the states, was done without any transparency. After the enactment of the Lokayukta Act in certain states and the judgement of the Supreme Court in the Vineet Narain case*, the procedure for the selection of the state lokayuktas and the central vigilance commissioner, which was hitherto opaque, became slightly more transparent, though not completely so. The selection of P.J. Thomas as CVC exposed the deficiencies in the process, and subsequent revelations in the Supreme Court case challenging his appointment revealed the complete lack of ethics in the UPA government in selecting a highly unsuitable candidate for this very crucial appointment that is meant to be the national instrument to check corruption.

A random check of the ombudsmen appointed at the centre, or states, indicates that a majority are retired persons from the judiciary or the administrative services. It can safely be assured that these appointees had not caused any inconveniences to the appointing government during their service, and managed the media by doling out catchy phrases and dramatic headlines, not necessarily reflecting the truth. Recall the corruption of the former minister for telecommunications, Sukhram. Has anyone discovered till date how and why N. Vittal, his secretary, failed to prevent his minister from indulging in corrupt practices? Subsequently, the same Vittal was appointed as central vigilance commissioner.

Needless to say, in the UPA 2 regime, post-retirement positions, constitutional and statutory, have become veritable entitlements of crony bureaucrats or active partners in corruption. This is clear on analyzing the appointments since 2009.

In this scenario, utmost care must be taken while drawing up the panel of shortlisted persons for election of the Lokpal. While unimpeachable integrity is the prime requisite, domain expertise and hands on experience of implementing anti-corruption laws should be the next important criterion.

It is imperative that the names of persons shortlisted by the Search Committee be placed in the public domain to ensure maximum transparency. Clearly, the integrity of the shortlisted persons would be known best by those who have had official interaction with them,

---

*Vineet Narain is a journalist and anti-corruption activist whose writ petition regarding the CBI's inertia in acting against the powerful mentioned in the Jain Diaries led to the Supreme Court directive regarding selection of the central vigilance commissioner and his responsibility for the objective functioning of CBI, thereby improving probity in public life.

and they would be most qualified to provide credible information touching upon the integrity of the persons under consideration. A time limit of a month may be set to elicit such information from the public. The Search Committee should not depend merely on the report of governmental agencies like the CBI, who will only give politically suitable opinions. A report from the public on the integrity of the candidates is the only method of bringing hidden facts out into the open, and provides maximum chances of getting the most suitable candidate, who like Caesar's wife, should be completely above suspicion.

After the end of the prescribed period of one month, a thorough investigation into any allegations by the public should be done, for which a time frame of another month may be fixed. The results of the verifications should also be made public. After this stage, no further allegations as to the misconduct or impropriety of past actions need be entertained. Such transparency and due diligence would avoid scandalous incidents such as the appointment of P.J. Thomas as CVC, or the lokayukta's resignation in Karnataka when a particular impropriety became public.

Postscript

The essence of a democracy is not controlling governance and the national exchequer through cobbled up numbers, as has been the UPA's fig leaf for staying in power, but through fulfilling the aspirations and ensuring the well being of the people through enlightened, responsible and accountable actions of elected representatives. Much of the support for Hazare has come because of the disgust and helplessness of the common man against corruption and patronage for corruption by the elected representatives, who have used their public offices for personal financial and economic advancement, at the cost of the common man. This corruption through a well-orchestrated partnership between the elected and the government functionaries, resulted in relentless harassment of the common man. Protesters saw government functionaries at all levels as kleptocrats in a rogue democracy. It is this phenomenon that has made a messiah of Hazare. In him the aam aadmi found a saviour and a cause through which they could at least be heard and gain relief. The message the aam aadmi is conveying is clear: elected representatives have lost their legitimacy in the eyes of their electors who have every right to use their own pressure groups to influence Parliament to enact legislation for public good. An effective Lokpal Bill without loopholes and exceptions is an example of the legislation demanded and there is nothing either unparliamentary or undemocratic about it. The government cannot logically expect the common man to trust corrupt legislators legislating tough anti-corruption laws. The angry, frustrated and helpless people trapped within the mockery of a democracy-turned-rogue have decided to make their power felt independently to influence Parliament. This is the real message of the Anna movement.

Genies once out of the bottle cannot be put back, and the Hazare movement is the first fundamental step towards questioning the conduct of the elected representatives of the people. Let us hope it gathers momentum and strength, and also reaches the poor, who really are the worst victims of corruption, but have neither the strength nor mobilisation to protest.

The citizens are ready and clamouring to strike against corruption and demand greater transparency, while the prime minister seems to be stuck on finding a magic wand to eradicate this malaise. He misses the fact that the magic wand he seeks is already in his hand in the form of political will. All he has to do is use it. In his Independence Day speech 2011, the prime minister stated, ' ...in the end, we can win the fight against corruption only when each and every citizen of India cooperates in it.'

The prime minister should be pleased, for this is exactly what the citizens are doing.

9
Bhopal—A Tale of Two Tragedies

Corruption, greed and self interest are endemic among the political masters of our country. They spare no one and in no situation are justice, humanity, compassion for victims, or the greater good for the people of our country, their guiding concern. Even a tragedy of the magnitude of the Bhopal disaster is not immune. Public posturing backed by political might is the weapon our elected rulers wield to hoodwink the nation, even in the gravest national disaster. A stark example of this is the government's handling of the Bhopal gas tragedy in general and the ignominious settlement of the Bhopal gas victims' claim in particular.

The Bhopal Gas Tragedy is one of the world's worst industrial disasters, horrific in its nature and magnitude. Late on the night of 2 December 1984, at the Union Carbide factory in Bhopal, water entered the tanks that stored a toxic gas, methyl isocyanate (MIC), used to make pesticides, and produced a dangerous reaction. The poisonous gas leaked out, and the prevailing wind-conditions pushed the fumes to the hutments surrounding the plant. The number of those who died immediately would have been far higher if the wind had driven the fumes into the congested city of Bhopal. The concentration of MIC gas was more than 25 parts per million, as against the recognized standard of tolerance, which is only 0.02 PPM. The long-term hazards of human exposure to this gas are not adequately known to science even today.

By October 1991 according to official estimates more than 4,000 innocent human beings were dead and tens of thousands physically injured and exposed to various degrees of pain, suffering and disease. Unofficial estimates are much higher.

Deliberately blind and criminally complicit

Rajkumar Keswani, a journalist working with a small weekly magazine called *Rapat*, wrote a prescient article two years before the tragedy titled *'Bhopal Jwalamukhi Kagar Pe'* (Bhopal on the edge of a volcano) warning the nation that the Carbide plant was in poor shape and there was likely to be a horrible disaster very soon. He wrote that the management knew about it, but was in no mood to make further investments on repairing the plant because the business was making huge losses. The management's mood almost seemed to be one of waiting and welcoming the disaster.

Despite these warnings, Arjun Singh, then chief minister of Madhya Pradesh, said on the floor of the legislature that everything was all right and there was no cause for any concern. If a journalist representing a small paper predicted the disaster, it is extremely disquieting that the state government and the union government armed with their enormous powers of inspection and control did not anticipate or take any steps to prevent it. It is not an unreasonable inference that all key functionaries including the Chief Minister Arjun Singh, had a very comfortable relationship with the management of Union Carbide, and it was unimportant and irrelevant in their priorities to make any ostensible effort to protect the life and health of thousands of their citizens.

The Brigands of Bhopal: how the government duped the people

The Union of India, while posturing to be the guardian of the victims whom it double crossed completely, divested the victims of their right to sue, appropriating this right to itself through legislation. The legislation made it a statutory trustee of the compensation due to the victims, individually and collectively. Thus the Government of India also appropriated to itself the victims' right to sue Union Carbide and those who in law were the effective and proximate cause of the tragedy. The victims were *sui juris* and had the right to be consulted before their property rights were negotiated and their consent was necessary to validate any dealings regarding their life and health.

The government filed a large number of cases in an American court on behalf of the victims and the Union of India became the effective prosecutor of these claims by 8 April 1985. It appeared before the district court in New York as a statutory assignee of the victims' claims. The American company was most anxious to avoid appearing before this court. Their plea of *forum non-conveniens* succeeded, and not without help from Indian lawyers, who swore that the Indian courts would be more convenient. What they really meant was that the Indian courts would be more 'manageable', which is what the history of this shameful episode in governance and, alas, judicial behaviour has proved.

After the initial rebuff from the United States of America court of Judge John F. Keenan, the Union of India filed its proceedings at the district court in Bhopal in 1986, claiming $3.3 billion (approximately ₹50,000 cr.) One must assume that the claim was quantified after careful calculation and competent legal advice. Yet, without fighting the suit and without any transparency, the government, by negotiation, the facts of which even today are a complete secret, settled the claim of the unfortunate victims for a ludicrously low sum of $ 470 million, that is ₹2,400 cr (and this at 1986 rupee values.) In the interlocutory relief petition pending before the Supreme Court, this overall settlement for $470 million was recorded by consent of the parties, on 14 February 1989. The victims of Bhopal could not have been betrayed more inhumanly and cruelly.

The terms of the settlement, as noted by the court, were:

'1. The Union Carbide Corporation shall pay a sum of US dollars 470 millions (Four hundred and seventy million) to the Union of India in full settlement of all claims, rights and liabilities related to and arising out of the Bhopal gas disaster.

2. The aforesaid sum shall be paid by the Union Carbide Corporation to the Union of India on or before March 31, 1989.

3. To enable the effectuation of the settlement, all civil proceedings related to and arising out of the Bhopal gas disaster shall hereby stand transferred to this court and shall stand concluded in terms of the settlement, and all criminal proceedings related to and arising out of the disaster shall stand quashed wherever these may be pending.'

The Court added that, 'A memorandum of settlement shall be filed before us tomorrow setting forth all the details of the settlement to enable consequential directions, if any, to issue.'

This was an extraordinary exercise of judicial power, to say the least. Apart from the meager settlement of the civil claim, criminal proceedings arising out of the disaster, wherever they may be pending, would stand quashed. What was surprising was that five Supreme Court judges, the learned attorney general of India, others taking daily interest in the litigation, and the press, which gets terribly hot under the collar about lesser matters, did not object to this unusual settlement reeking of corruption. This settlement, agreed upon without consulting either the victims, the NGOs working for their welfare, or their well wishers has been characterized by Prof. Upen Baxi, India's best scholar jurist, as an 'unconscionable settlement' by an unscrupulous Congress government.

Some more details were introduced in the order on the next day for the benefit of Union Carbide.

The Supreme Court thereafter developed a troubled conscience. It scented the anger which the settlement recorded by it had produced amongst the victims and some caring citizens and social workers. In another judgement delivered on 4 May 1989, that is less than three months after the earlier judgement, the court found it necessary to modify its declared reasons for the settlement which it had made a rule of the court. What it said was new: 'It appears to us that the reasons that persuaded this court to make the order for settlement should be set out, so that those who have sought a review might be able effectively to assist the court in satisfactorily dealing with the prayer for a review. The statement of the reasons is not made with any sense of finality as to the infallibility of the decision; but with an open mind to be able to appreciate any tenable and compelling legal or factual infirmities that may be brought out, calling for remedy in review under Article 137 of the Constitution.'

It then announced that it proposed to deal with two matters—justification of the figure of $470 million for an overall settlement and its failure to lay down the law applicable to liability arising out of such disasters as a matter of concern to all the democracies in the Third World. However, it did not touch upon the issue of how criminal proceedings came to be quashed. The anguish and agony of the kith and kin of the dead and disabled had not yet adequately reached the court.

The seventh paragraph of the Supreme Court judgement stated: 'The basic consideration motivating the conclusion of the settlement was the compelling need for urgent relief. The suffering of the victims has been intense and unrelieved. Thousands of persons who pursued their own occupations for a humble and honest living have been rendered destitute by this ghastly disaster. Even after four years of litigation, basic questions of the fundamentals of the law as to liability of the Union Carbide Corporation and the quantum of damages are yet being debated.'

In short, the court justified the settlement by arguing that it was compelled to ensure the survival of a large number of victims, implying that the sovereign nation of India and custodian of the victims' rights had no resources to provide the victims with immediate compensation, and hence stood in urgent need of American money. Shockingly, to secure this amount of 470 million US dollars, it was willing to give up seven times that amount. Obviously, this was suggested by the Union of India, in an attempt to provide a fig leaf for its betrayal.

The court noticed that the attorney general had informed it that attempts to make the settlement were facing public criticism. The learned attorney general was so much in favour of the settlement that he characterized the widespread criticism as 'uninformed and irresponsible'. Obviously, on instructions from the Union of India he pleaded for the settlement to be sustained. Counsel Fali Nariman, appearing for Union Carbide had offered $426 million as the maximum that his client could offer.

Union of India's law officer was satisfied with $500 million. The court appears to have taken the middle course and fixed the sum at $470 million. But neither the court nor the attorney general explained how a claim of $3.3. billion had been reduced to half a billion dollars. Those who constituted the Government of India at the time should be prosecuted for criminal breach of trust. They were the trustees of the peoples' property and their right to sue for it and recover it. They failed to do so as honest trustees. The manner in which the trust was criminally abused is apparent from the false excuse given—that the government urgently wanted relief for the victims, meaning thereby that if the Union Carbide had not parted with this small amount, all surviving, but injured victims would have been allowed to perish or live in agony for the rest of their lives.

Some public spirited lawyers like Shanti Bhushan and others were, however, not reconciled to this falsity. Their efforts led to a further hearing which resulted in another Constitution Bench judgement on 3 October 1991. The government recognised the right of the victims to compel the government to make up the deficit in the event of $470 million being insufficient to fully compensate and rehabilitating the victims. This is the duty of any democratic government.

What happened to the money Carbide paid?

There is enough circumstantial evidence to prove that the real settlement made by Union Carbide was different and most of the money clandestinely went into the pockets of national criminals who were then at the helm of affairs and are not difficult to identify.

The settlement was a fraud on the people of India. The spurious explanation that the money was urgently needed to provide relief to the victims makes it clear that a dishonest deal had been entered into. This was also clear from the manner in which Mr Warren Anderson, an accused on bail, was allowed to abscond despite his bail being conditional on his remaining in India. To add insult to injury, he used a state aircraft and had dinner with the bigwigs of the Congress before his flight from the country!

The *Sunday Guardian*, in its issue of 22 August, 2010 stated, on the basis of credible information, that a settlement took place at the Ritz Hotel in Paris and that it was worked out by Warren Anderson and a personal friend and representative of the then prime minister of India. Under this unofficial settlement, the government wanted to be paid secretly, under the table. When Union Carbide officers raised serious doubts regarding the Supreme Court's acceptance of this unfair and corrupt settlement, they were assured that the Supreme Court was not their worry. The negotiators would manage everything.

And manage, they did. The entire manifestly illegal and corrupt settlement did go through the judicial filter. A somnolent Supreme Court permitted composition of non-compoundable offences and quashed proceedings without falling under the well settled rule of quashing jurisdiction. Surely, if there was an honest and real negotiated settlement between Union Carbide and the Indian government it would require large and complex correspondence evidencing genuine bargaining prior to the settlement being finalized. Such huge claims are not settled by a telephonic talk of which no record exists.

It is worth recalling here an interesting *faux pas* that occurred in connection with the financial settlement of the Bhopal gas tragedy. When N.D. Tewari became external affairs minister, he went to the

United States to plead with potential investors to come to India. The consul general of India was present at the meeting addressed by the minister. The minister innocently referred to the Bhopal gas tragedy and the inadequate compensation received from Union Carbide. A Union Carbide representative present in the audience, stood up and caused consternation by declaring in public that Union Carbide had paid almost everything that India had asked for, but a large part of the amount was paid as out of court settlement, ostensibly for the purposes of the Congress party.

If the Indian government denies the truth of the story that some people in or connected with the government swallowed a big fortune, they must produce the documents which were exchanged during the pre-settlement negotiations and until their final termination. The government must produce them even now. The people of this country are entitled to know how a claim of $3.3 billion came to be settled for a paltry amount of $475 million.

However, neither has the government given any explanation, nor has the story been refuted till today.

Government did not dare to act against Anderson

Given the foreknowledge that the Bhopal plant was in bad shape and a disaster was imminent and given Union Carbide's reluctance to make more investment in the Bhopal plant, the offences of negligence were almost intentional murders and non compoundable. Thus, they could not legally be quashed by settlement. Yet, the attorney general and other law officers of the government got the proceedings quashed in blatant violation of the law. This cannot be explained away as honest error. At close of the case, the government pretended to be shocked by the disclosure of its complicity in letting Anderson go free. It shammed that it would institute extradition proceedings and get back Anderson but, as expected, the government did not dare proceed against Anderson or any other guilty persons in Union Carbide.

Proceedings against Anderson stood terminated with the first settlement. Even if the settlement is partially set aside after years, the dead proceedings will not be revived, at least not for extradition of Anderson. Any effort in that direction is going to be futile. Even in the October 1991 judgement of the Supreme Court, by which the court partially allowed a review of the earlier judgement and allowed criminal prosecutions to go on, the court noticed that the Union of India had not stirred itself to assail the judgement. This clearly confirms the government's commitment to Union Carbide to save it from all criminal penalties against any of its officers. This could not possibly be isolated conduct by some bureaucrats without the knowledge of the higher authorities. Obviously, Anderson had, during his stay in India, built powerful and fruitful relations with local politicians and bureaucrats who were true to their salt when they helped him flee.

The government also announced that it would take no action against Anderson in America and it has quietly put the blame on legal advisors who allegedly told them that the proceedings against Anderson were futile. Of course the advice is right, but it was not obtained by disclosing the true facts to the law officers. No court in America or the Commonwealth would extradite a person after 20 years when the government seeking extradition had originally consented to the proceedings being quashed. The government of course, will not produce the files containing the notings and the final decision to leave Anderson untouched. If any action had been taken as threatened, Anderson and Union Carbide would have publicly declared what they paid, how they paid and to whom they paid. That would have demolished the Congress government overnight and many of its leading figures would have landed in lock-ups and prisons.

While the Group of Ministers winked

The government, in answer to a question regarding the Bhopal settlement in the Rajya Sabha on 13 August 2010, informed the nation that they had, in their wisdom and out of great concern for the Bhopal sufferers, reconstituted the Group of Ministers (GOM) dealing with all aspects of the disaster and of relief and rehabilitation of the unfortunate survivors. The ministers generously recommended that for every dead victim, compensation of ₹10 lakh be given; for every permanently disabled victim ₹5 lakh and for those stricken with cancer ₹2 lakh. The government, out of public monies, a small part possibly contributed by the victims themselves, suggested giving about ₹700 crores, thus washing away their enormous crimes. It would do well to remember that in the dishonest settlement they gave away more than ₹47,000 cr.

Of course, the GOM will never reveal whose pocket that money found its way to. The pittance of a compensation offered adds insult to injury. The GOM is absolutely silent on the issue of who sanctioned the dishonest settlement.

The GOM must make public the correspondence and documents relating to the settlement of February 1989. Everyone who participated and contributed to the settlement abetted the breach of trust and must be delivered to an honest investigating force.

The inadequacy of the settlement is rendered more reprehensible when one considers that the paltry amount said to have been received from Union Carbide was not merely a settlement of civil claims but also of serious and non-compoundable criminal prosecutions. This term must have been insisted upon by Union Carbide itself. Who dealt with this and who accepted this term is the core issue in this case yet the government's reply in Parliament does not address this aspect. We live in hope that someday the attorney general of the time will tell us the truth.

The next issue is whether the settlement was arrived at by oral negotiations or by correspondence. It is impossible that our government could have carried out these negotiations orally. There must be at least some correspondence about how oral negotiations were proceeding and how they were brought to a successful end. Which minister finally put his imprimatur on the settlement and how the instructions to have the settlement recorded in the Supreme Court were passed on to the lawyers for the Indian Government are serious questions that must be answered by our *de jure* and *de facto* rulers.

The people of India are entitled to a disclosure of every part of this nefarious deal and no privilege from disclosure can be claimed, nor is a court likely to sustain any refusal to disclose this to the nation. It would be a denial of the Constitutional right of the people to know how government business is carried out and how the servants of the people are doing their job. So far the GOM has been contemptuous of the Right to Information Act and Article 19 of the Constitution.

Should they respond, the Group of Ministers will probably tell us that the representative of the government who negotiated this out-of-court settlement was an undisclosed agent of the late Narasimha Rao. Even India's illiterates are unlikely to believe that India's then prime minister, Rajiv Gandhi, did not know of this atrocious deal involving the Bhopal victims. Whoever sanctioned this arrangement must have received a fortune by way of illegal gratification, enabling the party to save the immaculate, spotless image of young Rajiv Gandhi and involving the old and wily Narasimha Rao in this murky business. The former is protected by his widow, Sonia Gandhi who controls India's state apparatus, but there is no one to defend the latter.

I would also like to bring to notice that the Group of Ministers appears not to have adverted to some telling facts that are now public knowledge. In fact, the GOM does not seem to have educated itself by reading the proceedings of the state legislature. I wonder if anyone has questioned Arjun Singh about facts that gravely implicate him; although his lies have been exposed by the press.

There had been a fairly serious accident in the plant in 1982, before the disaster of 1984. Union Carbide had in its possession an Internal Security Audit Report which said everything our government needed to win the suit and recover the full claim. Hence, there are a few more questions that must be asked of the GOM:

1. Is it true that the government's legal advisers never asked for the disclosure of this document, which Union Carbide was by law obliged to produce?
2. Did they use the 1982 episode and the US report during the negotiations with the Union Carbide or during arguments in the district court, High Court and Supreme Court?
3. What is the explanation for this collusive conduct by our lawyers?
4. Is the explanation total incompetence or corruption?

I am amazed at some of the recommendations made by the Group of Ministers. Is there one lawyer in India or America who has advised these ministers that the extradition of Warren Anderson is a legal possibility at this stage? Recommendations of a curative petition, a revision application in the High Court and an appeal in the sessions court are legal absurdities.

Deflecting public opinion

Doubtless, there are some individuals and organisations that have genuine sympathy for the victims of the Bhopal tragedy. Without meaning any disrespect to anyone, I think that all, or at least most, of them are on the wrong track. The poor victims are not waiting to see that some of the brigands of Bhopal should be convicted under Section 304 Part 2, instead of Section 304A; nor are they concerned about whether some Indian accused go to jail for two years or for more or not at all. They are not even waiting for justice for themselves.

It is also worthy of note that in the criminal court judgement which found some of the accused guilty of offence under Section 304A of IPC; the name of the chief executive of Union Carbide, Warren Anderson is conspicuously absent. Everybody's mind has been diverted from the real offence and offenders and instead been focused on how Anderson fled the Indian justice system.

This does not suggest that the matter is irrelevant; merely that it is peripheral and just another piece of circumstantial evidence in a wider conspiracy to rob the victims of their just dues. How the Government of India settled with Union Carbide that there would be no criminal prosecution of any kind anywhere against anyone who had anything blameworthy to his debit in the horrendous disaster has already been explained. This term mentioned in the February 1989 settlement was not disturbed in the May 1989 judgement. It is also relevant for the people of India, and the victims of the Bhopal gas tragedy in particular, to know that it is not only the non-executive directors of Union Carbide who are culpable, but also those whose statutory duty it was to detect gross non-compliance with safety regulations. It is their misconduct, coupled with incredible lies and recklessly false excuses that call for stern action for such criminals. The bureaucrats, the politicians and state and union ministers must be identified and subjected to speedy justice. Anderson is beyond our reach, but there is a stronger case against those who are still available and can be prevented from absconding.

As always, public attention has been cleverly steered away from the real issues.

As an intervener I appeared before the hon'ble Bench in January 2012. I was not concerned with who goes to jail for what offence and for how long. I was most anxious, as I said in my written submissions, to see that the court does not make any observation which makes it more difficult for the victims to secure from the state the compensation which is their just due. The $3.3 billion, which has by now become $10 billion, should be recovered from the corrupt government and all others who assisted in the corrupt deal. If the government has any humanity and morals left, it will not drive the victims to expensive and long litigation.

I drew the attention of the hon'ble court to a passage in an earlier judgement in the matter of Charan Lal Sahu vs UOI (1990) 1 SCC 613, which recognises the right of the victims to sue the two governments at the centre and in the state and others involved in the finalisation of the deal. I was most anxious that nothing should be said in the present judgement which will dilute the law laid down in that judgement. I am grateful to the court for refraining from doing that. The victims' only hope is the following passage in that judgement: 'It is common ground and, indeed, the learned Attorney General fairly conceded, that the settlement with the UCC only puts an end to the claims against the UCC and UCIL and does not in any way affect the victims' rights, if any, to proceed against the Union, the state of Madhya Pradesh or the ministers and officers thereof, if so advised.'

It is hoped that the friends and benefactors of the victims will now pursue this course of action completely and vigorously, without being concerned about imprisonment by a few fellow-Indians.

In fact it is my grievance against these well-meaning friends of the victims that they are helping to conceal the real crime of the government and involving the victims in controversies that hardly affect them. The victims and survivors are interested in rehabilitation and re-induction in normal life as useful and comfortable members of civil society. This can only be achieved by compelling the government to compensate the victims for the enormous fiscal injury that the government and its corrupt members and bureaucrats have caused them.

The crimes of the government who was the false friend of the victims of the Bhopal gas tragedy can be unambiguously stated as follows:

1. Helping Warren Anderson abscond from India in breach of the terms of his bail.
2. Settling with the Union Carbide that all prosecutions shall be quashed and claims for damages settled at a miserable figure of about ₹2,400 cr instead of ₹50,000 cr.
3. Callous neglect of the victims' relief and rehabilitation.

4. Concealing the identity of those who settled this matter, the manner in which it was settled, the documentary evidence about the settlement and the persons directly or indirectly responsible for the enormous losses suffered by the victims affected.

Supreme Court exposes government insincerity

I have always believed that the Americans are immune to any further action by Indian courts. I know that the Americans will not pay a single dollar to secure their Indian colleagues from imprisonment and further disgrace.

I had predicted in *The Sunday Guardian* newspaper that the government's curative petition was a big pretence and had no chance of success. It was intended to create false hope amongst the victims and temporarily keep them reconciled to their tragic fate.

The Hon'ble Chief Justice, speaking for all his four colleagues, delivered a unanimous judgement of the court dismissing the curative petition. Anyone having even a little knowledge of law should have been able to predict this result. The attorney general, who argued a hopeless case for the government, did his duty and did it well.

The judgement of the court is an indictment of the government which has been shedding crocodile tears for 14 years during which they have done precious little for the relief of the poor victims. The court has wisely left all other issues untouched. The government should easily be able to read in the judgement a gentle reprimand for its hypocrisy.

Is there any hope?

It is now time for the nation to protest in unison and destroy the pernicious political culture of deceit and corruption, especially when it concerns the welfare of the weakest *aam aadmi*. The ship of state is being steered by the corrupt and inhuman, and the protest must not stop until they are removed from their place at the controls. If we do not end corruption and eliminate injustice, there is bound to be a massive and imminent crash. The corrupt are more lethal to India than blind pilots of a plane, while those who preside over state injustice are as dangerous as any threat from outside.

Meanwhile, the people of Bhopal continue to deal with their dual tragedy—the destruction of life and health by the lethal MIC gas, and the treachery of the government that should have upheld and protected their best interests, both before and after the night of 2 December 1984. Is there any hope?

10
Black Money, State Collusion and National Fraud

'Garibi Hatao' was an old electoral illusion of the Congress, conjured by Indira Gandhi for the 1971 election. Yet, after three and a half decades, three million children still go to bed at night without a morsel of food, girls are sold into prostitution, farmers commit suicide, and half of our villages have no electricity or adequate clean water supply. Our hospitals are more like slaughter houses and half the population does not have the basic human right of a lavatory. More than half of the world's illiterates inhabit this unfortunate land of India. We need to create 10 crore new jobs just to sustain present levels of unemployment, a task beyond the capacity of this government. Sycophantic and well-paid preachers incessantly advise complete submission to, and prevent scrutiny of investigation of our politicians and their crimes.

A bright ray of light and hope, however, brought us some cheer a few years ago. R Vaidyanathan, a distinguished professor of finance at the Central Indian Institute of Management, Bangalore published a mind-boggling eye-opener in the April 2009 issue of the magazine *Eternal India*—that about $1,500 billion have been stolen from India and concealed in foreign banks. If this sum is retrieved, our national debt will disappear, we will have a tax free budget for 30 years and every Indian family will get about ₹2,50,000. Alternatively, we could play our part in the climate change debate by completely switching over to clean nuclear energy completely.

The Swiss Bankers Association Report of 2006 asserted that India tops the list of money launderers, with $1.4 trillion deposited in their banks. This is equivalent to ₹7,000,000 crore in Indian rupees. Apart from Switzerland, there are 70 other tax havens in the world. The government of this poor country should have exerted all its energy to discover the volume of stolen wealth and retrieve it.

Open accusations are being made that the present government is not interested in discovering the identity of the offenders hoarding money in Swiss bank accounts, obviously because some of them are in the government and exercise controlling power. If the government believes in democratic transparency, all documents and correspondence relating to their efforts to acquire control of this stolen wealth should be made public. If they do not, others will do it, and a day, not far off, will come when some top men would be facing the criminal courts of India. The lessons of Bofors should not be so easily forgotten.

Protecting identities—Government sanctum for those who plunder India

In an attempt to bring about accountability and action in the recovery of black money, responsible citizens filed Writ Petition No. 176/2009 before the Supreme Court of India in April 2009. Notice was issued to the Union of India, and an affidavit was filed by one Priya V.K. Singh, a director in the department of revenue, on behalf of the Union of India. Since the matter is still *sub judice*, I do not propose to comment upon the credibility of this affidavit. But it is pertinent to point out that the deponent has admitted that it's only since February 2008 that they started correspondence with the German Government to obtain the names of those Indians with illegal foreign accounts, even though credible information regarding this was available since 2006. The Germans, showing determination and honest pursuit of crime (characteristics that seem to have escaped Indian democracy), have been able to get some 200 names of people with secret bank accounts. They were, of course, after their own citizens; but in the process they got the names of about 50 Indians as well. The deponent admits that on 18 September 2008, the Germans provided this information to our government.

So what happened after that? Nothing. There is no indication that the government has taken any action against these persons. In fact, to heap insult upon injury, the government now claims that they will not reveal to the people or the court the names of the Indian culprits because they have received these names on condition of strict confidentiality.

Nothing could be more astonishing or devious, and there is reason to believe that this assertion by the government is false. Since when have the names of criminals been considered worthy of non-disclosure? The names are being concealed because, if disclosed, in my view, the information alone can bring down the government. There is reason to believe that the names implicate the highest in the land, and a dishonest effort is being made to protect them.

Let me now mention two more documents.

A very popular Swiss magazine, *Schweizer Illustrierte*, on 11 November 1991 did an exposé of 14 politicians from developing countries, who, it said, had stashed their bribes in Swiss banks. The magazine is not a rag. It sells over 200,000 copies and its readership constitutes 15% of Swiss adults. It had mentioned specific amounts held in secret Swiss accounts by different leaders with their photographs alongside. As the late Rajiv Gandhi was shown as one of the 14 most illustrious money launderers, it is a little strange that no one from the Gandhi family thought it fit to sue the Swiss magazine. Some patriotic Indians published these facts in a paid advertisement in the US in 2007. New York-based Indian National Overseas Congress Inc (INOC) filed a lawsuit in the Supreme Court of the state of New York to defend Sonia Gandhi's honour. The New York court dismissed the lawsuit in 2008 saying that the INOC was not the proper party and did not have the *locus standi* to bring a claim of defamation, because none of the statements were made about them. Sonia Gandhi had the option of filing the law suit herself but chose not to do so probably because subjecting herself to cross examination under US law would bring under scrutiny facts she would rather remained undisclosed.

Dr Subramanian Swamy, president of Janata Party and former union commerce minister, made several statements over the last few years containing serious allegations against the highest in the land. In an article published in the *Indian Express* in its issue of 13 July 2009, Dr Swamy alleges that there is a criminal nexus between the present ruling politicians and those controlling the inflow of participatory notes. When a citizen of India, who is also a former union minister, makes such serious allegations, the air needs to be cleared. Subramanian Swamy has also published these facts on his website. Since neither Rajiv Gandhi's widow nor his children have filed a defamation suit against Swamy, we must believe the statements to be true.

Allegations of foreign funds being gifted to Indian politicians have also been made by former KGB agents, who were obviously doing the gifting with the permission of their superiors. This money was not kept in an Indian bank, and certainly not in Russian banks. It went to a Swiss bank or to an account in a place like Liechtenstein, which does not care about the origin or colour of the money its banks get to stash.

When the government is unprepared to do anything about names in its files sent by the German government, it is highly unlikely to pursue independent trails that will create a sense of accountability in our system.

Everyone, including the Election Commission of India is complaining of criminalisation of Indian politics. But are criminals being ostracized by goverment or society? Instead, they seem to control the investigating agencies. We are indeed in the unhappy situation of criminals investigating accusations against themselves, and this sleeping nation seems helpless.

It is a matter of national shame that the custodians of the UPA government under the chairpersonship of Sonia Gandhi and prime ministership of Dr Manmohan Singh have chosen to conceal facts and documents from the people of India, to whom the money really belongs, and continue to protect those who have pillaged our country by refusing to disclose their names.

Huge stash hidden in a small country

Liechtenstein is a small but independent country in which if you absentmindedly jog a little longer than you should, you may end up across the border. Liechtenstein's bank, which has the same name as the country itself, has cash stashed by criminals, money launderers and tax evaders from all over the world. The Germans, by paying an employee of a Liechtenstein bank, managed to get the names of thousands of German tax evaders and money launderers. The Germans have offered friendly governments, including India, the names of these tax evaders. A spokesman for the German finance ministry, Thorstein Albig, indicated in March 2008, that they would give the information free. This official offer from the Germans reached India with further details, primarily because Indians were the largest number in the list of offenders, and their deposits of illicit wealth were over $1,500 billion. It is impossible to believe that the Germans have insisted that these names should be kept secret from the Indian nation. Surely the Germans wanted them to be punished, and not protected by the secrecy that the Government of India uses to protect a gallery of rogues.

The Americans, British, French and Germans have not only acquired information about their money launderers but have recovered heavy penalties from the banks involved. Our government meanwhile has done nothing as it is afraid of confrontation with the banks, and continues a cozy relationship with them lest they spill the beans. So far, and this can be easily proved, the UPA government not only has no intention of recovering the stolen loot, but is actually determined to make the funds irrecoverable.

One of the most damning statements regarding the government's apathy towards corruption and recovery of black money was made by the Swiss ambassador in March 2011. He publicly stated that the Swiss government had not received any requests from India for the release of data regarding money illegally stashed in Swiss banks during his tenure. So much for our government's determination to fight corruption!

Contrast this with the US, which has been proactive on the issue. It is reported that under pressure from federal authorities, Swiss bank UBS is providing information to the US authorities, disclosing hidden offshore accounts of its well-heeled American clients, transferring the assets to other banks or mailing cheques directly to account holders, who would then face the federal prosecutors. Portions of the money have been recovered, and UBS has committed to pay a fine of $780 million to settle the claim that it has defrauded US Internal Revenue Service.

The return of black money to India is, *per se*, a complex and laborious issue, encompassing concerted financial, legal and international processes and meticulous monitoring. The UPA government has done everything possible to complicate the maze further, so that no one except its creator can ever comprehend it. The fact that they themselves may get suffocated in the *chakravyuha* (as is happening today) is not their immediate priority. That is for the future. It is the present that must be defused and saved.

The UPA government has adopted the line of least resistance towards black money, and a determined political will towards concealing facts. Simply put, the government strategy is to wear out its opponents. The government is aware that its opponents cannot match its muscle and capacity to derail investigations and legal processes.

Legal obfuscation and amnesty schemes

The UPA government is trying to use every trick of the trade to provide escape routes for black money looters. Take, for example, the complex strategy being adopted to change the colour of money from black to white, with a unique 'Fair and Lovely' amnesty recipe. The press reported in 2011 that the Central Board of Direct Taxes (CBDT) was "seriously considering" recommending to the government a scheme on the lines of the Voluntary Disclosure of Income Scheme (VDIS) announced in 1996 to bring back black money stashed in tax havens abroad for productive use in India. It is reported that the source of the money will not have to be disclosed, but criminal action will be taken if the money (or the assets) pertain to proceeds of crime. How the two halves of the sentence can be harmonised defies logic.

In a democracy, every citizen is entitled to know the character and integrity of every other citizen, lest one day a crook manipulates a constituency of voters and colleagues in his party and occupies the office of prime minister. Concealing vast amounts of money and depriving a poverty-stricken nation of the revenue it badly needs is a criminal offence by itself. How would we find out whether or not one such criminal is already in office, instead of being in Tihar Jail? So all talk about criminal action to be taken if the money or assets pertain to proceeds of crime is nothing but an eyewash.

The motive behind this proposed amnesty scheme was supposedly patriotic—to encourage foreign remittances that are necessary for accelerating infrastructure growth in India. I learn that the captains of business houses have been proactive and influential in steering this proposal, so that idle funds lying abroad can be used for national development. Touching, indeed, was this belated concern about the idleness of unaccounted funds in distant shores, and their eagerness to restore it to the country after paying a levy. This matches the eagerness displayed when the money was stashed abroad illegally.

The proposed amnesty scheme was essentially unconstitutional, arbitrary and unfair, because it goes against the government undertaking given to the Supreme Court in the case of All India Income-tax Practitioner's Appeal (1998) that it would not float another amnesty scheme. It is arbitrary and unfair, as it chooses only grave money laundering offences for amnesty. On the same lines, can corrupt police or revenue officials or petty economic offenders return the bribe money with penal interest and demand the same amnesty as their more corrupt comrades who operate hundreds of crores as against their thousands and lakhs?

The result of the previous amnesty scheme, the VDIS of 1996, which resulted in a peanuts repatriation of ₹10,000 crores, proved that amnesty schemes do not have any impact on curbing the parallel black money economy in our country. The morality of schemes that offer relief to tax evaders and penalize honest taxpayers by default, is questionable. It amounts to the state government compounding the crime of plundering the national economy, and tainting the credibility of our taxation systems in the eyes of our law abiding taxpaying citizens.

Further, amnesty schemes promise complete confidentiality regarding the amounts secreted abroad, the amounts returned, and the differentials normally shared by all stakeholders. Can one trust a government that avoids sharing such information with the public? If at all an amnesty scheme is announced, its first feature should be complete transparency. Let an independent commission headed by an eminent sitting or retired judge be appointed to clear every case of settlement, with details available in the public domain, so that people can offer information regarding the credibility of the settlement offered.

While the front door amnesty scheme is presumably under process of finalisation, a backdoor amnesty scheme is already in operation through a crafty, subterranean sleight of hand. It flows out of Para 146 of the finance minister's budget speech of 2011: 'It has been represented that the taxation of foreign dividends in the hands of resident taxpayers at full rate is a disincentive for their repatriation to India and they continue to remain invested abroad. For the year 2011-12, I propose a lower rate of 15% tax on dividends received by an Indian company from its foreign subsidiary. I do hope these funds will now flow to India.'

Now you see it, now you don't

The government had to resort to camouflage in the background of the undertaking given to the Supreme Court that it would not float another amnesty scheme in future. Hence, the sleight of hand through amendment to the Income-Tax Act the newly inserted Section 158BBD, with effect from 1 April 2012, to legalise remittances to Indian companies from abroad at a concessional rate of 15%. Its implications are clear: any Indian company with illegal money abroad could set up a subsidiary in one of the innumerable tax havens, transfer its illegal funds to this tax haven, and re-transfer the money by way of dividends of fictitious activities to the Indian holding company.

A part of the money safely stashed in Liechtenstein and other safe havens has been brought into India and its stock markets in the shape of participatory notes. These exotic instruments are issued by anonymous entities not regulated by SEBI.

In other words, the government and its agencies would not know whose money was circulating in the Indian markets; it could belong to international terrorists or spies.

Let's also look at the case of the UN Convention against Corruption which the Indian government signed in the year 2005. The government has been boasting that it has demonstrated its commitment to fight corruption by ratifying this charter on 9 May 2011, seven years after signing it. One does not need to wonder at the sudden desire to ratify the Charter. It is well known that this was done because of pressure by the anti corruption wave led by Anna Hazare and Baba Ramdev, which was gathering overwhelming momentum. However, what is not well known is that the ratification is accompanied by a notification 'that international cooperation for mutual legal assistance under Articles 45 and 46 of the Convention shall be afforded through applicable bilateral agreements, and where the mutual legal assistance sought is not covered by a bilateral agreement with the requesting state, it shall on reciprocal basis, be provided under the provisions of the Convention.'

Let me now expose the fraud of frauds. The following describes the brilliant scheme of a fake ratification without any useful result.

The Supreme Court was to reassemble after its summer holidays on 4 July 2011. The judgment in the foreign money case was expected to be delivered on that day. The nation was apprised of the stinging criticism of the government's apathy in tracing the money and the criminals. The government must have expected that judgment and, therefore, it pretended to ratify the Convention only a few weeks earlier, on 9 May 2011, to deflect attention.

The UPA-friendly *Times of India,* on the next day, reported the prime minister's statement: 'The ratification of the United Nations Convention Against Corruption is a reaffirmation of our government's commitment to fight corruption and to undertake vigorously administrative and legal reforms to enable our law-enforcement agencies to recover the illicit assets stolen by corrupt practices.'

To this statement the newspaper added the following flattering comment: 'The move will help the Manmohan Singh government blunt the Opposition's charge of UPA dilly-dallying on this agreement. The government has been under pressure not just from its political opponents but also from the courts which have cracked the whip in several cases such as the 2G scam.'

Now let us look at two brilliant actions designed to make a mockery of this delayed ratification. The attempted explanation for the delay is itself false and fraudulent. The prime minister said that his explanation for the delay was that ratification had been under active consideration since September 2010, when a Group of Ministers was deputed to oversee the process. This does not explain why India signed the Convention in early December 2005 while the Group of Ministers to ratify the Convention was created five years later, in September 2010. There is no excuse for the delay of five years which had elapsed after India put its signature on the Convention. That the Group of Ministers created in September 2010 was not considering a genuine ratification, but was engaged instead in how to make the ratification totally worthless and incapable of rendering any meaningful assistance is even more atrocious. Yet, through a sleight of hand, the ruling UPA government jettisoned its primary obligation—Constitutional, political and moral—to get our nation's stolen wealth repatriated to India. Foreign banks, of course, have not, till recently recognised any such duty, but it is surprising that the entire Cabinet, Congress leaders, Sonia Gandhi and heir-apparent Rahul Gandhi are silent regarding this matter. Colluding in this conspiracy of silence were the print and electronic media, who are usually so keen to bring scandals and scams to their viewers. Members of Parliament, who are vocal in their demands to treble their allowances and salaries, remained tongue-tied too, a few exceptions apart. All this naturally provokes the question: Are we just indifferent or are we sold out?

Government blocks information on black money

Examination of the events of August 2010 show that on the 30th of that month, a few days before the Group of Ministers was created, the government entered into the Amending Protocol between the Swiss Confederation and the Republic of India for the Avoidance of Double Taxation with respect to taxes on income. This document was thus a continuation of an earlier fraud by which information about the stolen money was not being demanded under the Convention, but under a Treaty for the Avoidance of Double Taxation on Income.

The amended Double Taxation Avoidance Agreement came into force in October 2011 on completion of some internal procedures by the Swiss. The full text of the protocol is not easily available, however, a one-page document describing the salient features of the protocol was circulated to both Houses without any question or discussion in the Upper House and some fleeting clarification in the Lower House. The salient features of this protocol are:

1. Article on Exchange of Information has been amended to bring it in line with international standards.
    a. Under the current DTAA between India and Switzerland, India has not been able to obtain banking information from Switzerland. The protocol now seeks to amend the Article concerning Exchange of Information to enable exchange of such information.
    b. Information which is foreseeable relevant for carrying out the provisions of this agreement or to the administration or enforcement of the domestic laws concerning taxes can be exchanged under the DTAA, whereas earlier information which was relevant only for carrying out the provisions of DTAA could be exchanged.
    c. Information exchanged is to be used for tax purposes only. However, the new Article also provides for use of information for such other purposes which are allowed under the laws of both states and the competent authority of the supplying state authorizes such use.

d. There is a specific provision to ensure that information will be exchanged even if there is no domestic interest.
   e. There is a specific provision for providing banking and ownership information.
   f. The new provision will be applicable only for prospective information and not for past information.
2. At present the income from international shipping is not covered...

This protocol is plainly absurd, its objective malevolent, and it should have been rigorously attacked. It is my opinion that the silence of the government, parliamentarians and media on this issue speaks very loudly.

In the first place, the controversy about concealed funds has nothing to do with double taxation. We are not dealing with cases of honest businessmen who have business spread out in more than one country and who are, therefore, liable to pay tax to more than one state. We are concerned with those who have acquired illicit assets—the product of criminal activities and money laundering. The notorious case of Hassan Ali of Pune is an illustration—there is no ostensible business from which he could have earned more than $8 billion in a few years and whose last deposit of more than $2 billion in the Swiss Bank expressly carries the legend 'arms deals'. It could be theft, breach of trust, bribery, prostitution, drugs and even fraudulent evasion of taxes which is a criminal offence in India.

To speak of DTAA is to throw dust in the eyes of people and create total confusion. The present Protocol only compounds the misdeeds of our ruling party. The protocol, by clause 1 of sub-clause f—which says, 'the new provision will be applicable only for prospective information and not for past information'—expressly blocks out information about past activities. Thus the evil purpose of the protocol becomes manifest. Why would a Government take this step except in obedience to compelling orders from a superior authority?

Sub-Clause 1b—which says, 'Information which is foreseeable relevant for carrying out the provisions of this agreement or to the administration or enforcement of the domestic laws concerning taxes can be exchanged under the DTAA, whereas earlier information which was relevant only for carrying out the provisions of DTAA could be exchanged'—makes no sense. It is what is contemptuously called gobbledygook. Obviously, the government would want the text to be as verbally obtuse and incomprehensible as possible.

By accepting sub-clause 1d—which reads, 'there is a specific provision to ensure that information will be exchanged even if there is no domestic interest'—read with 1f, we have almost completely surrendered our right to know, and recognised complete Swiss obduracy in the matter of yielding any information. The government welcomes it for good reason.

Sub-clause 1c—reads, 'information exchanged is to be used for tax purposes only. However, the new Article also provides for use of information for such other purposes which are allowed under the laws of both states and the competent authority of the supplying state authorizes such use'. This shows that any information furnished to us will not be used to prosecute the offenders either criminally or even for recovery of tax penalties. The exchange of information is not compulsory. It depends upon the whim of the supplying state. The bureaucrats in that state can even block the use of that information for tax purposes if they so decide.

When the Leader of the Opposition tried to raise a discussion in Parliament on the DTAA, he got the following cryptic answer from Minister of Finance Pranab Mukherjee: 'The Swiss do not give any information in respect of their banking transactions. Only once in 1945 they disclosed the assets of the Nazi leaders. Before and after they have not revealed any such information. This will provide us an opportunity to have the relevant bank information for tax purposes.'

Even the last sentence is not accurate. The supply of information even for tax purposes depends on the complete discretion of the supplying state. He admitted that we cannot give that information even to the Enforcement Directorate for a money laundering case. The 2 September 2010 issue of prestigious British magazine, *The Economist*, published on page 29 an article with a large photograph of Prime Minister Manmohan Singh. Below the picture was the caption 'India's Disappointing Government'. The word 'disappointing' is an understatement. The epithet 'criminal' would have been appropriate.

As a criminal lawyer of long standing and with some facility in dealing with circumstantial evidence, my reading of the Protocol to amend the Double Taxation Avoidance Agreement, signed by India and Switzerland in August 2011, leads me *inter alia* to the following conclusions:

1. That the condition of confidentiality has not been imposed by the supplier of the information but is being dishonestly pleaded to block disclosure of the names of the criminals to the prosecuting agencies and the people of India.
2. That the United States government, by putting pressure on the employees of a Swiss bank, managed to get the names of thousands of defaulters and the process of discovery is still on. The officers of the bank are on conditional bail. India could do the same, but it does not wish to act because it will expose those who are running the government.
3. That the British, French and Germans have been able to gain access to plenty of secret accounts, but we are either too stupid, apathetic or reluctant to do the same.
4. The Western press, with high credibility, has published that the late Rajiv Gandhi was a recipient and account holder of more than $2 billion dollars, an amount that has possibly been inherited by his heirs.
5. Total inaction in getting back this money and exposing the identity of the account holders convinces me that VVIPs are involved, and that is the compelling reason why the names are being withheld. Almost conclusive evidence of this is the failure to disclose the correspondence and documents on which the claim of confidentiality is founded.

In other words, through the amended Protocol, India gave up for all times the right to obtain information for any transaction prior to 1 April 2011. Having already made a dead letter of even the DTAT, the government perpetrated a further fraud when it pretended to ratify the UN Convention against Corruption in May 2011. While ratifying the Convention, Government of India made the following reservations:

'The Government of the Republic of India does not consider itself bound by paragraph 2 of Article 66 of the Convention...

'The Government of the Republic of India declares that international cooperation for mutual legal assistance under Articles 45 and 46 of the Convention shall be afforded through applicable bilateral Agreements, and where the mutual legal assistance sought is not covered by a bilateral agreement with the requesting State, it shall on reciprocal basis, be provided under the provisions of the Convention.'

The essence of the Convention is legal assistance in detecting criminals and evidence of their crimes. This reservation nullifies the provision by providing that mutual legal assistance will not be sought under the Convention if any bilateral agreement exists. The only bilateral agreement is the Double Taxation Avoidance Treaty (DTAT) in its new version under the protocol of 2010. For this fraud alone those who perpetuated it should be locked up in Tihar Jail; but may be not Manmohan Singh, because he is an honourable man.

The Black Money case and government's contempt

On 4 July 2011, the Supreme Court passed its judgement in the *Ram Jethmalani and Others vs Union of India and Others case*. It is popularly known as the Black Money case. The operative portions of the order are: a) that the existing High Level Committee constituted by the government to oversee and coordinate investigations into cases of money laundering and stashing black money in tax havens be forthwith appointed as a Special Investigation Team; b) the SIT would be headed by two former eminent judges of the Supreme Court; c) the SIT would be responsible for ongoing and future investigations regarding unaccounted monies in the cases of Hasan Ali, Tapuria, and other known instances, and all other matters with respect to unaccounted monies being stashed in foreign banks that may arise in the course of the investigation; d) that the SIT would be responsible to the court.

The Supreme Court also ordered that the government shall forthwith disclose to the petitioners all the documents and information secured from Germany regarding the Liechtenstein names, with some reasonable conditions, and that the SIT shall expeditiously investigate the same.

The Supreme Court order records the reluctance and disinclination of the government to take stringent action in the Hasan Ali case. The government is seen in an utterly pathetic light, with its culpability slowly but surely being exposed, indulging in (and I quote the words of the court) evasion, confusion and denial, slow investigation and lack of seriousness, inadequate and unsatisfactory replies to the court on critical issues, such as, granting licence to UBS, whose antecedents were suspect.

Perhaps it was the persistent obstructionist attitude of the government, which appeared hell bent on protecting Hasan Ali that prompted the learned judges to record the introductory Part 1 of the order, which goes into details about the neo-liberal paradigm of government, and its implication on Constitutional governance. The behaviour of the government during the hearings appears to have confirmed all the negative-governance manifestations of the neo-liberal paradigm. Anyone who has read the order will note these reaffirmations in its main body.

Several questions arise from government's suspicious, indifferent and self-destructive behaviour, actively inviting upon itself yet again a stinging judgement from the Supreme Court. Did it not learn from the CVC case that the Supreme Court is not a forum where illegalities and omissions of government can be glossed over? Was opposition to the SIT so critical to the government that it was willing to sacrifice the entire credibility of the finance ministry and the law ministry in the Supreme Court? And why did government oppose the SIT so resolutely? It had certainly not opposed it in the Gujarat case, and there are several other precedents of SITs quoted in the order.

Judging from the desperate behaviour of the government, the only inference that can be drawn is that this SIT had to be opposed at any cost, because important people controlling the Congresss empire were involved in the larceny.

The government's obduracy in this matter clearly reflects its growing shamelessness and brazenness about corruption. It continues to show contempt and apathy to the Supreme Court order, and instead of starting the process of implementing the order, it is focusing on how to get it reviewed, recalled or diluted, including contesting the order and seeking its recall.

The silence of the guilty

Any self respecting person, and more so a person in high office, should be anxious to keep his image and reputation impeccable, and if unfairly accused of wrong-doing, should leave no stone unturned to clarify the misconception. Apparently, this is not true of those who hold high political office in India. When I read Dr Subramanian Swamy's article that I mentioned earlier, I sent a notice under Rule 188A of the Rajya Sabha Conduct of Business Rules of my intention to mention this matter of public importance on the floor of the Rajya Sabha. The notice read:

'The worst scam in the history of India has taken place involving stolen funds approximating ₹7.5 million crore.

The allegation is frightening. If it is false it is a vicious libel and if true it means that there exists a criminal conspiracy at the apex of power.

This statement assumes sinister importance in the background of a bureaucrat swearing that Government of India has received the names of many Indians with illegal bank accounts from Germany, but the names cannot be disclosed. Why?

The people of India are entitled to this information and any excuse is a fraud on the people's right to know.

The government should immediately make a full and frank disclosure of the information received so that the suspicion, which now hangs over the heads of possibly innocent people is dispelled, and the real culprits become the target of effective and honest investigation.'

It is unfortunate that this notice of Special Mention was rejected on some unintelligible technical excuses. Both the government and the Congress president should have been anxious to use the opportunity it afforded to explain their case to Parliament and soothe the suspicions of the poor masses.

Recovery of black money should be a top priority of custodians of high public office. Hence, an anxious nation waited for the President of India, Mrs Pratibha Patil, to show leadership in this matter in her address to the joint session of both Houses of Parliament in February 2011. We hoped to hear of some credible steps being taken to bring back the black money. Unfortunately, the speech proved disappointing, with only one reference, that too hidden in the 15th paragraph. In the next paragraph it was mentioned that the government had been able to recover income tax of ₹34,601 crore and detected an additional income of ₹48,784 cr. It is in this paragraph that one finds evidence to convict the entire government of a gigantic fraud on the entire nation and raises the following questions which the government should answer:

1. While demanding information from the countries or the banks in which this money is suspected to be stashed, has the Indian government told them that it is investigating the serious offence of money laundering, and the moneys

stashed away are the proceeds of criminal activities and are not the proceeds of any legitimate trading activity?
2. Is it true that after the German government received the names of these dacoits by bribing an employee of the Liechtenstein bank, the German government announced that they will share this information with every friendly government which is interested, without any cost or condition?
3. Did the German government supply the Indian government with the names of these grand criminals without insisting on any condition of confidentiality?
4. Is the government prepared to make public the document under which it claims the condition of confidentially was imposed by the Germans?
5. Is it not true that against the notorious Hassan Ali and his Calcutta accomplices, the government had only slapped a demand of tax amounting to about ₹71,000 cr, based upon the amount lying to his credit in only one account?
6. Is it not true that Hassan Ali has four accounts, not one, and the Indian government has never revealed to the German government or any other government that these are the products of crime and are not cases of mere tax evasion?
7. Is it not true that the Swiss were prepared to give India full information and that they informed us in early 2007 that they would give India all the information required to investigate money laundering?
8. Is it correct that for nearly four years the Indian government has not responded to this request?
9. Is it true that the government has approached the Bombay court and obtained Letters Rogatory on the footing that Hassan Ali and his accomplices have made this illicit money out of arms sales, particularly in transactions with Adnan Khasogi, a notorious arms dealer?
10. Is it true that the Indian government has been deliberately using the Double Taxation Avoidance treaty when it does not apply?
11. Is it true that the government did not ratify the United Nations Convention against Corruption for nearly five years after signing it? What is the reason?
12. Is it true that even Switzerland has signed and ratified it?

13. Is it true that the delay in ratifying it was because it meant the confiscation of the money involved, whereas the Indian government was busy evolving a scheme of amnesty to enable high-powered Indian dacoits to enjoy their ill-gotten wealth on payment of even less than what the Income Tax Act Law would bring to us?
14. Having admitted that the government received names and is busy collecting taxes from them, why are their names not being revealed to the people of India?
15. Lastly, has the government read the statement presented by Matthias Bachmann of the Permanent Mission of Switzerland to the United Nations, New York, on 20 October 2010, which makes it clear that the Swiss are willing to give the information but the Indian government is not willing to receive it?

Another eloquent bit of evidence is that during the run-up to the parliamentary elections of 2009, Dr Manmohan Singh had promised that the government would take effective steps to retrieve black money funds within a hundred days. The people of India are entitled to ask the prime minister what steps have been taken in this direction till date, and why the government is not revealing the names of persons holding illegal accounts, which they received from the German government. However, the government's obduracy and hubris in concealing these facts persist as patriotic Indians struggle to gain freedom from a reign of corruption and venality.

Manmohan Singh's lost opportunity

The anti-corruption agitations of 2011 provided a wonderful opportunity for the prime minister and his government to start the process of purging the system of corruption and retrieving black money illegally stashed away in foreign banks. The government had two options to get our money back. The first, to behave like a responsible, honourable and strong nation and demonstrate political will to fight corruption using the ample machinery available through international and bilateral legal instruments, the Tax Information Exchange Treaties (TIEAs), Double Taxation Avoidance Agreements (DTAAs) and the Organisation for Economic Co-operation and Development (OECD) automatic exchange route.

The Swiss have volunteered cooperation; and India can follow the example of the US and UK, and get India's stolen money back to the country. Or, the government can take the other option and behave like a banana republic and a failed state, plunder capital from their own country through a UPA-sponsored version of imperialism, perpetuate poverty and backwardness by denying the people of this country their rightful development dividend while repeatedly rewarding and incentivizing the looters with amnesty schemes.

Mr Singh's government has continuously concealed information on black money by fooling the people of our country, shielding the corrupt and guilty who have illegal bank accounts in foreign banks, and by creating obstacles for any progress in the matter instead of taking proactive measures to obtain the information from the foreign governments concerned.

Prime Minister Manmohan Singh could have chosen the former option and gone down in history as a great patriot and leader of our country, a pioneer against corruption. But sadly, he has lost the opportunity and chosen such, that history will remember him as having presided over the greatest frauds practised on this poor and gullible nation.

Codicil

On 21 May 2012, Finance Minister Pranab Mukerjee tabled a White Paper on Black Money in the Lok Sabha. It is an amazing document that seems to conceal rather than reveal information. Mr Mukherjee gives absolutely no information to the public regarding the legal sword of Damocles hanging over his government's head, in the form of the Supreme Court judgement announced in July 2011, in the Public Interest Litigation that I filed in the Supreme Court in 2009.

The Supreme Court judgement in its operative portion ordered that:

a) the existing High Level Committee constituted by the government to oversee and coordinate investigations into cases of money laundering and stashing black money in tax havens be forthwith appointed as a Special Investigation Team;

b) the SIT would be headed by two former eminent judges of the Supreme Court;
c) the SIT would be responsible for ongoing and future investigations regarding unaccounted monies in the cases of Hasan Ali, Kashinath Tapuriah, and other known instances, and all other matters with respect to unaccounted monies being stashed in foreign banks that may arise in the course of the investigation;
e) that the SIT would be responsible to the court. The Supreme Court also ordered the government to forthwith disclose to the petitioners all the documents and information secured from Germany regarding the Liechtenstein names, with some reasonable conditions, and that the SIT shall expeditiously investigate the same.

The UPA government, instead of implementing the Supreme Court order—which would have been the defining indicator of *its bona fides* in retrieving the black money looted from the people of India— instead demanded a recall of the order. This establishes its complete *mala fide*, connivance and conspiracy, and confirms that it has no intention of taking any substantive steps to recover the black money stashed away abroad, or take any serious action to combat this grievous economic crime impoverishing our nation— the 21st century version of UPA imperialism.

The nation should be informed that no investigation has taken place regarding the issues before it since the Supreme Court judgement, but the finance minister chose to conceal these extremely pertinent facts in his Paper.

The White Paper coyly discussed the dimensions of black money stashed away abroad by quoting statistics that are more than a decade old, saying that these are being researched upon by three agencies whose report is expected in September 2012. From this it would appear that the government had no knowledge of the quantum of black money lying abroad. One wonders why the government presented the paper at this stage. Interestingly, the Paper officially disclosed a figure regarding Indian accounts held with Swiss banks, at around only US $213 billion (as against $88 billion projected by the International Monetary Fund, and $213.2 billion by GFI), down 60% between 2006 and 2010. A reasonable conclusion that can be drawn is that black money holders, in anticipation of international and national public pressure (not governmental) transferred their money to other safe havens, the safest, it is said, being India. The last two years have seen several enabling statutes and mechanisms to stealthily repatriate the ill-gotten wealth back to India.

I am also given to understand that there is evidence of a huge disparity between export figures, particularly of metals quoted by the government, and actual exports through data available from independent sources. The same applies to figures regarding FIIs. The game is clear. Use every government tool and instrument available to repatriate the money to India, without disclosure, culpability or punishment. There must be ways, and ways that we can never fathom or document, but the black money holders control legislation, either through being important politicians, or big businesses, who can buy safe passage, necessary loopholes and escape routes through statute or legislation.

The finance minister through his negligence and active cooperation with the criminals allowed the stolen money to be removed from the accounts in which it was held and only a small fraction now remains, which too he is determined to place beyond the reach of the people of India who are its legitimate owners. Although the powerful often consider themselves above and beyond the law, I would remind Mr Mukherjee, who is now our honourable president, that there is a greater law, of nature or of the gods. Several seemingly invincible powerful families have met their retribution tragically because there is no escape from the divine wrath of god or nature that awaits the wicked and corrupt.

Meanwhile, the White Paper on black money provides no fresh insights, information, or analyses on this mammoth national plunder. In fact, it meanders and misdirects, pointing fingers at real estate owners and jewellers as major culprits, without explaining that they are merely the jugglers and not the generators of black money. Even social sector schemes, such as the NREGA are not spared as possible suspects. But most tragically, it provides not even a faint shadow of political will to recover the black money and use it for national development. Truly, it is not even a 'bikini', as Mr Jaswant Singh has called it. It is more like a shroud burying the entire issue. A Black Paper on Black Money.

Section 4
An Ode to Humanity

11
Fanaticism, Religion and the Contemporary World

11 September 2001 has become a tragic date, and will be remembered as a watershed in the cultural history of mankind. Figures vary on the number of lives lost—2900 or 3500? Or more? Regardless, the tragedy was of unprecedented magnitude, executed in an unprecedented manner, with unprecedented loss—human loss, financial loss, the loss of tolerance, the loss of reason...one could go on enumerating the dimensions of the 9/11 attack. In it we saw stark images of the ability of fanatical miscreants to mislead innocents and invoke violence in the name of a greater god and a greater good. Have these incendiary zealots become the new messiahs, the upholders of the faith, as their followers claim?

I think not. They are international criminals who have hijacked religion to misguide youth and preach hatred; deliberately twisting and misinterpreting social and religious tenets to propel their nefarious objectives. And as the World Trade Center attack changed the nature of discourse in the American media, the dominant question became: What is wrong with the Islamic world that it failed to produce democracy, science, education, its own enlightenment, and instead created societies that breed terror?

Political philosopher Stephen Bronner offered one answer: The 11th of September only highlights what should have been obvious; the need remains for an unrelenting assault on religious fanaticism not merely of the Islamic variety, but of the sort promulgated by 'born again' Christians, biblical literalists, protestant sects intent on converting the Jewish infidels, and all those who would bring their revealed certainties—contested by others with other revealed certainties—into the mainstream of public life.' He could have added some Japanese and Indian fanatic groups as well.

As cultures get more and more polarized, the troublesome question that faces the civilised world is : can we confront and conquer terrorism? The answer is, yes we can. We should clearly understand that the terrorism the world faces is not a fight for the legitimate rights of Palestinians or Kashmiris or Chechens, but a conspiracy to impose on the whole world the hegemony of a faith-based toxic system, wherein unspeakable crimes can be committed and human rights suspended in the name of religion. Hence, terrorism cannot be conquered only by the use of superior military power wielded by the state and its agencies. The intellectual challenge today is to understand the scourge of religious fanaticism, identify its roots and analyse and expose them with moral clarity and honesty. Let us be clear that our war is not against Islam. It is against a group of evil, inhuman beings who are deliberately misguiding us. In truth it is this evil group that is pitted against Islam and all that Prophet Mohammed taught and practised.

When Islam was born in the 7th century, the Arabs were given a simple and direct doctrine. There is no god but one god, and Muhammad is His Prophet. The duties of being a Muslim were a simple package: belief in god and His Prophet, prayer, alms giving, fasting during Ramadan, and pilgrimage to Mecca at least once in a lifetime. With this new and intelligible doctrine Muslims went out into the Arab world. They conquered Syria and captured Jerusalem. Khalifa Omar himself journeyed to Jerusalem in order to play a decisive part in the peaceful settlement which followed the Islamic conquest. The Christian inhabitants were promised complete security—for their lives, property and the True Cross. The Prophet of Islam himself never sought warfare outside the Arabian peninsula. Indeed, in his youth he had traded with Christian cities and experienced a significant moment of spiritual enlightenment in the cell of the Nestorian monk known in Christian literatures as Sergius, and in Muslim texts, as Bahira.

The root of fundamentalism

Corrupting a faith is not difficult. For all its liberal foundations, Islam has perhaps been the worst victim of exploitation at the hands of its supposed defenders. The 17th century produced, in a remote village of east Central Arabia, an ideologue who has become the scourge of the 21st century—Mohamed ibn Abdul Wahhab, founder of a sect called Wahhabi. He misunderstood the gentle religion of Prophet Mohammed, a religion which by its name, stands for peace. He misunderstood the causes of Muslim decline and the political and military ascendancy of the Christian west. He concluded that the degeneration of Muslim empires was caused by their abandonment of first principles. Wahhab misconstrued what the Prophet had preached, picked up stray lines and convinced himself that his faith decreed death and annihilation to all *mushrikhun*, i.e. polytheists. By his definition, Christians, Jews, shias and Hindus, among others, are polytheists, who have forfeited their right to live. He wanted to use jihad as a 'cleansing' war against fellow muslims. The Holy Quran clearly forbids aggression: 'fight in the way of god against those who fight against you, but do not commit aggression' (Quran 2:190-92), and proclaims that the ink of the scholar is more valuable than the blood of a martyr. Such edicts of the Quran were completely ignored as they did not support the ideology that Mohamed ibn Abdul Wahhab propounded, and in the spring of 1802, 12,000 Wahhabis invaded the southern part of Ottoman Iraq, entered Karbala, massacred 4,000 Shias and ransacked holy Shia shrines, including the tomb of Hussein, the martyred grandson of the Prophet himself.

Latif, a Saudi judge and descendent of Wahhab, promoted a similar religious movement called Ikhwan. The Saudi royal family saw great merit in both—Wahhabi Islam, which would be useful for uniting the warring tribes of their emerging state, and Ikhwan, which would be useful as their instrument for moulding the new Wahhabi society. They enlisted both. There may have been ups and downs in this relationship, but it continues. King Ibn Saud was the architect of this alliance, his descendant, King Faisal, went a step further and gave Wahhabi religious leaders control over Saudi religious education. The founder of Jamaat e Islam, the India-born Maulana Mawdudi offered a parallel ideology. These influential leaders denounced secularism in education and condemned it as an aggression against Islamic legitimacy. Such thinking spawned the Muslim World League, which soon set up office in Peshawar, Pakistan. This office became a recruiting ground for Osama bin Laden's followers.

Osama bin Laden, a Saudi by birth, was a Wahhabi. Since he was more dangerous than his preceptor, he was not happy with the Saudi regime even though it was committed to Wahhabism. He even accused the Saudi regime of not being sufficiently Wahhabi. His extremist actions and support of terror networks led Riyadh to revoke his Saudi citizenship in 1994. Osama masterminded and sponsored innumerable acts of terror, creating an image of Islam that was far from that given by its founder. The rise of terror, intolerance, chauvinism and dogma in the 21st century can all be attributed to him, but perhaps his worst crime was that he misinterpreted Islam and adopted a counterfeit creed, a direct negation of the teaching of the Holy Prophet. He indoctrinated young men and led them to commit diabolical crimes against humanity, he encouraged the Islamic world to lose its gentle acceptance of other creeds and kinds, and most importantly, Osama bin Laden legitimized and created an identity for terror within Islam.

He deserved his ignominious end. Meanwhile, his fellow fanatics and followers, like Afzal Guru and Ajmal Kasab, have been indoctrinated over a long time to believe that killing innocent persons in cold blood will earn them post-mortem bliss. Their timely hanging by the Indian State, after due process and trial, should send a message to other champions of terror that the chimera of eternal bliss is suspect whereas temporal justice and pillory are a certainty for those who commit crimes in the name of religion.

Anna Hazare and the Shahi Imam

While we saw a spontaneous movement of youth providing a groundswell of support for Anna Hazare in his campaign for the Lok Pal Bill, and pledging participation and sacrifice in the movement to free the country from what the prime minister describes as the 'cancer of corruption,' it is somewhat depressing to note that participation of Muslim youth, though visible, was somewhat inhibited. So much so that Zia Haq was constrained to write in *The Hindustan Times* of 21 August 2011, 'Slowly Muslims are shedding Anna apathy'.

But the Muslim youth cannot be blamed. They had to face a diktat from Syed Ahmed Bukhari, Shahi Imam of Delhi's Jama Masjid, calling upon Muslims to stay away from the Anna movement, because Anna's war cries—'*Vande Mataram*' and '*Bharat Mata*

Ki Jai'—were against Islam! Islam, he argued, does not condone the worship of the nation or land. It does not even condone the worship of the mother who nurtures a child in her womb. How can Muslims then join his stir with a war cry that is against the basic tenets of Islam? 'I have advised them to stay away', he told the *Times of India*. Does the word of the Prophet deserve such narrow interpretation? Contrast this with the actions of Hafiz Ghulam, a humble restaurateur who volunteered to deliver hundreds of food packets to Anna's followers at Ramlila Maidan, and you will see that the humble provide a more compassionate interpretation of Islam than its designated spokesmen, who seem to be more intent upon hijacking the faith. I think the Shahi Imam does not deserve his title or office because he seems to be ignorant of both what Islam teaches and the spiritual meaning and message of *Vande Mataram*. In fact Hafiz Ghulam, the humble restaurateur, understands Islam and its Prophet's message far better than Syed Ahmed Bukhari.

I will now make an attempt to educate the foolish fanatic-cleric and his ilk regarding the nobility of Islam, a religion that he preaches though does not appear to understand, and the duty of every Indian citizen. I admit I am a little pessimistic that he will pay me any heed.

14 and 15 August 1947 were great days in the history of India. The nation had come of age. It had emerged from the era of slavery and was taking the reins of governance in its own hands. On the morning of the 14th, the fifth session of the Constituent Assembly of India commenced its sitting in the Constitution Hall, with Dr Rajendra Prasad in the chair and almost all members present. The first item on the agenda was the singing of the first verse of *Vande Mataram*. Sucheta Kripalani sang it in her melodious voice and all members without exception stood in reverence and listened to it. The president's address followed thereafter. He ended his speech with a message to the minorities—he gave the solemn assurance that they would receive fair and just treatment and that there would be no discrimination in any form against them. Their religion, their culture and their language would remain safe and they would enjoy all the rights and privileges of citizenship. He did not shirk from reminding them, however, that India expected them in their turn to render loyalty to the country in which they live, and to its Constitution.

Jawaharlal Nehru made his famous *Tryst with Destiny* speech and moved a Resolution that when midnight struck, every member would take the following oath : 'At this solemn moment when the people of India, through suffering and sacrifice, have secured freedom, I... a member of the Constituent Assembly of India, do dedicate myself in all humility to the service of India and her people to the end that this ancient land attain her rightful place in the world and make her full and willing contribution to the promotion of world peace and the welfare of mankind.'

The Shahi Imam and his misguided followers will notice in this short passage reference to the dedication to the service of India and her people. *Mataram* is a name for India and her people. Nehru's dedication was commitment to serve her with reverence and gratitude.

Significantly, no Muslim member objected to *Vande Mataram* being sung. Chaudhari Khaliquzzaman seconded Nehru's resolution, which was then duly adopted, and as the clock struck 12, every member made the prescribed pledge.

There was a tussle between Rabindranath Tagore's *Jana Gana Mana* and Bankimchandra Chattopadhyay's *Vande Mataram* for recognition as the National Anthem. The selection was made on the basis of superior musical qualities in favour of the former, but on 24 January 1950, two days before our Republic was born, the president of India made the following announcement: 'The composition consisting of the words and music known as *Jana Gana Mana* is the National Anthem of India, subject to such alterations in the words as the government may authorize as occasion arises; and the song *Vande Mataram*, which has played a historic part in the struggle for India's freedom, shall be honoured equally with *Jana Gana Mana* and shall have equal status with it.' There was resounding applause in the House when this announcement was made. No Muslim member thought his religion was being assailed. For a long time nobody made such a ludicrous suggestion. And the president's announcement has as much sanctity as any section or article of the Constitution.

The proceedings of 14 August 1947 and 24 January 1950 constitute a contract between the nation and its minorities. The Constitution will be respected and *Vande Mataram* will be sung with reverence and joy. This is a requirement for national solidarity and integration. The Shahi Imam's repudiation of *Vande Mataram* is an act of betrayal of a solemn pledge that can amount to sedition and treason.

Another bit of mischievous religious propaganda, albeit by the so called 'secular' Congress party of India, is the deliberate misconstruction of the term 'Hindutva'. Just as *Vande Mataram* is not a BJP slogan or an RSS song, Hindutva too is not a communal slogan of the Hindus or a religious concept. It is a national slogan, the secular essence of our Constitution, which citizens of all faiths and creeds swear allegiance to. It is a concept that separates state and religion, gives fundamental rights for religious and cultural freedom, and treats all citizens equally. In 1995, the Supreme Court of India held that Hindutva was not religion, but an ideological concept, a way of life which comprises a code of conduct to be observed by every individual in every sphere of personal and national activity, and includes respect and equal treatment to all religions. Yet the Congress is teaching the minorities that Hindutva is Hindu communalism, just because the word starts with Hindu.

I appeal to the minorities as well as the Scheduled Castes, Tribes and OBCs that Hindutva is their shield, guarantor of their security and dignity. Let them do nothing to weaken it.

Every nation has the right to expect loyalty from its citizens. India is entitled to expect from every citizen of India, irrespective of his religion, respect for the National Anthem and an equal respect for the song that provided the inspiration for the freedom movement of which every citizen is a beneficiary.

The Holy Quran tells us: 'And the earth we have spread (like a carpet); set thereon mountains firm and immovable; And produced therein all kinds of things in due balance....And We have provided therein means of subsistence, for you and for those for whose sustenance Ye are not responsible.' Therefore, must not one respect the earth which takes your excreta and converts it into the food you eat for nourishment and without which you will be dead? Remember that Anna is fighting to retrieve the stolen wealth of poor Muslims and Hindus alike. The crowds that gather at Ramlila and other places are soldiers battling corrupt rulers. Why should Muslims be deprived of their right to participate in this movement?

If mischievous and anti-national ideologues like the Shahi Imam continue to wallow in their misunderstanding of the teachings of the Holy Quran, then logically he and his cohorts should treat India as Daru-ul-Harab, and consequently, migrate. There are certain obligations which follow from living in the tolerant pluralistic society of Bharat. Participate or quit. India would be perfectly justified in depriving Shahi Imam of his citizenship. What the Imam should be teaching his followers is the oft-quoted poem of Kabir:

> *If Khuda lives only in the masjid/ who looks after the rest of the world?*
> *If Ram is lodged in the temple idol/who takes care of the universe?*
> *Is east the abode of Hari/and west that of Allah?*
> *Search in your heart for both of them,*
> *There live both Karim and Ram.*
> *They are one and the same, Creator of the universe*
> *Men and women are His image and Kabir is son of both Ram and Karim*
> *His preceptors are Guru and Pir alike.*

Who is responsible for alienating Indian Muslims?

Why do Indian Muslims feel alienated today? Almost a hundred years ago, it was the sheer vastness, the heterogeneity and plurality, the pervasive human warmth and the miraculous unities of humanity that inspired India's great poet and philosopher Allama Iqbal to write his ode to India, *Saare Jahan Se Achchha*, that he published first in 1904, and then as *Tarana-e-Hindi* in 1924. Mohammed Iqbal was a Renaissance man of his time, with a brilliant education in India and Europe, deeply influenced by Kant, Hegel, Nietzsche and Bergson. He had a farsighted, insightful vision of society, encompassing tolerance, compassion and a great patriotic love for India. From *Sare Jahan Se Achchha* to his poems of reverence towards Hindu gods, calling Ram the Imam-e-Hind, Iqbal devoted much of his work in praise of India's composite culture. In his 1930 Allahabad address, he told the Muslim delegates of the Muslim League with great emphasis, 'We have a duty towards India where we are destined to live and die.' Later, when he was misunderstood as a supporter of Pakistan, he promptly wrote a letter rejecting this idea and stated that he had not presented the idea of a separate Muslim state; rather he wanted a large Muslim province by amalgamating Punjab, Sindh, North West Frontier Province and Balochistan into a North-Western Province within India. There is debate that as an ardent Indian nationalist, he experienced frustration at the inflexible, rigid stance of the political leadership during the Independence Movement in the 1920s and 1930s.

Despite the existence of such visionary and nationalist Muslims, a strong religious divide developed in the Independence Movement, eventually culminating in the creation of Pakistan. The onus of alienating the Muslims in pre-independence India can only rest on the Indian National Congress—for their repeated inability to deal successfully with the Muslim League, and their greed for power during those years—so much so, that large sections of influential Muslims went to the extent of exchanging their patriotism for the Two Nation call. Gandhi had left no stone unturned to enlist Muslims in the freedom movement. Ignoring Jinnah's sensible advice, he even joined the Khilafat Movement. Unfortunately for the Muslims of India, Turkey itself made short work of the Khilafat. When it collapsed, one of the Mohamed Ali brothers even abused Gandhiji in language so foul as to be unworthy of any respectable gentleman. It is then that the RSS was born in the belief, by no means unreasonable, that Indians will have to fight for freedom without any help from the majority of Muslims.

The unpardonable and irreversible blunders of the Congress are documented in history, their refusal to share power with Muslims for one-third seats in the Central Legislature, or address their political security demands, the failure of the Nehru Report of 1928, under the chairmanship of Motilal Nehru with Jawaharlal Nehru as secretary (note the beginning of dynastic rule), and the ensuing 'parting of ways' with Jinnah and his 14 points as a Muslim leader, and finally succumbing to the Two Nation Theory and creation of Pakistan.

The shock of 1857, where Muslims and Hindus had united, never left the British. Such a unity should never happen again, and must be prevented at all costs, through any means, fair or foul. This became the fundamental principle for governing India, and kept gathering strength in proportion to the strength of the Independence Movement. It started with separate electorates and reservations of the Indian Councils Act 1910, progressing further in the Government of India Acts of 1919 and 1935.

At the time when the Congress should have negotiated these principles in the interest of national unity, in a spirit of give and take with the minorities, it failed to do so, playing right into the hands of the imperial powers. It remained rigid and stubborn, leading to a religious divide and eventually Partition. It is ironic that it is exactly these same principles that it employs today in the name of vote bank politics to stay in power. Reservations, and religious and caste politics are presently the most potent multiple-use political weapons in Indian electoral politics. Today, the unholy alliance in our political system of democracy, caste and religion that has evolved over the last few decades, is deepening social divisions in a most dangerous manner. How this trend can be reversed before it completely destroys our national fabric, is one of the most serious challenges the nation faces.

Pluralism under attack

Our Constitution makers refused to imitate the Muslim world where every new state made Islam the dominant faith and almost every newborn state called itself Islamic. In short, India opted to be secular but until the Emergency of the mid-seventies, the word secular did not exist anywhere in our long Constitution. It conceded to everyone the right not only to profess and practice his religion but to propagate it too. Every religious belief and practice will compete in the free market of truth. The final judge for its validation will be the human brain, the seat of reason and logic. Tolerance and equal opportunity underpinned the Indian ideal of the time.

Today, we have a somewhat different situation, largely because Congress has never explained what Indian secularism means. It has subverted the vision of our Constitution makers to its vote bank politics. This is why neither Sonia Gandhi nor Rahul Gandhi nor a single minister in the UPA Cabinet had the moral courage to reprimand the foolish cleric for objecting to Muslims singing *Vande Mataram*. They were all willing to swim with the sharks, not caring that Indian secularism and Indian tolerance are being eaten alive. Today, Indian secularism is facing a mortal threat fuelled by Congress duplicity and doublespeak.

At the same time, it behoves the BJP to acknowledge that demolition of the Babri Masjid was a crime. Historical wrongs cannot be avenged by unilateral violence of today. The story of Ram is a fascinating product of Hindu religious imagination. We must wait patiently till the ordinary Muslim shares Iqbal's view of Ram as the Imam-e-Hind from an inner conviction. Construction of a temple in Ayodhya can wait until Muslims out of reverence for Ram lovingly join in its construction.

India's pluralist multi-polar society can march forward only by demolishing dividing walls and cultivating a dominant Indian identity. This is best secured by a rational secularism that makes the need of the Republic paramount, with power to trump religious beliefs and practices. Article 25 of our Constitution, correctly understood, requires every Indian life to be guided by reason and logic and inspired by love and charity. In the distribution of economic, political and social rights, the state shall remain neutral and treat all as equals: religion of a citizen shall never justify any hostile discrimination. No one will be permitted deviation for electoral advantage. If one scripture ordains 'Go forth and multiply', an overcrowded nation can legitimately propagate birth control. If a young man refuses to recite *Vande Mataram* as being opposed to his religion, the state may respect his choice but can well deny him admission to a public school.

India's progress does not require more mosques and temples. Controversies like a Ram temple in Ayodhya on the site of the Babri mosque must be totally outlawed. Instead, at the disputed site, a university of secular education and religious harmony should be established. It is a pity that we pride ourselves on being secular without giving such education to our youth.

Anti-Semitism is a slur on religious tolerance

With the dominance of fanaticism, intolerance has become a canker that pervades the relations between Islam and all other religions, and is at its most pathological in relation to Judaism and the State of Israel. It is well known that I have been totally opposed to all those forces that are plotting to wipe Israel off the map of the world. More than 20 years ago I had written, 'No one, however hard-hearted, can deny that the story of the Jews between the Diaspora and the creation of Israel is a tragic epic of world history. Add to this moving account the horrendous story of Hitler's Final Solution, the gas chambers, the killing fields of Nazi Germany and the murder in cold blood of six million of this unfortunate race... Yet the PLO's charter, in its Arabic version, even today proclaims as its prime political objective 'to wipe Israel off the world's map'. This, despite Arafat having generously declared that he will, after all, allow Israel to exist, but on his own terms.'

The policies of successive Congress governments which refused to establish full diplomatic relations with the State of Israel were condemnable. Though India had accorded both *de-facto* and *de-jure* recognition to the State of Israel from the moment of its birth, Israel was prevented from having an embassy in Delhi. It had to be content with a consul located in and confined to Bombay. The decision was sordid when taken and became increasingly ridiculous until the Late Prime Minister P.V. Narasimha Rao bravely put an end to it. Treating Israel as a political outcast was both cruel and immoral. That we should do this when we had full diplomatic relations with China and Pakistan, countries with which we have been at war and who are in occupation of Indian territory, only highlighted our partisan policies. With our contacts and influence in the Muslim world, we should have strived to establish peace in West Asia. Only if India had been neutral and impartial, the peace talks between the two would have been held in New Delhi. Israel is part of the Orient and it wants desperately to be so recognized. During the Chinese attack on us it acted like a friend. It offered all help during the Bangladesh War. But we remained ungrateful and refused to acknowledge Israel's gestures of friendship. It is a matter of great satisfaction that we have now established a relationship of friendship and cooperation even more cordial than with many other states. It is a step that is good for international peace and helpful in the fight against terrorism. The volume of trade between the two countries has been steadily rising.

When I attended The Ottawa Conference on Combating Anti-Semitism in Canada in 2010. I was not the only Indian. The venerable Imam Ilyasi, who had for many years shown tremendous wisdom and objectivity in dealing with the Israel-Palestine dispute and made public his abhorrence for the rising tide of hatred against Israel and Jews all over the world, was also present and made a significant contribution to the understanding of the minds and attitudes of the Muslims of India. It was sad to hear at the Ottawa meet that in many civilised countries anti-semitism is rearing its ugly head, particularly in university campuses among the young generation. While deploring the earlier attitude of the Government of India towards Israel I could assure the vast gathering that India is a country which has never in its long history provided any hospitality to the spirit or practice of anti-semitism. Our Jewish citizens rose to the highest positions in the fields of education, art, movies and the armed forces.

Enlightenment amidst the discourse of hatred

Despite a record of vibrant tolerance and acceptance of Muslims, including a substantial degree of cultural integration, Indian Hindus too have not escaped the special attention of the motley crowd of fanatics who are the known face of Islam today. In the middle of 2002, Saudi Arabia's national television TVI broadcast a sermon from the Imam of the Grand Mosque in Mecca, spewing poison against Hindus, Christians, Jews and secularists of all kinds. He said 'The idol-worshipping hindus indulge in their open hatred against our brothers in Muslim Kashmir threatening an imminent danger and a fierce war in the whole Indian subcontinent'. All this substantiates the point that the war on terror to which India has become a party cannot be won until the ideological motivation for Osama's teaching is extinguished and the centres of evil indoctrination closed down by persuasion, diplomacy and low-scale military activity. Democracies must create a powerful anti-terrorist alliance and armed front, if possible with the sanction and cooperation of the UN Security Council. Once it does dawn on terrorists that there is no chance of success, they will desert the sinking ship. They can see that Americans are thriving after September 2001 and so are Indians after November 2008. But till this dawns on them, no one is spared the fanatics' venom.

This is not to say that Islam has not had its visionary leaders who have sought peace and reconciliation, overcoming national egos in their attempts to nurture world peace. Egypt in recent times produced a statesman of the highest caliber, President Anwar Sadat, the predecessor in office of President Hosni Mubarak. President Sadat overpowered the hatred which Muslims generally feel against jews and their tiny homeland, Israel, although Egypt was the worst sufferer in the six-day war with Israel. The territory it lost was huge and the humiliation that it suffered was galling. The Americans persuaded President Sadat to settle for an honourable peace. Israel responded generously. All territory conquered with all

Israeli investments in development infrastructure were returned to Egypt and a new era of friendship and co-operation began between the two warring states. Sadat defied the advice of other Arab states involved in the conflagration. That was a measure of his greatness. After all, he had imbibed the essence of the pristine Islam of the Prophet as also the value system of Egypt's ancient pre-Islamic civilisation.

President Hosni Mubarak inherited this great intellectual and spiritual legacy. It must, however, be said that Mubarak did not provide Egypt with a genuine democracy and ruled almost as an uncrowned but autocratic emperor until he was overthrown. Like India, Egypt too has not been able to cure itself of the cancer of corruption and finally the disenchantment was seen in the Arab Spring of 2011, that overthrew President Mubarak. I cannot say however, that the future looks bright for Egypt today.

Being one who firmly believes that in the present day, civilised existence is not possible without a secular democracy protecting human rights listed on the UN Declaration of 1948 and its two covenants of 1966, protected by an honest and independent judiciary, I would welcome a change which ensures the installation of such a political dispensation. However, I am not convinced that the revolution the world is witnessing is heading in that direction. Many revolutions have taken place in the world's history, which have not improved the social and political existence of the citizens. The protestors are not always lovers of democracy and fighters for human rights. I suspect that the revolution that is taking place in Egypt has not much to do with establishing a democratic regime.

The Muslim Brotherhood of Egypt is not different in its ideology and teaching from the Wahhabis. In 1928, the Egyptian schoolteacher Hasan-Al-Bana founded a similar movement called the Muslim Brotherhood. Both Wahhabism and the Muslim Brotherhood had tremendous ideological affinity. It will be a tragedy if Mubarak's displacement should be the harbinger not of the rise of a secular democratic state, but a mere replacement of a secular despot with an intolerant, bigoted zealot. Such an occurrence would be a tragedy for the world and for those Muslims who retain their faith in the original and pure religion of Islam, in tolerance and in the right and need for all mankind to peacefully coexist. As Ellen Glasgow says, 'All change is not growth, as all movement is not forward.'

Consecrate tolerance

Combating intolerance and protecting the freedom of speech is a growing concern in today's world. In a civilised democracy, bad speech cannot be allowed to be conquered by the sword or the bomb. It must be neutralised by better speech. The great Ameer Ali in his famous book *The Spirit of Islam* wrote that the 'Prophet has consecrated reason as the highest and noblest function of the human intellect. Our schoolmen and their servile followers have made its exercise a sin and a crime.' Muslims produced brilliant kings like Harun-al-Rashid, the greatest of medieval philosophers, like Avicenna, the greatest of medieval physicians like al-Razi. It is they who brought about the enlightenment in Europe and literally brought civilization to it. None of this is possible without the application of reason, without questioning established ways of thinking or without forbearance.

Some years ago, His Holiness the Pope of Rome made some unfortunate remarks about Islam and Muslims. He provoked serious anger and even threats of violence. But it was fortunate that His Holiness tendered a public apology. The Muslim world, more or less, accepted it gracefully but there were some who attacked churches in retaliation. Amongst them was the Al Qaeda. In an internet statement, they declared jihad until the 'West is defeated'. Hardliners, as ever, commandeering the moderate voice. For liberalism to survive this growing swell, it needs must be enshrined in the statutes of every nation and actively supported by every rational human being.

Society is frequently confronted with profanity of thought or word. How each society manages such profanity defines whether it is liberal or narrow minded. Donald Findlay QC, one of the best criminal lawyers of Scotland, was famous for his irreverent sense of humour, which made him a favourite after-dinner speaker. He never pretended to possess any great reverence for religious leaders, the Pope included. He was once the guest speaker before a Catholic dominated group. During his speech he lit his pipe, blew some smoke, coughed and spluttered. The media later reported him as saying, 'It is very smoky in here tonight. Has another (expletive deleted) Pope died?' He breached the tolerance levels of the headmaster of the local Catholic school, a certain Lynch, when he continued with a joke about nuns. Lynch promptly reported

Findlay to the disciplinary tribunal of the Bar. Findlay pleaded that he had been misrepresented: the point of his joke was not to laugh at the death of the Pope, but at the practice of blowing smoke out of a Vatican chimney to signal the election of a new Pontiff. For good measure he added that he was an atheist and that he had made many less respectful jokes about many leaders of other religious denominations. But Findlay was fined and admonished, in my opinion, wrongly.

Doubtless he made jokes which some did not like. Whether they were funny, depended on the listener's sense of humour; whether they were offensive, depended on the auditor's sensitivity. A Catholic witness told the tribunal that it had no right to assume that all Catholics were as humourless as complainant Lynch. The lawyer had said nothing to condone or encourage sectarian violence. There was no present and imminent danger of breach of peace. In the words of the Indian Supreme Court 'it was by no means a lighted match and gunpowder keg situation'. The witness convincingly argued that he did not question the complainant's right to think of Findlay as an 'uncouth moron', but if every lawyer was expected to conform to the Lynch standard there would be few lawyers left to defend clients. If it became an offence to lack charm, display bad table manners and possess dirty fingernails, he continued, most barristers' chambers would have a large number of vacancies.

There are vital reasons for tolerance of speech in every civilised and democratic nation, even if a particular speech is distasteful to some. India faces a serious threat from religious fanatics who refuse to tolerate critical comments about their faith.

If we are proud of being a secular society and a democratic republic, we must understand that religious beliefs are not entitled to protection from any and every criticism or ridicule. In India, Article 25 of our Constitution makes the right of a citizen to profess, practise and propagate his religion subject to public order, morality and public health. Implicit in this Article are two corollaries:

First, every religious belief, dogma and practice must compete in the free market of reason.

Second, any one or two of them or even all three are liable to yield to and be trumped by national interest in maintaining order, morality and health.

Unfortunately, politicians hungry for votes from the irrational and ignorant have let the entire Article to be trumped by fleeting electoral gains. It is these politicians who deserve to be disqualified and outlawed from politics.

Taslima Nasreen, persecuted in her own country for the legitimate exercise of the right of free speech, sought refuge in India where Freedom of Speech and Expression are enshrined in the Constitution of the land. Yet, we readily disgraced our Constitution by becoming agents of her persecutors back home. Whether Taslima Nasreen's exhortation to women to shun the burqa was misreported or not is immaterial. What is relevant is that the Mangalore edition of the daily newspaper that carried the news item was vandalised by some hooligans and Taslima's resident permit was for some time jeopardized. Fortunately the fanatic babble was not given credence.

Every woman in India has the right to decide what she wears in and out of home. Restrictions on this right will be only those arising from express enacted law. A woman cannot be compelled by social pressure to be a walking tent. If some men are titillated by the sight of a patch of female body, it is the men who should wear the burqa. The practice of a tent-like burqa has no sanction from the Quran Sharif and it is directly opposed to what the great Prophet of Islam taught.

The teachers of Islam must let the community know that incontrovertible historical evidence portrays women of Medina (where the Prophet established the first Muslim state) raising their heads from slavery and violence to claim their right to join as equal participants in the making of Muslim history when the Prophet was the political leader. Women fled from Mecca (then ruled by non-Muslim Arabs) by thousands to enter Medina because Islam promised equality and dignity for all men and women alike. Every woman who came to Medina could gain access to full citizenship, the status of Sahabi, companion of the Prophet. Women freely entered into councils of Muslim ummah to speak freely to the Prophet, to dispute with the men, fight for their happiness and to be involved in the management of military and political affairs. The Prophet's widow Ayesha, years after his death, took to the battlefield at the head of a male army which challenged the legitimacy of Khalifa Ali. Neither during the life of the Prophet nor after his death did she wear a veil or a hijab (as we know them today). Thus Muslim clerics, terrorists and their followers who would condemn women to perpetual inferiority and compel them to conceal their countenance behind a veil or hijab are a disgrace to the Prophet and insult to his beloved wife. Ayesha cannot be written out of the history of Islam. The life of Ayesha is a lesson for Muslim women to stand up and fight.

Young Muslims must appreciate the majesty of Article 14 of the Indian Constitution. No hostile discrimination is permitted against women just because they are women. I am one of those who believe that women made civilisation possible. Woman domesticated man by constructing a home and tilling a field. She can rightly claim that man is woman's last domesticated animal!

While the civilised world is migrating from darkness to light, from the regime of blind faith to the rule of shining reason, the hooligans of Mangalore and their like elsewhere want humanity to shift into reverse gear. M.F. Hussain, one of our greatest artists, and Taslima Nasreen's right to freedom of expression must be protected. It is tragic that private pornographers pretending to be public purists have persecuted them, demanding apologies for their free and refreshing artistic independence. No citizen has the right to ask another citizen to apologize. That is the function of law and judiciary. Prof. Herbert Hart, the foremost legal philosopher of the 20th century, taught us that law must strive to prevent harm to society and never just enforce conventional morality. So although Lenny Bruce, a famous American comedian of the 1960s, convicted in 1964 for using obscene language during a nightclub performance, died a convict despite his attorney's passionate pleas for Voltaire's words: 'I may not agree with what you say, but I will defend to the end your right to say it,' to be heard, the Supreme Court of the United States has now ruled, definitively, that even obscene speech enjoys Constitutional protection unless it is utterly without redeeming social importance and is only an appeal to prurient interest.

12
A Refreshing Change—Kate and William

Progress demands change. Religious and social norms have to adapt to changing times. I unabashedly savoured the glamour and romance of the wedding of William of Windsor and Kate Middleton; something that could never have happened fifty years ago. I admit I am an octogenarian with a young heart. Romantic weddings of young lovers move me greatly, and what better than a grand royal wedding of a future king of England and his beautiful, demure bride to stir in me my best sensitivities? Everyone loves a wedding, but a royal English wedding of the son of the Prince of Wales, second in line in succession to the throne, with all its pomp and pageantry, spectacle and splendour, historical tradition and the quaint affinity that my generation holds with the former imperial power of India, compels a special comment.

Plenty has been written about it in every newspaper in the world—the beauty of the bride, the style of the wedding dress, was it an imitation of Grace Kelly's (a great beauty of my time), the nature and quality of hats (absolutely compulsory for every royal wedding), attire of the celebrity guests, comparisons of all kinds with Princess Diana and Duchess Camilla, and of course serious discourses regarding the great kiss on the Buckingham Palace balcony, and comparisons between Charles' somewhat reluctant kiss and the eager one of his son. Even the derriere of the bride's sister (who was viewed mostly from behind as she was the maid of honour holding the bridal train) was held in high estimation.

My years made me nostalgic. I thought of several other royal weddings that should have happened but never did. I could see the faces of Wallis Simpson and Edward VIII, two people completely in love, but she was twice divorced and he was king. The times were different and less tolerant (1936) and the entire constitutional machinery decided that this was just not acceptable. Edward VIII abdicated the throne to be with the woman he loved, adding a sombre and bitter chapter to the monarchy.

Another wedding missed was that of the beautiful and vivacious Princess Margaret with Group Captain Peter Townsend, both completely in love, but he a divorcee. The romance was terminated by constitutional guardians. Princess Margaret later married a photographer, Antony Armstrong-Jones, had children, divorced, drifted and died prematurely. Peter Townsend rebuilt his life, remarried, remained non-controversial and died in 1995. Let us hope they are happily united in the other world.

Since then, divorce has plagued the monarchy. All of Queen Elizabeth's children divorced, except her youngest son Edward. The Prince of Wales, Prince Charles is a divorcee, as also his wife, Camilla Parker Bowles, now known as Duchess of Cornwall. We hope there will be another significant constitutional moment when Prince Charles becomes King and Camilla the Queen, despite their respective divorces.

So along with the pageantry, along with the pomp and splendor is a serious comment to be made on the wedding of William and his Kate, a comment that has significance for all those who aspire for tolerance, liberalism and positive change as the wedding marked a constitutional moment in the unwritten Constitution of England. For the first time, a direct successor to the throne married a commoner, without murmur or protest from any constitutional guardians of the palace, clergy or government. This was indeed a significant constitutional moment, a moment for the world to take note of, when the British ruling class put their frosty traditions, prejudice and irrationality behind them, and embraced modernity and egalitarianism in true democratic spirit.

Let all the fanatics and obscurantists take notice and emulate.

Postscript

A book like this is always out of date. Between the last stroke of the author and editor's pen and the time it reaches the reader's hand, the events become dated. So I will not even attempt to update them. Instead, I will share with you some impressions, of the chaotic times that we are passing through, as I look back at what I have written.

If I shift myself away from the noise, anarchy, contradictions and lost opportunities of India's society and politics a little, and dispassionately observe all that is around me, I see not merely crossroads, but an interlinked, distorted web of them, with directionless forces moving in all directions, without an inkling of how to propel the nation forward along the right path. There are roundabouts along which we have been aimlessly circling, though what we should really be doing, very consciously and carefully, is breaking the circle at the right place and advancing forward. I see flyovers where the privileged, fortunate, industrious and crooked have been able to ascend to riches or power or fame, often at the cost of the nation and the multitudes trampled to the ground. And then there are tunnels, where the poor, hungry, and ignorant remain trapped, even after sixty-five years of independence, without ever seeing the light at the end.

Indeed, there are not two, but three Indias. The first is of the growing rich and famous, whose wealth and ostentation matches, if not exceeds, that of the wealthiest on the planet. They make their presence felt in lists of the richest people in the world. Like their counterparts elsewhere, they control governments and their institutions through their wealth. They have enormous leveraging power not only to protect, but to expand their financial and economic clout, often at the cost of national interest and common good.

The second India consists of the new middle class, which has been growing unobtrusively over the last few decades. Its might hit our social and economic fabric during the IT boom about fifteen years ago, when it made India a world leader in the IT sector. This India is well educated, works hard, earns well, boasts of gender equality, and has contributed handsomely to the economic growth of our country. As reported in the *Economist,* it is this India that has the talent to lead in the mobile internet, as it did in outsourcing, provided the government gets its telecom sector in order. To it belong the malls and bars and hotels, the brand names and designer clothes. As their numbers expand, the middle class is changing the landscape of urban and peri-urban India—its architecture, traffic, economy and demography. It also effects change indirectly in the social dynamics of rural India, attracting a large rural-to-urban migration to serve its domestic and official demands. The malls, department stores, hotels, restaurants, spas and gyms that cater to the middle class also require manpower from the stage of construction to maintenance. Migration from all parts of rural and north-east India is more than evident, which is a good thing in terms of livelihoods. I am told that the size of middle class India has now reached 160 million individuals, nearing 20% of the population in 2015, and increasing to 37.2 per cent by 2025-26.

Even today the middle class holds a vital key to any national election, directly affecting electoral outcomes in at least 40% of constituencies, now urban or semi-urban. But, the middle class must first find a political voice and a political party through which it can articulate itself, just as its counterparts in 18th and 19th century England had, through the Radical and Liberal Parties.

It is indeed paradoxical that the Indian State appears to be failing in direct proportion to the burgeoning of the middle class and the economic growth it claims to have achieved. The Indian middle class wants things which every citizen of a modern country wants, but which our failed state is incapable of delivering anymore, such as, proper governance, civic amenities, law and order, public safety, freedom from corruption and harassment by politicians, bureaucrats, and touts. Cash and booze, white goods and caste reservations—the only electoral language that present day politicians know—mean nothing to them. The middle class has become the milch cow for the State's corruption and the victim of its failure. Hence its strong empathy and sustained presence during the anti-corruption protests of Anna Hazare and his team, that took the corruption opiated government by complete surprise. It had, for the first time, found a platform from where it could speak.

The middle class has never been pampered in India. It lacked the numbers, couldn't influence electoral outcomes, and therefore, had no clout. This fast expanding new political force now desperately requires its own political outfit to protect its interest. And this is precisely what the existing political parties are trying to thwart, as they know the risk that lies in it for them. But, it is inevitable that their political formation will come. As Victor Hugo has said, 'all the forces in the world are not so powerful as an idea whose time has come.'

The third India is the India of the poor, the ignorant and the hungry. One sees families of them in every Indian city, living on the streets, under flyovers and bridges, their women and children begging at traffic junctions. In rural areas, they are at the lowest rung, doing menial jobs, emaciated and ill, indebted and without assets. This third India never gets reached, never seems to change, and is always left behind. It persists, and perpetuates itself, whether the economic growth rate is 4% or 8%. These are the feeders and fodder of India's democracy, generally viewed as a bunch of ballot papers—the unlimited and eternal sea of votes that every political outfit lusts after. Leaders of ruling political parties realized that keeping them this way is the surest way of maintaining captive vote banks, and thus remaining continuously in power.

Unfortunately, even the Communists of Bengal fell prey to this inhuman strategy for power. They ruled Bengal for more than three decades. Yet, the economic development and human development indicators of West Bengal are among the worst in the country. Compare this with how the Russian Communists transformed their country into a military and scientific super power within the same time. Can anyone answer why constituencies like Amethi and Rae Bareilly, pocket boroughs of the Nehru-Gandhis, nursed by a string of prime ministers, have some of the lowest human development and economic indicators in the country? The answer is simple—obviously, because it is intentional.

These three Indias coexist in our rogue democracy that today is strung together in an unholy alliance with corruption, caste and crime. Take the number of politicians with criminal records in our parliament and legislatures. Their democratic defenders unabashedly state that having FIRs or charge sheets is not conclusive evidence of guilt, that can only be pronounced by a court of law after several levels of appeals and stay orders, something that can take decades.

This rogue alliance of corruption, caste and crime has become the motto of the state and further passes on to governance. The brunt of it is borne by the middle classes and the *aam aadmi* of the third India, despite the slogans of equity, inclusiveness and development our rulers boast about *ad nauseam*. No prizes for guessing who should be held responsible before the court of the people. Except for a short period of about 13 years, the Congress Party has ruled the country since Independence.

This depressing state of our society and nation, for which the blame rests squarely on those who have controlled the state for the last three generations, is what we bequeath to the youth of our country. Not that we didn't have men of mettle and integrity whose actions were dictated by national interest, like Sardar Patel, Lal Bahadur Shastri, Atal Behari Vajpayee. But the collective might of those who were surreptitiously ushering in the subversive process into our synthetic democracy always appeared to prevail.

Politics today is considered a lumpen profession and the word politician is pejorative, associated only with brokering power or pelf. This process of lumpenizing politics was a conscious design of Indira Gandhi to keep herself in power after the great Congress split of 1969. Integrity, efficiency, rule of law and democratic governance were thrown to the winds, and replaced by loyalty, money, corruption, and dynasty. As this paradigm of governance steadily evolved, innovation in subversion of democracy became a profitable occupation amongst politicians who were now becoming more aggressively involved in the financial and administrative aspects of government. New political-bureaucratic models were set up, not to serve the people more efficiently or in national interest, but for facilitating corruption, so much so, that the permanent Civil Service of the Westminster model was converted into a permanent spoils system. The politics, politicians and administrators of today are a highly evolved product of this governance model. And the engine that fires it from start to finish is money.

As politicians became cannier, and administrators more spineless or purchasable, democratic norms and parliamentary practises in India have gradually become tightly knit with money. Democratic tradition in India today quite frankly accepts that an aspiring legislator must pay the political party for getting an election ticket, (the assumption being that if elected, the 'representative of the people' gains access to great political licence and power for rent seeking and siphoning off money from the treasury). Our democratic tradition also accepts that votes can be purchased from the voters through cash, booze, promises and white goods. It is also now a firmly established democratic norm, that once elected, the honourable representative of the people acquires several entitlements, the first being that he becomes exempt from the laws of the land, be they traffic rules, land laws or criminal statutes. This is guaranteed through yet another privilege he acquires, namely, that he can demand of the government that his henchmen and cronies be appointed as key police and land revenue officials in his area. And through his captive *babudom*, he and his minions control the local administration, dole out rewards and punishments, meddle with title deeds, grant licences and permissions, normally of a dubious nature, and to cut a long story short, become rich in the shortest possible time.

Though as custodians of their constituencies, the first responsibility of the representatives of the people is to act for public good, for honest and equitable implementation of all laws and development programmes, and as champions against corruption, it is clear that under no circumstances can our subverted democracy permit this, as the conflict of interest involved is too great. Understandably, therefore, 'representatives of the people' do not place much priority on representing their constituents' sentiments for freedom from corruption and harassment, or improving service delivery.

Our democracy is legitimizing itself only through the chicanery of arithmetic, cobbled up through every undemocratic means. As long as the Congress Party had its majority governments, 'floor management' was not a major parliamentary expertise. Today, in the era of coalitions, it has become a specialization supporting a high degree of innovation of the most unethical kind. The UPA's 'floor management' skills, especially after the government turned into a minority government, have added a new chapter to the subversion of democracy. Just as it has become legitimate in our democracy for the representative of the people to buy voters, it appears to have become equally legitimate for governments to buy 'representatives of the people' to get special legislations through. The infamous cash-for-votes scam, and Foreign Direct Investment in Retail have given us a fairly convincing sense of this. Innovative 'floor management' requires multiple strategies—inducements and rewards, political and budgetary quid pro quos, walkouts by amenable opposition parties at the right time to defeat legislations like the Lokpal Bill, and the CBI stick, of course.

In this political theatre, can any honest citizen expect the rule of law, justice, or law and order to prevail? Everything is on sale, from legitimate personal dues to a citizen from any level of government, receiving services paid for by the taxpayer of India, obtaining basic documents and certifications from the bureaucracy, such as, tax-paid receipts, property documents and certificates of all kinds. The social norm that emerges from this political theatre is 'might is right' and 'survival of the richest'.

The helpless citizens feel completely trapped. They are aware that their 'representative', is in cahoots with the law breakers of the area, if not a law breaker himself, be they the land mafia or the sand mafia, or the several other mafias that have mushroomed in our country, duly protected by the representative's specially appointed cop and *patwari*. A complete lack of fear of the law, wilful disobedience to it, and a general defiance of legitimate authority by law makers, law enforcers, and the rich and privileged is the form of democracy that our youth see today.

This is nothing but governance failure of a failed state. The standard alibi that the UPA government gives to any mis-governance reality is that they have adequate laws in place—a complete *non sequitur*, as it is these very laws that are being defied and violated by law makers, law breakers and law enforcers. Yes, laws abound in our country, on every subject under the sun, as making a law is the softest option, especially if it is reactionary. The comprehensive law against rape was idling in various wings of government for more than a year, and had to be rushed through only because of a horrific tragedy.

The failed state is not merely afflicted by policy paralysis, but even more serious, from an implementation paralysis. It is implementation of law that requires political will, bureaucratic commitment and accountability, and the administrative stamina that can only be triggered by honest leadership committed to the national interest. And in the absence of all of this in the ruling government, there is always someone else they can blame—the state government, the bureaucracy, or a simple 'systems failure', often used and the most obfuscatory.

India today belongs to the youth who form around 30% of our population. Our generation has left a very onerous burden on them, for which they have every right to condemn us. We have failed them on several counts and left a shameful legacy—of a wrecked democracy functioning on money, of a depraved and rapacious ruling class, of a society getting deeply divided on caste and religious lines thanks to vote bank politics, of an economy that is focused more on helping the rich than the needy, of a complete distortion and breakdown of governance.

The legacy that the unscrupulous and corrupt rulers of today leave for our youth and middle class, is the responsibility of once again purifying democracy and de-lumpenizing politics. Politics must again be made respectable if it has to attract the best talent of the country, and this is only possible if money and touts that oil the wheels of our democracy are banished from start to finish. Committed and patriotic men and women who place national interest at the forefront must enter politics to repair our wrecked democracy and reconstruct the nation.

It is shameful and tragic that young India inherits a country enveloped in corruption that has become India's cancer and is blighting the lives of its people. This corruption has grown into something so severe and chronic, so deeply rooted and intertwined that no single quick fix can purge it. Like a strong mesh, it has spread laterally and vertically, and developed several interlocks that protect and support it from all sides. This kind of institutionalized, internalized corruption cannot be eradicated by slogans and laws. As long as the implementer of the law is corrupt and owes his position to a politician who is also corrupt, corruption will persist and the rule of law will be flouted. To eradicate corruption, every link in the mesh needs to be broken in a multi-pronged process by continuous involvement and pressure from the people. And the process must start from the very top.

Political parties must ban charging money for giving election tickets. Bureaucratic and police regulatory appointments from lowest to highest levels should not be made through political patronage, cash or cronyism, but on merit, integrity and fairness. The CBI should be freed from political control. Exemplary punishment should be awarded to the corrupt. The Judiciary should finalize all cases of corruption or misuse of power within the shortest time possible, even if there are stays and appeals. Even these few measures will send shockwaves through the corruption nexus and start bringing some relief into the life of the common man. But the determination and enduring commitment to attack corruption must come in the clearest terms through political will of the highest political and governance levels. It is possible, and I am confident that Narendra Modi has the commitment, patriotism, experience and knowledge to do it.

The UPA government's grand conspiracy over the last decade to politically assassinate Narendra Modi failed miserably. Their slander, fabrications and Goebellesian lies were completely exposed and demolished before the Special Investigation Team, and in the report it submitted to the Supreme Court. The UPA seems rather bankrupt as to how to attack him next, and have been reduced to using the blanket slander against him that they reserve for the BJP in general, that of 'non-secularism' or 'communalism.'

The past decade of UPA rule has witnessed an unprecedented series of financial scandals that merely prove the obvious, that corruption has invaded the state, and the state has failed. Starting from the Oil for Food scam, in which the Congress Party was reportedly a major beneficiary, we have been through the Cash for Votes scam, IPL scam, Sukna land scam, the Black Money scam, the 2G scam, the Commonwealth Games scam, Adarsh Society scam, ISRO Devas scam, Coal mines scam, the Tatra scam, the multiple scams of Robert Vadra, the Agusta Westland scam, to name only some of the more notorious ones.

We leave behind for our youth a country looted by its own citizens. A sum of around US$1,500 billion, amounting to ₹82,462,500,000,000 approximately stolen and secreted in off-shore tax havens. The Congress led UPA government has shown no political will to recover it, even though they have been directed by the Supreme Court to do so. The German and French governments have shared information about the major money launderers. Yet, not a rupee has been recovered, no information has been provided to me even though ordered by the Supreme Court, and the Special Investigation Team ordered by the Supreme Court was never constituted. I have written copiously on this subject in this book.

Young India also inherits a precarious security situation, both internal and external. The youth and intelligentsia should try and understand India's long term and short term strategic requirements, and keep a watchful eye over government's actions or inaction. Security is an area that successive governments have allowed to turn from bad to worse, particularly during the last decade. Just as the Congress Party believes that vote bank politics is their profoundest contribution to protecting our national interest, it also seems to believe that appeasement of China is the most effective means of protecting our north-eastern border. The result is that the Chinese have persisted undeterred in aggressively encircling India by land and sea, fully encouraged by our passivity and appeasement. During the last decade China concentrated on encircling India over land, and establishing a strong presence in all our neighbouring countries. During the present decade, it is determined to encircle us by sea as well, and is strengthening its presence over the South China Sea and Indian Ocean. India has yet to get its act together to counter China's expansionistic and hegemonic design with intelligent and effective action.

Security analysts and think-tanks currently believe that striking India once again before the end of this decade is on the Chinese agenda. It is highly unlikely that our border dispute will be settled through bilateral negotiation. I have always believed that the entire border dispute between the two countries must be settled by the International Court of Justice, unless the Chinese are prepared to accept arbitration by some world dignitaries enjoying the confidence of both countries.

Two of our neighbours possess the capacity to wage a nuclear war. Only recently, when a small dispute between India and Pakistan over water could not be settled by our ministers and their officials, two Pakistani politicians, notorious for their audacity, made statements of a blood curdling nature. One of them said that if water does not flow the Pakistan way, rivers of blood (obviously Indian) will flow. The second threatened a nuclear war. My life-long commitment to Indo-Pak friendship is under severe strain.

Our Chinese neighbour with its huge arsenal of nuclear weapons, has also acted as Pakistan's nuclear assistant and supervisor. What makes the nuclear button more dangerous is when it is controlled by the mind and will of a single individual in a despotic state. A step urgently required is to prevent nuclear armaments from falling into the hands of governments that are despotic or theocratic, that finance and command terrorist organizations. Pakistan would fall under this definition, with its weak democracy, and the Army and ISI undoubtedly nurturing and controlling the Taliban.

All the secular democracies of the world must recognize the menace and pool their resources, economic, military and diplomatic to exterminate this threat. During the last few years, India and the USA have definitely understood the danger which civilization is exposed to from this source, yet there is no unity in action. India must make a serious diplomatic effort to impress upon the USA and other democracies of the world, a few glaring facts. It has been known for a long time that the Taliban was originally an instrument for Pakistan's colonization of Afghanistan. Pakistan has repeatedly double-crossed the Americans on sheltering the Al-Qaeda terrorists like Khalid Sheikh Muhammad, and Osama bin Laden himself. It is more than obvious that Pakistan continues to play its perfidious game with the US, and yet the American taxpayers' money continues to be pumped into virtually the pockets of Pakistan's army. We have not yet been successful in impressing upon the Americans that this money is financing terrorism against India. India's other democratic friends should also be persuaded to mount the strongest possible diplomatic pressure on the US government to stop this blatant misuse of its bounty by Pakistan. I strongly believe that India must fully support the sanctions on Iran and in turn the US and India must enter into a treaty of mutual defence, not only against war, but against the use of terrorism.

Our internal security situation is also precarious. The nation is enduring periodic terrorist attacks, and we still have no effective preventive or punitive systems in place, nor political will and national legislation to combat terrorism. It is almost as if India is determined that it shall not combat terrorism, shall not have enabling legislation as enacted by the US, such as the Homeland Security Act 2002, and the Prevention of Terrorism Act 2005 of UK and similar legislations in European governments. India is determined not to have an effective national agency on the lines of the Homeland Security Department of the US. The ramshackle National Investigation Agency showed itself a complete failure during the terrorist attacks on Mumbai, Hyderabad and Bangalore. Our anti-terror agencies remain effete, scattered and unmonitorable, even by the Home Ministry itself.

Our youth also inherit a world threatened by another dark age, heralded by the new barbarian, the late Osama bin Laden, and being propelled across the globe through his heirs and blood thirsty followers. The priceless jewels of democracy and secularism, the social and political values that we enjoy today, paid for by the blood of countless citizens of the world over the ages, are under attack by the new barbarians created by Osama bin Laden, the father of Al Qaeda. The Economist of Sepember28, 2013 states that the Al Queda terrorist network 'now holds sway over more territory and is recruiting more fighters than at any time in its 25-year history.'

They have a universal agenda soaked in blood and hatred; they have unlimited supplies of petro-money; they have an evil mission to create a multi-national 'jehadi' army of millions of mental and moral dwarfs, and indoctrinate them to murder innocent humans and destroy every relic of civilization, for which humanity has fought for centuries. They catch them young, they catch them vulnerable, and according to some reports, they ensnare them through sex. And then they start the great brainwash, until the victims are left with no discernment or reason, and become so indoctrinated that their belief becomes unshakable – that they will bomb, kill and murder innocent people, and immediately acquire the assured passport to paradise. This is the Al Queda, founded by Osama bin Laden, funded by Saudi and their extremist followers in the world, inspired by the Wahabis. They shoot little girls on the face, if they dare to go to school; they flog women mercilessly or even kill them if they dare to complain of rape; they stone them to death for adultery, imaginary or real. Amputation or shredding of limbs is a common form of punishment, as citizens watch on, without voice. For, if they dare raise it, nothing short of stoning to death for blasphemy will befall them too. Can the world ever forget the fate of young Malala, who fortunately survived by the grace of God, or of the Governor of Punjab, Salman Taseer, who was assassinated, reportedly because of his defence of a Christian woman sentenced to death on a false charge of blasphemy. The only Christian minister, Shahbaz Bhatti, was assassinated in March 2011 for similar reasons.

Al Queda's core beliefs internalized by their members are generally that all 'non-believers' of Islam have forfeited their right to live and exist on this planet, particularly, Jews, Hindus, Christian, Sufis, Shias and open minded intellectuals. They believe that if they kill even a few of us, God is waiting to reward them by a 24 x 7 paradise, with unlimited pleasures of all kinds. Several Muslim leaders like Anjem Choudary, a leading Muslim radical, leader of Islam4UK, take strong exception to the description of Islam as a peaceful religion. Samuel Huntington's clash of civilizations sounds tame and benign. For, what we see today is not a clash of civilizations but a clash between the world's collective civilization and the savagery of terrorism. This clash has become the gravest challenge to the contemporary world, for which no antidote has yet been found by the international community or affected nations.

Secular democracies of the world must come together to defend and preserve our liberal and enviable civilization through a global coalition. India should take a diplomatic lead on this issue. If the world really wants to combat and extinguish terrorism, which has now become a global network, any antidote must begin by the global coalition of secular democracies to choke the source of its funding, resources, men and arms. The US which is the world leader of secularism and democracy must resolve its contradictions and serious conflict of oil and security interests with its oil rich strategic partner Saudi Arabia, which is the source for funding, recruitment, indoctrination and training for terrorism, and influence them to cry a halt. Today, even as American drones try to exterminate this monster called terrorism, Obama's government, afflicted with acute financial embarrassment, is thoughtlessly pouring the American tax payer's wealth into the pocket of the Pakistan army and through them to their terrorist allies, whose declared enemy is US, the donor country, India, Israel and western nations. India must insist with the US that they extract a guarantee from Pakistan that US funds given to them to fight the Taliban should not be diverted towards terrorism or jehad against India. India must also insist that Pakistan shuts down their terror training camps that are targeting, not only India, but the donor himself. So far, we have not succeeded in doing this.

External diplomacy through a global coalition must be accompanied by internal engagement. India should start a process of creating appropriate platforms for liberal Muslim leaders and intellectuals to be heard and give confidence to peace loving Muslim community of India and reassure them about the true tenets of Islam and its practice. There are several peaceful and influential Muslim organizations that can act as interlocutors and instill the true teachings of Islam to the misguided brainwashed victims of jehadi ideology, and convince them to end their war against humanity. We have succeeded in doing this with the dacoits of the Chambal, with the Nagas, the Mizos, the Bodos, though the dimensions of conflict may have been different. I have no doubt that with determined political will, we can do the same in defeating bin Ladenism in India.

There is enough space in the world for all people to practise whatever religion they want, if it is based on love, compassion, mutual respect, tolerance, and peaceful coexistance. Civilization has finished its chapter of battle with religious fanaticism and force, and has no place today for creeds that preach violence and intolerance.

I would like to impress upon our youth that our nation must be guided by true secularism, the tenets of which must be included in the education systems of the country to educate young minds. We have not yet done so. Whatever definition of 'secularism' is adopted, its non-negotiable common factors are:

- complete neutrality by the state in matters of religion, neither supporting, nor opposing it;
- treating all its citizens equally regardless of their religion, without favouring or giving preferential treatment to any particular religion or non-religion;
- constitutional bar against the state adopting any religion as its state religion;
- since religion is a matter of personal faith, there should be no mixing of religion and politics for vote banks.

Undoubtedly, social values of all countries are bound to trace their origins to religion, but these must pass the test of rationality and public good before they are accepted as social norms.

In its famous judgement defining Hindutva, our Supreme Court has held that 'Hinduism' in truth and substance is not a religion but a way of life. If 'Hinduism' is only a way of life and not a religion like the other denominational religions, Hindutva is much less so. It stands for a uniform culture by harmonizing differences between all the cultures co-existing in the country. It stands for communal harmony and national unity, obliterating the distinction between Ram and Rahim.

The so-called critics of Hindutva, do not see the beauty and majesty of Hindutva as thus understood, for the very word 'Hindu' by itself, or any of its derivatives, is anathema to them. The Supreme Court's tribute to Hindus is that Hindutva does not depict hostility, enmity, or insolence toward other religious faiths. However, the communal propaganda machinery relentlessly disseminates 'Hindutva' as a communal word, something that has also become embedded in the minds of leading TV anchors. I earnestly request them to discover the true meaning of the word 'Hindutva' as defined by the Supreme Court, before they use it with communal overtones, as they are repeatedly doing, even now. It would also be in national interest, if all political parties advocated this ennobling and magnificent vision of Hindutva to the voters of India.

Our minds must also turn to Article 25 of our Constitution. While conferring on every citizen the right to profess, practice and even propagate his religion, it makes this right subject to public and order, health and morality, all of which represent vital and superior interests of our society and state. A conflict between the exercise of this right and the conditions it is subject to will be resolved not by *fatwas* of death or practice of mayhem and murder, but by peaceful and friendly intellectual argument in the free market of ideas. I believe that India's secularism mandates a life guided by reason and logic, but inspired by love and compassion. I respect all religions, but my own religion is a very simple one: 'Make as many people happy as you can while you live'.

I end on an optimistic note. All political parties have women and men of mettle among them. They should unite and pledge that their first commitment is towards national interest, economic, political and strategic. They should act as role models and mentors which our youth today are desperately but unsuccessfully seeking, and who seem completely absent in today's political action. Loyalty to a political party is a virtue as long as it is in the interest of the nation. If the political party's policies and actions are damaging the nation, loyalty to them becomes equivalent to a crime against the nation. The interest of the nation must always be paramount in politics.

APPENDIX

British Official Secrets Act 2 Defence

(1) A person who is or has been a Crown servant or government contractor is guilty of an offence if without lawful authority he makes a damaging disclosure of any information, document or other article relating to defence which is or has been in his possession by virtue of his position as such.

(2) For the purposes of subsection (1) above a disclosure is damaging if—
   (a) it damages the capability of, or of any part of, the armed forces of the Crown to carry out their tasks or leads to loss of life or injury to members of those forces or serious damage to the equipment or installations of those forces; or
   (b) otherwise than as mentioned in paragraph (a) above, it endangers the interests of the United Kingdom abroad, seriously obstructs the promotion or protection by the United Kingdom of those interests or endangers the safety of British citizens abroad; or
   (c) it is of information or of a document or article which is such that its unauthorised disclosure would be likely to have any of those effects.

(3) It is a defence for a person charged with an offence under this section to prove that at the time of the alleged offence he did not know, and had no reasonable cause to believe, that the information, document or article in question related to defence or that its disclosure would be damaging within the meaning of subsection (1) above.

(4) In this section "defence" means—
   (a) the size, shape, organisation, logistics, order of battle, deployment, operations, state of readiness and training of the armed forces of the Crown;

(b) the weapons, stores or other equipment of those forces and the invention, development, production and operation of such equipment and research relating to it;
(c) defence policy and strategy and military planning and intelligence;
(d) plans and measures for the maintenance of essential supplies and services that are or would be needed in time of war.

Selected Speeches

The Clash of Civilizations, as Samuel P. Huntigton very wisely asserted, underpins international relations and the balance of power in the post cold war period. The world has changed greatly in the new millennium and there is no doubt that the clash is deafening, power equations between nations are changing and a new alignment is taking place along the fault lines of religion, culture and terrorism. Each society, each culture has taken a different path of development from its inception to the garb it wears today and too often, culture and society are defined by religion.

Like every other aspect of civilization, religious groups have also gone through their own zeitgeist. The golden age of Islam was the dark ages of Christianity. Today, the development of the Muslim world, the architecture on which it has been built and the face it wears have significance not only because it is the world's second largest religion, but because in the interlinked world, the developmental path of one group has hugely significant ramifications for all people—be they Christian, Muslim, Hindu, Jew or of any other religion. The non-violence of Mahatma Gandhi that shaped India's history and converged a common brotherhood between Muslims and Hindus to win us freedom from colonial rule is not the answer to the problems of today's vicious world. We need to seek answers. We need to find a new way.

Understanding the history and fundamentals of society holds the key to a peaceful 21st century. It has been my privilege to speak at various fora and I have shared my thoughts on this seminally important aspect. Although the gist of many of my speeches have been mentioned in various chapters of this book, I reproduce some of them in their entirety here in the hope that they may shed more light on our world dynamics.

Aligarh Movement in the new millennium and education of minorities in India

28 July, 2007
Cleveland, Ohio

It gives me great pleasure to be here today amongst distinguished ladies and gentlemen who owe a good part of their intellectual development to the quality of teaching of distinguished scholars at the Aligarh Muslim University in India.

I was born in 1923 and Sir Sayyid Ahmed Khan had finished his glorious tenure of eighty years on this planet a quarter century earlier. I became a qualified lawyer in 1941 and it is, as far as my memory goes, at or about that time that as a student of Indian history, I had valuable and refreshing information about the venerable and enviable life of one of the great Indians our country had produced in the previous century. He lived between 1817 and 1898.

Most of you are perhaps more familiar with the details of his life than I have ever been. Therefore, I will not regale you with those, however interesting their recall to memory is even today.

I will refer to only a few, which in my opinion, greatly influenced his thinking and course of action. This sensitive young man could not have failed to be influenced by what was happening to one Islamic country after the other. European powers were grabbing, subjugating and exploiting them as was the wont of colonial powers of the time. France occupied Algeria in 1830, Britain occupied Eden in 1839. Tunisia was occupied in 1881, Egypt in 1882 and Sudan in 1889. This humiliating process continued even after the death of this great man. Libya and Morocco were occupied in 1912 and in 1915. The Sykes-Picot agreement divided the territories of the moribund Ottoman Empire which had committed the crime of being on the side of Germany during the First World War. Muslims in the Balkans, Russia and Central Asia became subjects of the new Soviet Union. Apart from this subjugation the west managed to establish control over the economy, the oil, and other resources of vast areas in the Muslim world. In 1948 Palestine was divided by the United Nations and the international community.

Sir Sayyid Ahmed Khan doubtless shared fully the feeling of humiliation of all thinking muslims. They were seized with fear that something terribly tragic was happening in Islamic history. The suicide bombers of modern times show at least to some Muslims that the community is pitted against hopeless odds. The Muslim experience inside India was equally depressing. Though there was a titular Moghal ruler in Delhi, he was a king without troops and without subjects. The real ruler was the East India Company which propagated the fiction that it was ruling on behalf of the Mughal kings. Everybody knew that he had neither power nor riches. The Muslim nobility and professional elite—the Sharif—would drown their sorrows by privately sneering at Britain's presence. Some turned to sycophantic poetry and others nostalgically recalled the by-gone days of phenomenal Muslim glory.

The decline of the Mughal emperor and the annoying arrogance of the British officers of the Company had a peculiar impact on the Muslim theologians, the Ulema. They were habituated to political patronage for more than five centuries. They had always avoided conflict with the temporal rulers. Now that the Christians had occupied the centres of temporal power, the world of the Ulema had almost been turned upside down. Writing of this period Jawaharlal Nehru has recorded:

'Moslems were especially affected as they were, as a group, more feudal than the Hindus and were also the chief beneficiaries of the 'muafis'. Among the Hindus there were far larger numbers of middle class people engaged in trade and commerce and the professions. These people were more adaptable and took to English education more readily. They were also more useful to the British for their subordinate services. Moslems avoided English education and, in Bengal, they were not looked upon with favour by the British rulers, who were afraid that the remnants of the old ruling class might give trouble. Bengali Hindus thus acquired almost a monopoly in the beginning in the subordinate government service and were sent to the Northern provinces'* By contrast, the Muslims resorted to rebellious actions. They viewed the growing British influence as a direct threat to Islam.'

As one eminent historian has recorded: 'A new element had come to be introduced into the social situation of the Indian Muslims; it was the well known Pan-Islamic Movement initiated and organized by Jamal-ud-din Al-Afghani (1839-97). The declared objective of this Movement was the union of all Islamic states under a single Caliphate and a strong Muslim empire which should be able to liberate all Muslims from western cultural and political domination and resist western economic intervention and exploitation. Jamal-ud-din Al-Afghani visited India and went round a number of places meeting a good many leaders of the Indo-Muslim society'#.

It is in this background that one must now look at the events of 1857 when Sir Sayyid Ahmed Khan was just forty years old; events which have come to be retrospectively described as India's 'first war of independence'.

In my view it was nothing of the kind. Out of the vast territory of India, the area involved in these events was a small part of Indo-Gangetic plain roughly the land between Lahore and Lucknow. The Sikhs, the Gorkhas and the Rajputs not only did not participate but fully helped the Company's forces to suppress the rebellions. The igniting match was neither India's

---

*Jawaharlal Nehru, *Discovery of India*.
#Parmanand Parashar, *Nationalism: Its Theory and Principles in India*.

independence nor even consciousness of threatened Indian Nationhood. On May 11 Indian troops in Meerut mutinied, killed their officers and marched on to Delhi. Hindus resented the threat to the caste system and low emoluments. Most of the third Cavalry Regime refused to handle new cartridges which they thought contained cow and pig fat thus offending both Hindus and Muslims.

Incredible acts of cruelty took place on both sides. Delhi was recaptured by British forces in September. Lucknow held on till March of the next year. Considering that the Nawabs of Lucknow, who were notoriously fond of the exquisite and exotic and had been dissipated like most oriental despots, should have shown such tenacity is remarkable. Two notable non-Muslim figures deserve mention not because they showed any deep involvement with the Hindu majority, but because they were just exceptional. One is Nana Sahib and his protégé Tantya Tope and the other is Rani Laxmi Bai of Jhansi. The former operated in Kanpur and eventually escaped to Nepal. The Rani was a remarkable woman respected by all who came in contact with her. She was comparatively young and possessed considerable feminine charms and a remarkably fine figure. She hardly played a significant role in the rebellion but she had to fight rival claimants to her husband's defunct title and some neighbouring Rajput Rajas who invaded Jhansi on behalf of the British. She raised troops and fought them. Her military talents and leadership came to the fore not in fighting the British, but fellow Indians. When the British captured Jhansi the lady was nowhere to be found. But she was then seen fighting in Gwalior where she died a hero's death, which she undoubtedly was. While walking the ramparts of the city she was hit by a spray of bullets as the British launched their attack. She was cremated nearby, 'the only man among the rebels', according to one of her British admirers and adversaries.

The net result of the rebellion was that Victoria became the queen of India and India's Governor General became her Viceroy. The fiction of Mughal Rule thus finally ended. The unfortunate Mughal king was jailed in Rangoon and died composing heart rending poetry.

What was Sir Sayyid Ahmed doing during these tumultuous times? Sir Ahmed was a Munsiff Magistrate at Bijnor. Many English officers and Christian men, women and children had sought refuge in the town in fear of being done to death by the Muslim insurgent Mohammad Khan. Sir Ahmed worked night and day to save the lives of these fear-stricken foreigners.

To him Sir Sayyid Ahmed Khan had said earlier 'By god, Nawab Sahib, I say that the British sovereignty cannot be eliminated from India'. Sir Ahmed was plainly right but fortunately his prophecy lasted for 90 years only.

The British quickly rewarded him and for years spoke of him as their 'foremost loyal Mohammadan'. This however did not make Sir Ahmed happy. His misery was part-guilt and part-sorrow. He had, after all, taken the British side against his own people. He had encouraged Bijnor's Hindu landlords to defeat Nawab Mohammad Khan. He was so bitter that he not only rejected the offer of a estate by the grateful British but seriously contemplated migration to Egypt, a decision which he did not execute explaining that he remained to share the troubles of his *kaum*.

This word *kaum* is an ambiguous word but Sir Sayyid Ahmed obviously meant the Muslim community, and neither the Indians in general, nor Ummah—the moslems of the world. He expressly rejected the sovereignty of the Turkish Khalifate over the Muslims of India. They were the worst sufferers when the mutiny was suppressed.

Sir Sayyid Ahmed Khan had arrived at one conclusion: that his *kaum*'s future lay in reconciliation with the British which he thought was for India's good too.

In his short epigram called *Asbabe Baghavate Hind* he pointed out with great candor the errors of the British Raj. He pleaded for the ruler-subject cordiality of the Akbar Era. Two years later he produced another booklet called '*Loyal Mahomedans of India*', pleading with the British that not all Muslims were guilty of sedition and rebellion. He even founded the society which came to be known as the Scientific Society of Aligarh through which he hoped to bring knowledge and literature of the nations of the western world within the reach of the immense masses of the people of the East. The Duke of Argyll, Secretary of State for India, was its patron. The declared motto was 'Educate, educate, educate'.

I hope these words sound a bell. Archangel Gabriel visited the Prophet in his desert cave on Mount Hira. Did he not tell him to read? When the Prophet said he could not read, did he not repeat—'Read! Read! Read!'. I am sure this familiar story inspired the University motto.

It is at or about this time that Sir Sayyid Ahmed Khan, when reprimanded, declared to his friend Shakespeare, a local British bureaucrat:

'Now I am convinced that both these communities will not join wholeheartedly in anything... On account of the so-called "educated" people, hostility between the two communities will increase immensely in the future. He who lives will see.'

I do not believe that Sir Sayyid Ahmed Khan had accepted the inevitability of a parting of ways by Hindus and Muslims of India. Nor was he predicting, much less pleading, for the partition of India. His later actions showed that he wanted the bridge to be gulfed between the two by intensive modern education of the Muslims. He was most anxious that Muslims should not be humiliated like the last Mughal Emperor. His remark to Shakespeare was only an angry portrayal of the prevalent ground reality. Even his anger was not totally without good cause. He was rightly incensed by irrational hostility to growth of Urdu by some Hindi fanatics.

No wonder that very soon he undertook a trip to England to learn more about British culture, society and politics. There again he made a remark which should be considered irresponsible and unfortunate. Said he:

'Without flattering the English, I can truly say that the natives of India, high and low, merchants and petty shopkeepers, educated and illiterate, when contrasted with the English in education, manners and uprightness, are as like them as a dirty animal is to an able and handsome man'.

These remarks were published in the Aligarh Institute Gazette. They certainly diluted Sir Sayyid Ahmed Khan influence and appeal. But he drew no distinction between Muslims and Hindus. It must also be said that Anglomania had overtaken almost the entire social and intellectual elite of India. Derision of Indian culture was a common failing and token of their Europeanisation. Macaulay's reforms of 1830 had ensured this development. All education was already in English. Ram Mohan Roy had initiated this change. A reaction set in much later when someone realized that Europeanisation would not convert India into Europe but result in a distorted India. The British, continued to see in him a reconciler between them and the Muslims of India. They assisted him in bringing to his community the blessings of modern education in western science and literature.

Governor Miur released 75 acres of land in Aligarh City and Lord Northbrook, the Viceroy made a generous financial contribution. Lord Lytton, his successor, laid the foundation stone in January 1877. The Sikh ruler of Patiala and the Hindu ruler of Vizianagaram and other less prominent Hindus made their humble contribution to the founding of the Mohammedan Anglo-Oriental College which offered arts, science and law courses in English.

Sir Sayyid Ahmed Khan was totally opposed to this education being imparted in the local vernaculars. He wanted English to forge the unity of India. He could visualize the dangers of linguistic and regional chauvinism.

Sir Sayyid Ahmed Khan clarified that he did not wish to impose his understanding of Islam on anybody and that the education in the college will be without prejudice to the religion of the students. He rigorously opposed the interference of government in the running of the college.

I would be less than honest if I fail to mention Sir Sayyid Ahmed's views which greatly impinged upon later Indian politics and lend some plausibility to the charge that Sir Ahmed was a separatist. At one point he declared:-

'Now suppose that all the English were to leave India. Then who would be rulers of India? Is it possible that two qaums—the Muslim and Hindu—could sit on the same throne? Most certainly no. It is necessary that one of them will conquer the other and thrust it down'.

When Lord Ripon's Local Self-Government Bill was before the Council, Sir Sayyid Ahmed made a successful plea for separate nomination of Muslims to local boards and district councils. His speech on the occasion deserves to be quoted at some length:-

'The system of representation by election, in countries where the population is composed of one race and one creed, is no doubt the best system that can be adopted.

But, my lord, in a country like India, where caste distinctions still flourish, where there is no fusion of the various races, where religious distinctions are still violent, where education in its modern sense has still not made an equal or proportionate progress among all sections of the population, I am convinced that the introduction of the principle of election, pure and simple, (to) the local boards and district councils would be attended with evils of great significance...

The larger community would totally override the interests of the smaller community.... And the measures might make the differences of race and creed more violent than ever.'

My view still remains that this was his response to existing reality which he hoped radically to change through the institution he was giving birth to and the kind of education he proposed to provide.

In dealing specifically with the subject of education of minorities, you will excuse me for dealing with only the Muslim minority. Each minority has its own traditions, its own beliefs and superstitions, social attitudes and religious dogmas and rituals. All these are relevant to evaluation of the educational reforms needed for a particular minority. I do not have either the time or the energy to deal with all the minorities or even the prominent ones. Having lived with Muslims all my life I find it comparatively easy to speak about them.

I hope you know that I was born in a small but important town called Shikarpur in the north of Sindh, now in Pakistan. It was a Muslim majority area but it had the distinction of a gentle culture born out of the synthesis of the two cultures Hindu and Muslim, in which on the hindu festival of Deepawali, muslim children got new clothes and Hindu children got them when Eid was being celebrated. It was the land of the Sufis where Hindus worshipped at Muslim Khankas and shrines and Muslims worshipped at the Asthans and Deras of Hindu saints.

I must hasten to explain my personal attitude to religion. Marx told us that religion is the opiate of the people. I think he was wrong. Opium suggests something which numbs you, makes you sluggish and often puts you to sleep. Far from being an opium, it is an aphrodisiac for horror, a Benzedrine for bestiality. All the fleets of the world could easily swim in the spacious comforts of the ocean of innocent blood which has been spilt in the name of religion. The Crusades, the Inquisitions, the ignorance of the dark ages, terrorism and war are huge on the debit side of its balance sheet. I concede that religion has brought some hope to the frustrated and forlorn and some comfort to those suffering from the intensity of pain and cruelty. Religion has been at best a Placebo. I believe that kindness is all that this sad world needs. I have therefore a one line religion: 'we must live a life governed by reason but inspired by love'.

When people ask me 'do you believe that God exists?' My honest answer is I do not know. As a criminal lawyer I am willing to give him the benefit of doubt; he perhaps exists but certainly not in the shape in which he is presented in the movies or in the minds of millions of men and women. I must share with you an interesting anecdote based on the story of the Philosopher and Theologian. Sneered the latter: 'Philosopher is like a blind man in a dark room, looking for a black cat which is not there'. The Philosopher then retorted 'That may be, but the Theologian would have still found the cat'.

I prefer the Philosopher to the Theologian. I have still not been able to find answers to the three old questions which Epicureans asked many centuries ago. Is god willing to prevent evil but not able? Then He is impotent. Is He able but not willing? Then He is malevolent. Is He both able and willing? Then why does evil still exist?

I am tempted to relate a significant incident in the life of Gautam Buddha. His cousin had shot a bird flying peacefully in the sky. The arrow had penetrated its body. Bleeding, it fell to the ground. The cousin claimed it by conquest but Buddha gently took up the bird, smoothened its ruffled feathers, removed the arrow and applied soothing honey to the smarting wound. He brought the bird back to health and let it fly away free. It is the highest religion, earnestly to strive to reduce the sum total of the world's suffering. We are to take things in our own hand. The Cynic said:

'I turned to speak to God
About the world's despair
But to make bad matters worse
I found God was not there'.

If He does exist, he has obviously forgotten that we humans exist. It is an interesting reflection that perhaps the great god suffers from Alzheimer's.

I have two preliminary observations to make and then we get to the main theme.

India is a Democratic Republic and the Preamble of its Constitution proclaims that it is a Secular Republic. Our Supreme Court has held that secularism is a basic feature of our Constitution and is a feature which cannot be destroyed or diluted even by the unanimous vote of both Houses of our Parliament. India as a state has no religion, in the normal sense in which the word religion is used, but we have not abolished religion. People of all faiths including agnostics and atheists are entitled to all the rights and privileges of a citizen. Every person is entitled to freedom of conscience and the right freely to profess, practice and propagate religion. These rights are, however, subject to public order, morality and health.

Minorities with a distinct language, script or culture of their own have the right to conserve the same and have the right to establish and administer educational institutions of their choice. Hostile discrimination against anyone on the ground of his religion is outlawed.

It should be a matter of some interest to you that when the first draft of the constitution was prepared, this right was confined to professing and practicing one's religion. But at the instance of the minorities, the right to propagate was also conceded to them. Of course this only means the right to convert others without the use of force or fraud. Obviously a secular republic cannot spend the tax payers money on religious education of any kind. Religious minorities however can, if they so choose, but public funds cannot be employed for the purpose. It is my view that it is the right and the duty of a secular republic to turn the minds of the young away from irrational religious beliefs and inculcate in them the spirit of genuine secularism. More than the majority, which obviously means the Hindu majority, it is the religious minorities in India who place a high value on its secularism as a protector of their identity, equality and dignity.

Fanaticism and fundamentalism are inconsistent with Indian secularism. If any religious dogma or practice offends morality, obstructs the prevention of disease and promotion of health, or is productive of social divisiveness, hatred and violence, it must be vigorously suppressed.

The second observation that I have to make is that Indian democracy is as dear to the majority as to the minorities, perhaps more so to the latter. Democracy is an exercise of equality and an exertion of people's sovereignty. The right to vote, freedom of dissent and the right of even vicious attack on the rulers are totally useless unless the individual citizen is armed with knowledge of how the country is being governed and whether it is being governed in the interest of the people, or for filling pockets of corrupt rulers and counterfeit mediators between men and the gods.

A successful democracy requires the highest education of the citizen. It is trite that 'democracy without education is hypocrisy without limitation'. Right to education is, therefore, more fundamental than any other right. The Constitution of India so declares it. But the obligation of the state to provide free education is subject to its economic capacity. The right thus exalted to the level of fundamental right is in practice hardly capable of being enforced against the state which wastes its resources on corruption, war and weapons, and pretends that it has not much to spare for enlightening the citizens. Education is that which nourishes the spirit of liberty. It is that spirit which seeks to understand the mind of other men and women; that attitude which weighs the interest of the other's side against its own without bias or prejudice. All this does not make the nineteenth century vision of Sir Sayyid Ahmed Khan irrelevant in the twenty-first. It still retains its vigour and dynamism.

Let me now turn to the legacy of Sir Sayyid Ahmed Khan and share with you what I believe were the chief components of this priceless legacy:-

First: Religion and its teachings are not inconsistent with science and its view of the universe. He obviously meant—though with a view not to offend his audience he used the mildest terminology—that in its peculiar domain science will prevail over the belief systems of religion. He did not accept the fatalistic Hindu belief that the stars alone determine our destiny as well as the Muslim belief in kismet. His attitude to religion was that of a rational sceptic. I am sure he had read Gibbon who wrote 'The various forms of worship, which prevailed in the Roman world, were all considered by the people to be equally true, by the philosopher as equally false, and by the magistrate as equally useful'.

He was perfectly aware of the history of religion. It had consistently been on the side of political power. The Vatican supported Mussolini and the overthrow of Spanish democracy by General Franco. He dreaded a spiritual police state. Writing in the *Khut bat-e-Ahmedia* he advocated a critical review of the Hadith to ascertain their authenticity.

Second: He was clearly of the view that Muslims must revert to the old rationalist interpretation of the Holy Quran of the Mutazila School and turn their backs on any inconsistent teaching. In this Sir Sayyid Ahmed Khan incurred the opprobrious epithet of 'Nechari' for the Aligarh movement and the wrath of Egyptian Al Afghani. The latter indulged in violent denunciation. 'Nechariya' he wrote 'is the root of corruption, the source of uncountable evils and the ruin of the country... The Necharis present themselves before the eyes of fools as the standard bearers of science but only give a wider range to treachery.'

This did not break Aligarh, or Sir Sayyid Ahmed Khan; quite the contrary. But it certainly raised a serious dilemma for Indian Muslims. If they turned their backs on international Islamic solidarity they would inevitably become full-fledged citizens of a united India and a powerless minority in the very land they had ruled as absolute masters.

Ashraf Muslims—and to a lesser extent the Ajlaf too, could not digest this. This dilemma led to the partition of India and should no longer worry the Muslims of India. We should not forget that in the 40's, AMU did get involved in the Pakistan Movement and became a center of Muslim League politics. Through the rough course of Indian History, the two communities doubtlessly misbehaved with each other. Partition was a punishment. Only history will decide who has fallen under the most severe and cruel part of it. Wisdom requires that every Muslim and every Hindu should not be implicated in the event of the past. Deep civic engagement will dull the painful edges of historical memories.

Syed Ameer Ali's powerful book *Sprit of Islam* is a classic of modernism and stands out as a luminous lighthouse of rational Islam.

Third: Indian Muslims must no longer look out of India and waste their energy on recovering their Arab, Turkish or Persian roots but strive to be the most beautiful flower in India's bouquet of numerous religions, races and tribes.

The supreme and inexorable law of change is synthesis arising out of thesis and antithesis. Resistance to change is wholly contrary to the teaching of Sir Sayyid Ahmed Khan. It will be futile and perhaps suicidal.

I have no objection to muslims looking back and trying to recapture their lost glory. But what was it that made Islam glorious? In just one sentence let me answer this question : It was their intellectual curiosity and the pursuit of knowledge; certainly not their rule over others by war, plunder, bloodshed and rape.

A few days before Prime Minister Tony Blair of England gave up his office, he spoke to a gathering of Muslim intellectuals said to be moderates. He told them that the true meaning of Islam had been hijacked by some extremists and the authentic message of Islam needed to be heard loud and clear. Now while still in office he could not avoid polite and dull diplomatese; otherwise he could have told them that the hijacking he mentioned had taken place many centuries ago. The Prophet of Islam established his unique superiority over other godmen by being the only one to preach that 'those who walked in search of knowledge walked in the way of God; that the ink of the scholar was more valuable than the blood of a martyr; fight against those who fight you but do not commit aggression'.

Muslims were at the zenith of their glory when they seriously heeded his sublime message. Islam civilized the west and rescued it from the darkness of the middle ages. Arabic literature had presented the best of Greek philosophy. For three centuries Christianity saw Islam advance, saw it capture the Christian people and lands one after another, dominate Christian trade and commerce. Christians even suffered the humiliation of being called infidels. Unfortunately they jettisoned the message and their decline started, which ended in the enslavement of virtually the entire Muslim world.

In 1150 Caliph Mustanjid at Baghdad ordered the burning of all the philosophic works of Avicenna, forty-four years later Emir Abn Yusuf Yaqub-al Mansur, then at Seville, ordered the burning of all works by Averroes; he forbade his subjects to study philosophy and urged them to throw into the fire all books of philosophy wherever found. Ibn Habib was put to death for studying philosophy. Contrast the great Sadi and Gazali and you will understand the tragedy that was overtaking Islam. After 1200, Islam shunned speculative thought. In the next century Muslims lost most of Spain; in the east the Crusaders captured Jerusalem and the Mongols took and destroyed Bagdad. Civilized comfort attracts barbarian conquest. Islam suffered a devastating blow to its magnificent civilization.

It was bad luck for Muslims and the rest of the world that in the late 17th century Arabia produced an evil person—Mohammed Ibin Abdul Wahhab. Though he rightly concluded that the decline of the Muslim world was attributable to a departure from the true word of the Prophet, he grievously misunderstood the 'word'.

Picking on a stray line in the Holy Book he convinced himself that the Book had decreed the death and annihilation of all Mushrikhun. He then included amongst them Christians, Jews, Shiites, Hindus and many others. All these had forfeited their right to live. In the spring of 1802, twelve thousand of his followers invaded southern Ottoman Iraq; entered Karbala, massacred 4000 Shiites, ransacked their holy shrines including the tomb of Hussain, the martyred grandson of the Prophet himself. They looted the city and carried off its wealth on the backs of 4000 Camels. One of his descendants, Latif, a Saudi Judge promoted a religious movement with the same philosophy and called it Ikhiwan.

In 1928 was born the Moslem Brotherhood in Egypt with tremendous ideological affinity. Maulana Mawdudi of Pakistan was a follower and collaborator.

The Saudi Royal family patronized all these with massive financial and other supports. Osama bin Laden attacked the Saudi government for not sufficient commitment to the Wahabi teaching. Only when he became a nuisance he was deprived of Saudi nationality in 1994.

What happened on September 11th 2001 was a declaration of war on the entire free world—more dangerous than the Japanese attack on Pearl Harbour. Fifteen of the attackers were indoctrinated Wahabis and Saudi nationals.

How does one account for suicide squads, each member convinced of immediate entry into paradise and the company of enchanting Huris? A deadly combination of opium called Religion and Hashish can alone accomplish this. I have not investigated nor have I been informed by any one what awaits the female suicide bomber in Paradise! If you do believe in god, then for His sake do not believe He is running a brothel. Martyrdom is the only way in which one can become famous without any ability or character.

Sir Sayyid Ahmed Khan wanted to recapture the past—the glorious one during the first three centuries after the Prophet was no longer on this planet. This recapture of the spirit of dynamism of a vibrant Islam does not mean forgetting the knowledge science has given us and becoming as ignorant and ill-informed as humanity was in the dark ages. Let us have the courage to recall that not one founder of the three major religions of the Middle-East knew that the earth was round and revolved round the sun, that we did not fall off the earth due to a force called gravity, that most disease is caused by bacteria and viruses, that the 21st century will be the century of computers, cell phones, fax machines and man-made satellites roaming in the vicinity of distant stars, or that the world one day would wait in mortal fear of a nuclear holocaust.

What the education of the Muslim minority urgently needs is a dramatic improvement in the qualifications and character of teachers. It is unfortunate that most of the available teachers almost justify Oscar Wilde when he quipped 'those incapable of learning have taken to teaching'.

The modern teacher must be a convinced secularist committed to maintaining a pluralistic society. Sir Sayyid Ahmed Khan imported teachers from England. They had their British imperialist prejudices but they were the best the school or university could afford.

The sum total of the teachers' religious beliefs must be the barest minimum; a religion whose parameters are limited to answering questions which our small mammalian equipment called the brain cannot answer. He must know that philosophy raises some questions that cannot be answered and religion furnishes answers that cannot be questioned. Why was this universe created? Who created it? Where did humanity come from and where does it go after death? Is there a surviving soul and is there a cycle of births and deaths? Only on such questions it may be pardonable to take, on faith, answers by religious leaders without any scientific evidence in support.

These teachers must also be aware that poverty, extreme inequality within a society and growing gaps between the rich and poor as well as false religious indoctrination are the causes of conflict and brutal violence. The young minds must be trained to concentrate on removing these causes.

It is unfortunate that one of the shortcomings of democracy is that people and political leaders only debate short term issues which are likely to influence the course of the next election. The short term and the long term aims which the teachers must concentrate upon are reasonable prosperity for all, global peace and human security. The teacher must by his moral influence persuade the politician to do likewise.

The teacher must let the community know that incontrovertible historical evidence portrays women of Medina raising their heads from slavery and violence to claim their right to join as equal participants in the making of Muslim history when the Prophet was the political leader.

Women fled from Mecca by thousands to enter Medina because Islam promised equality and dignity for all men and women alike. Every woman, who came to Medina could gain access to full citizenship, the status of Sahabi, companion of the Prophet. Women freely entered into Councils of Muslim Ummah to speak freely to the Prophet, to dispute with the men, fight for their happiness and to be involved in the management of military and political affairs. Years after his death the Prophet's widow Ayasha took to the battlefield at the head of a male army which challenged the legitimacy of Khalifa Ali. Neither during the life of the Prophet nor after his death did she wear a veil or a Hijab. Thus Muslim clerics, terrorists and their followers who would condemn women to perpetual inferiority and compel them to conceal their countenance behind a veil or hijabs are a disgrace to the Prophet and insult to his beloved wife. Ayasha cannot be written out of the history of Islam. Keeping women out of Muslim politics has been a favourate pastime of even some known historians like Syed Al Afghani, whom I have mentioned earlier. The life of Ayasha is a lesson for Muslim women to stand up and fight.

Young Muslims must appreciate the majesty of Article 14 of the Indian Constitution. No hostile discrimination is permitted against women—just because they are women. I am one of those who believe that woman made civilization possible by constructing a home and tilling a field. No civilization was possible in the hunting stage.

Education is not imparted only by the teachers. It is also the duty of the intelligentsia. Those who are proud of the Aligarh movement must show the courage to warn all their compatriots that a society that produces suicide murderers in quantity is essentially committing suicide. Iran and Saudi Arabia are funding the entire world terror infrastructure. They cannot overlook the certainty that one day the terror that they spread will end up in their own backyard. Just look what is happening to Pakistan. The people of Pakistan are my kith and kin. I grieve in their misfortunes and wish them a better future. But they too must abandon the way of terror and war. They too have to emerge from the darkness of superstition and Jahaliat.

The scriptures are full of pleasing fables. Enjoy these stories but do not allow your intellect to be subverted. That is the greatest tribute you can pay to a man whose memory you are commemorating at this convention, and whose legacy you want to preserve for posterity in the centuries to come.

I am an optimist and let me conclude with the melodious tarana by Majaz Lakhnawi, a distinguished product of AMU

Jao saara kajam la spz yahan
Aur saare jahan ka saaz yahan
Jo abar yahan se uthega, wo saare jahan par barsega

On Anti-semitism

Anti-Semitism World Conference
November 2010
Ottawa, Canada.

My gracious hosts and distinguished fellow guests assembled here tonight.

We meet when much of the world is struggling to recover from the after effects of the economic meltdown of two years ago, and what is more relevant to this conference, during the disappointment caused by the protracted impasse in Israeli-Palestine peace talks.

At the outset I must dispel your understandable curiosity about my qualification for the honour of being amongst you during this conference.

I am here because I am from India—a country which never in its history provided any hospitality to the practice of anti-semitism, a country in which our Jewish citizens rose to the highest positions in the field of education, art, movies and the Armed forces.

For many years my home in Delhi was the unofficial Embassy of Israel and my part in establishing the most open cordial and cooperative relationship between India & Israel is well recognized by both countries. I do not claim any higher credentials.

I take this opportunity to pay sincere and respectful homage to the Jewish people assembled here or settled anywhere else in the wide world.

Anyone who has even a perfunctory knowledge of your long history of suffering, your magnificent struggle for survival and your breath taking contribution and achievement—with your incomparable genius in every field of human thought and endeavour—must bow to you in admiration and empathy.

Only the sons of Satan would wish you ill or plan your annihilation. It is a shameful blot on the civilized world of today that there still exist such malignant characters and their number and capacity for mischief are by no means insignificant to be ignored as innocuous.

Your troubles started soon after the birth of Christianity. Within seventy years the holy city of Jerusalem was captured by the Romans and that started the long saga of Dispersion. For four thousand years before that event you were the Chosen People of God. It is strange that your tragedy did not invoke the compassion and fellow feeling even of those who professed belief in the Sermon on the Mount.

Spinoza, one of the greatest Jews, though excommunicated from the synagogue for his refreshing freedom of thought, had reached the conclusion that Christian persecution gave you the unity and solidarity that was essential for your continued existence and survival.

Then came the birth of Islam in the country of the Arabs of the Middle East, some six centuries later.

Both Christianity and Islam are products of Jewish scriptures and their world memories. Their hostility is not rationally explicable; though in fairness it must be recognized that in earlier times you were better off in the easy world of Islam's ascendency.

The prevailing feudal system debarred you from owning land; the powerful guilds excluded your from trade and commerce. Outcast and excommunicated, insulted and injured, condemned to the peripheral Ghettos of urban existence, you were mobbed by the commoners and robbed by the kings. A typical example is the Spanish King Ferdinand of the late fifteenth century. Historians record that Columbus discovered America and Ferdinand discovered the jews.

How you managed to preserve your racial and cultural integrity, guarded with jealous love your ancient rituals and traditions, patiently and resolutely awaited the day of your deliverance, have evoked the admiration and earned you the sympathy and reverence of all the good people of the world. But the wicked, wallowing in religious fanaticism, have been burning with malice and hatred. Like the pusillanimous child that tries to crush the insect it dare not look at, they spawned a Hitler who planned your genocide but ended in his own shameful suicide.

After more than 2000 years of wandering your friends have watched with profound admiration your restoration to your ancient but never forgotten home. What drama could rival the grandeur of your sufferings and the justice and glory of its end. 'What fiction could match the romance of this reality', wrote Will Durant, the historian.

The Christian world has owned its wrongs of the past and is even busy making recompense and providing protection against those who are still planning your extinction as a free people. Those who genuinely follow the pristine and peaceful Islam of the Prophet are not amongst them. It is the followers of a counterfeit version known as the Wahabi faith generated from Saudi Arabia in the late 18th century by an evil being—Ibn Wahhabi. The core of that faith is that all *Mushrikun* have forfeited their right to live. According to his teaching the *Mushrikun* include Jews, Christians, Hindus, all nonbelievers and Muslim Shias too. According to him jihad against these and their destruction is a religious duty.

Osama bin Laden is a Wahhabi and his quarrel with the Saudi regime is that it is not sufficiently Wahhabi.

All the secular democracies of the world, and Canada is one of them, must come together and master this menace to all civilization—not only Israel or the Jews.

No government that spawns terrorists and terrorist organizations is fit to be a member of the United Nations. To prevent such governments from acquiring access to nuclear weapons is a categorical imperative of our survival.

Diplomacy, dialogue and delay are only steps towards suicide. Prevention is much easier than cure. Anti-semitism has to be wiped out before it destroys its victims and their friends too—which practically means the whole civilized world.

You need foolproof insurance against the trauma of another holocaust. I know you have powerful friends. But friends can become fickle depending on the sacrifice friendship needs and the kaleidoscope of conflicting interests when the critical time arrives.

Your faith in your Prophets, your will, your valour, your nukes and nuclear submarines are more reliable policies of insurance.

On non-violence

Bhartiya Vidya Bhavan
7 June 2012
New York

I am flattered by your invitation to speak this evening at a great institution and to a wonderful audience. The well-deserved name Bhartiya Vidya Bhavan—the mansion of Indian wisdom—reminds me of my limitations and lack of qualifications to receive this invitation. What surprises me is my false courage, call it bravado if you please, in not only accepting but actually appearing in flesh and blood before you all.

I must recall my first appearance in the Chief Court of Sindh before Sir Godfrey Davis and Justice Constantine. I was so full of the facts and law involved in my case that I was going too fast for the judges.

The chief justice asked: 'Are you trying to catch a train'?

I said, 'No, my Lord.'

'Are you feeling nervous?'

I again said no.

And this evoked a surprising response. They replied 'For God's sake, do feel a little nervous!'

Ever since then I have taken to a reformed style of public speaking. I speak carefully and in measured tones and, believe you me, I do feel reasonably nervous.

Let me now clear some misgivings about myself. I am neither a spiritually evolved soul nor known for any deep study of moral philosophy or even religious scriptures. I am basically a lawyer and I plead guilty to the charge of being a politician. Both the professions are at the low water mark of social acceptance and respect these days. In fact they have never fallen so low during the entire 65 years of Indian Independence. I speak of India and not this great country of the United States.

A word about politicians: we have not produced one prime minister from the Nehru dynasty with the moral height of Lal Bahadur Shastri—a pm who clearly diagnosed that corruption had infested the highest decks of our political life. Today, except for sycophants and flatterers, politicians are objects of public ridicule and contempt.

Lawyers too have been under attack. Shakespeare wanted them all killed. An American president blamed them for all the ills that ail the nation. The pharmaceutical laboratories in the United States have decided to use lawyers instead of rats in their laboratory experiments. Lawyers are more numerous than rats and there are things which lawyers do that even rats will not, is their stated reason for this change.

The choice of subject—somewhat esoteric and ambiguous—'Relevance of Non-violence and Teachings from Ancient Civilizations', suits me. It is not terribly restrictive and I am free to share my thoughts with you. But make no mistake, I am no expert on non-violence though it is a matter of concern to us today as it has been for thousands of years of human existence on this planet. During about 4000 years of recorded history, only in less than 300 years there has been no war. Experts get lost in the jungle of their thoughts and they get confused by the excessive stock of their wisdom. I suffer from no such handicap.

I am not a seeker of power nor do I crave it. Power often gives one a distorted view of the world as well as of oneself. Such men are found in every lunatic asylum. Some think of themselves as kings and still others think of themselves as miracle makers and some even god. Similar delusions expressed by educated men in obscure language make qualified professors of philosophy in reputed universities.

Each one of you present here is my judge—I hope you will be able to certify that you are more clear in your understanding of the subject than when you entered this hall. If that happens, I will consider myself an expert for all times on this non-legal subject.

Indians of the 20th century became familiar with the doctrine of non-violence not so much from Indian scriptures or history but from the writings, speeches and political actions of Mahatma Gandhi. I have great reverence for the Mahatma and if any single individual can claim all honour and reverence for bringing Independence to India and the graceful exit of the British it is this great son of India whom we rightfully call the 'Father of the Nation'. Gandhiji was a Jain and I have no doubt that non-violence and pacifism were a part of his genetic structure. But according to him even he had been influenced by Jesus' Sermon on the Mount. I have no doubt he was.

But whence came this inspiration to Jesus himself? His own Hebrew background and Jewish philosophy provide no satisfactory clue. Jesus himself, a Jew from Nazareth, had no access to any teaching except that of the prophets of the old testament which taught 'an eye for an eye and a tooth for a tooth'.

It is only now that respectable western scholarship has traced the source of Jesus' actual inspiration to Ashoka's teaching and the contact established by his missionaries with the Greeks and Macedonians who settled in India after Alexander left and some encountered in the Middle-east particularly the Assenian community located in Jerusalem. This community got the concepts of sexual chastity, non-violence and 'love thy enemy' morality from the missionaries sent by emperor Ashoka, and Jesus borrowed it from them. The Dead Sea Biblical manuscripts fully support this conclusion.

I do not allow my critical faculties to be paralyzed by admiration of the great or the fear of being considered an iconoclast. In spite of Gandhiji's Jain heritage and the influence on him of Jesus and his teachings, I do not believe that Gandhiji accepted non-violence as a moral imperative or spiritual mandate. He had read the Bhagwad Gita and it clearly ridiculed the doctrine of pacific resistance or 'ahimsa' as Gandhiji later called it.

The Bhagwad Gita starts with a spiritual conundrum of how to reconcile absolute spiritual faith with the outer actualities of man's life and actions. On the one hand there was the dharma of the man of action, a prince and warrior like Arjuna and, on the other, the demand of the safety of thousands of soldiers with no direct interest in the outcome of the Kurukshetra war. Make no mistake—Arjun was not a votary of non-violence. He did not want to kill his friends and relatives and revered Gurus like Bhishma and Dronacharya. Krishna advocated war and advanced what appears to some as an incredibly foolish argument that Arjuna was killing those whom the Lord had already killed. True, the Gita did recognize that non-injuring and non-killing are the highest law of spiritual conduct. On the other hand was the duty of the warrior to bring about a just and moral order, gravely disturbed by a kingdom and a wife lost in gambling and a demand for five villages for the Pandavas contemptuously rejected. This was his genius. Gandhiji dismissed the entire Gita as an allegorical fiction. He recognized that the unarmed Indian had no option of violence to exercise. The British Ruler, with his sophisticated technology and weapons, could never be defeated or ousted in a violent fight. Some Indians would certainly have laid down their lives if Gandhiji gave a call. But he was too intelligent to know that the average Indian was too timid to die under the fire of British guns.

He had known the British closely and he knew that they were not like the Nazi butchers. He knew that they were too honorable to shoot down innocent freedom fighters and he knew their commitment to the Rule of Law. Indians had shown no active resistance to the armies of Kassim, Gazni, Gori or Nadir Shah or even the East India Company. They had meekly submitted to foreign rule. At best some defence had been put up by the Kshatriyas but the rest of the population raised not even their small finger to resist being slaughtered.

An appeal to British conscience and character was the only solution and the mild suffering of the Satyagrahi in the shape of a brief sentence of imprisonment would be adequately covered by the fig leaf of Satyagraha.

In dealing with teachings of the Bhagwad Gita and the lessons of India's ancient history, he practised a clever double diplomacy. The response of the masses in such large numbers joining the freedom movement and taking to a life of austere simplicity was not a miracle produced by Mr Gandhi but it was a new religious faith conjured up for the occasion by not a Mr Gandhi but *Mahatma* Gandhi. No wonder he retained that honorary title without any serious demur till the last day of his life. He was a clever lawyer, an astute politician and a great expert in mass psychology. He knew perfectly well that in his earlier incarnation as Mr Gandhi, his non-violent struggle in South Africa had proved a total failure so much so that even 50 years later the small Indian minority in that country was in a worse condition than it had been at the turn of the century.

This is not to belittle his great success in India but it must be known that his strategy succeeded with the British exhausted by a horrendous war, a coming into power of a brand of honorable Labour Party statesmen who were ashamed of the moral incongruity of fighting the Nazi and fascists in Europe but retaining their unwanted Colonial rule over Indians. The last conclusive action that won freedom for us was not a non-violent one but the Naval Mutiny in Bombay which made the Labour Government and the British public realize that they could no longer rely on the loyalty of the armed forces to protect and preserve their Indian empire.

No one can doubt than Mahatma Gandhi was a great student of world history and in particular the story of civilizations. He was familiar with what my friend Andy refers to in his letter of invitation to me as the teachings from the ancient civilizations of India. Those of you who have read my friend Bhagwan Gidwani's book *The Return of the Aryans* must indeed be anxious to know what this history has to tell us about non-violence. One need not go beyond the arrival of Alexander the Great in the region of the west bank of the Indus. It is there that he met what the western historians describe as the Gymnosophists of India. These were the ancestors of our Sindhis who had discarded worldly attachments and almost lived like people in the state of nature. In other words, they hardly wore any clothes.

Alexander prided himself on being a philosopher and he was a student of Aristostle. He engaged these holy men in a long dialogue. They naturally asked him why he had come that far fighting wars and killing people. When he told them that he was on a mission of world conquest they laughed and laughed incessantly in his face. They told him that however far he went he would still see that which he can neither capture nor control. They warned him of death hovering over his head all the time. These philosophers of India did finally persuade him to abandon his insane project. The warrior king then tried to persuade atleast some among them to go with him to Macedonia. They refused the tempting offers he made to them. Finally one Kolynos agreed to go with him. While going through Persia Kolynos developed a high fever. He explained to Alexander that with an infirm body he had no right to live. His religion taught him that. To the amazement of the Greek army he lit up a fire and immolated himself without batting an eyelid. He did however confess to Alexander that they would meet very soon. Alexander died in Babylon and never reached his native Macedonia. Western historians are wrong in their conclusion that Alexander went back because he thought he had reached the end of the world. He was not such an idiot.

I have often wondered who moulded the minds and thoughts of these Gymnosophists. I believe they were the followers of Buddha. Buddha was the greatest prophet which humanity has produced so far. His age symbolized the end of an overgrown culture and disgust at avoidable and superfluous metaphysical speculation.

He adopted the atheistic and rationalistic views of the Sankhya philosophy and added to it virtually the entire thinking including the virtual Nihilism of the Nastik Movement. He was not concerned with politics, art or science. His teaching was mainly psychological, dedicated to the liberation of the individual human being alone.

His four noble truths placed before mankind the tragic existence of human suffering, indicated its origin and cause, provided the glimmer of hope that it could be ended and went further on to indicate the technique of its extermination. He was a pessimist and pessimism paraded his culture and philosophical exposition. In that sense he perhaps unwittingly added to the sum total of the world's unhappiness.

As Sir Edwin Arnold; in the great poem *'The Light of Asia'* says,
We are the voices of the wandering wind,
That moan for rest but rest can never find,
Just as the wind is, so is mortal life,
A sigh, a sob, storm and strife."
This sums up his thought.

Buddha's teaching made Indians fatalists and totally indifferent to the world, reflected in the life and philosophy of the Gymnosophists. They were echoing the Buddhist teaching.The suicidal pacifism and pessimism of Buddha by no means made India strong.

Fortunately for a while, but a while only in the eternity of India, his influence was diluted by the rise of Chanakya—the author of *Arthashastra*, an almost immoral compendium of practice and principles to be followed by successful princes. He was the ancient Machiavelli of India. He helped Chandragupta to found the Maurya empire by conquering the remnants of Greek power in the north . His son Bindusara annexed more territory and his son, the well-known Ashoka, conquered the Kalinga empire in the eastern part of India. India became strong and united not by practice of Gandhian morality and non-violence but by immoral practices and use of war and violence. It is strange that Ashoka was remorseful about his great achievement and became a Buddhist. He certainly did a lot to make Buddhism a world religion but the empire he built melted away within a few years after his death. The vast population of India relapsed into dreams of Nirvana or the more attractive Swarga.

Some thing was also happening to Christianity. It became an enemy of rational thought and scientific development.

The church prohibited bath as a sin. An attractive body or garment meant the entry of Satan in man's soul. St.Paul said it in no ambivalent terms: 'Purity of body and its garments means impurity of the soul'. Lice were called the 'pearls of god' and to be covered with them was an indispensable mark of a holy man. Disease was caused by sin, so medical science could not grow. Women were burnt on stakes as witches and so were scientists. Bruno was among them and Galileo was compelled to recant his discoveries by a crazy Inquisition. Teaching of Darwin's *Origin Of Species* and theory of evolution was a criminal offence even in educated America for a good part of the twentieth century. I would request you to read about the Monkey Trial and the famous cross-examination of Father Bryn, a religious fundamentalist, by the famous lawyer Clarence Darrow.

Things were not so bad in India but the paralysis of religious faith was taking its toll. Let me give a few examples.

Sindh was conquered by Mohamad bin Kassin in the eighth century. The Hindus had tortured the buddhists and naturally they took no part in defending Sindh. The rest of India heard about this new menace from across our borders. It did not even occur to them to unite and plan resistance. They had four hundred years to plan but they only declared Sindh a polluted territory of no concern to India and its future. Then the Turks of Central Asia stepped into the scene. When Subkutgin of Ghazni crushed Raja Jaipal of Bhatinda; no one bothered. His son Mahmud of Ghazni further humiliated us. He destroyed the Somnath temple. Nehru in his *Discovery Of India* omitted this disgraceful act of fanatical religious faith and glorified Ghazni as a lover of good architecture. It was then that the great Muslim historian Alberuni described the social and political scene. He wrote of the vicious caste system and the Brahman attitude to life and death. Every intelligent reader of this great treatise was convinced that India was ready for conquest.

Gandhi learnt all this from the history of India. He pretended to forget it. He never mentioned it. There was none to contradict him or to recite the lessons of Indian history to the masses. Gandhi brushed aside, or attempted to brush aside, all the monstrous growths that had sprouted on the protoplasmic body of Hinduism over the centuries, choking it like giant creepers strangling a mighty tree. Gandhi's fanatical belief in ahimsa—non-violence—was derived by a very unorthodox interpretation of the Bhagwad Gita . In fact, this specific temperament of his was probably due to a potent permeation of his whole being by the Jain philosophy of his native Gujarat rather than to the more martial influence of Lord Krishna . But this ahimsa is,to an extent, in the tradition of Hinduisim itself, which has deliberately set itself out to decrease the vitality of its devotees—through starvation diets and taboos of all kinds—in order to keep them in line and avoid excessive temptations. Inheriting from Gautama Buddha's teaching its emphasis on the negative rather than the positive aspect, Hinduism has encouraged its followers to lower their vitality in order to eliminate temptations rather than run the risk of intense conflicts between vice and virtue.

The static nature of ahimsa goes hand-in-glove with a certain form of moral turpitude, a certain cowardly flight from the dangerous struggles of life which has been overlooked by its admirers. Gandhiji was not blind to this aspect of the problem and warned time and again: 'I have often noticed that weak people have taken shelter under the Congress creed or under my advice, when they have simply, by reason of their cowardice, been unable to defend their own honour or that of those who were entrusted to their care...Non–violence is not cover for cowardice but it is the supreme virtue of the brave.'

Did not Gandhiji plead for use of violence at least in self defence? True enough, but the fact remains that this view of non-violence was an ideal, saintly one, and that its appeal for the masses lay rather in its passive and negative character. This vitality-sapping character of ahimsa was not conspicuous because of the overwhelming number of Indians who made it a practical success in India against the British.

There are enemies who need to be destroyed before they destroy us. Why should we love our enemies? Do we not place ourselves at their mercy? 'Love those who hate you'. Is it not the despicable philosophy of the poodle that comes back to you when it is kicked? It is sensible to be a terror to your potential destroyer. When he retreats he will have some additional wisdom in his head, and your immortal spirit will live, not in an intangible paradise but in the brains and muscles of those who respect you. 'Love those who deserve it'. You cannot love everyone ; it is foolish to imagine that you can. Never turn your other cheek to a vicious aggressor.

Non-violence is not and never should be the ruling precept of governance in the Kal-yuga of today. What is going to be its duration, no one knows. Another stark and frightening possibility stares us in the face. Before it ends mankind may well decide to end itself—this entire planet might disintegrate or some primary unicellular organisms might be left to restart the history of human evolution all over again, with no certainty that creation of man as he is today will be the dominant purpose and propelling force of nature.

It is futile to look that far into the inscrutable future. Let us concern ourselves with India and the remainder of the current century. Nature is angry with us. Forests and farmlands are fast disappearing. Vast tracts of the earth's surface are turning into desert. Nature refuses to replenish the water we consume—every year sixty billion tons of water are being denied to us. Wars over water—and nuclear ones at that—are highly probable. The future is bleak indeed.

The solution is not non-violence by India or a few states. Complete universal disarmament is a mirage. Even if that happens, humans will still fight with sticks and stones true to their genetic structure of hunting animals and the Natsiya Dharma. Democracies and peace-loving nations must pool their resources—spiritual, economic and military—in vigilance and readiness to defend and die for the survival of civilization.

We must build our bodily strength and not allow ourselves to be sapped by the debilitating thoughts and deeds which have led to the conquests of the civilized world by barbarians possessed of superior vitality and will to subjugate and enslave the comfort-loving weaklings. We shall not imitate them though and become aggressive predators like some of our ancestors.

You must pardon my pessimism.

Acknowledgements

Writing a book is never a one-man show. It requires the support and encouragement of many, and I am fortunate to have been surrounded by people who have provided both.

I would like to thank my good friend and colleague, M.J. Akbar who has been an ally in the crusade to bring about probity in public life; my children, Shobha, Janak and Mahesh, for their unfailing interest and support, my dear daughter Rani, who sadly left us before her time, whose greatest commitment was to the cause of women, whether in the courts or in social fora; and my colleague, Lata Krishnamurty, for providing continuous motivation to write this book.

My junior colleagues, Karan Kalia, Ashish Dixit and Pranav Diesh provided great help in researching various issues that form part of this book, and my assistants Sanjay Ahluwalia and Pawan Kumar spent many extra hours at the office on this project.

The articles in this book are based on my writings in *The Sunday Guardian* and I am grateful to Neena Thomas for patiently editing and helping me give shape to *Maverick Unchanged, Unrepentant*.

Lastly and mostly, I am grateful to Kapish Mehra of Rupa Publications for his great enthusiasm and support in bringing out this book.

Ram Jethmalani